MIDCENTURY AMERICA

MIDCENTURY AMERICA

 *Life in the 1850s*

Compiled and Edited by

CARL BODE

SOUTHERN ILLINOIS UNIVERSITY PRESS
Carbondale and Edwardsville

Feffer & Simons, Inc.
London and Amsterdam

TO VERNON STERNBERG

Contents

List of Illustrations

The Midcentury American

IF YOU were the average American (and nobody ever is) living in the 1850s, you would, I think, be worse off physically and better off mentally than you are today. This is a paradox and an unprovable one, the sort that historians love to leap on with a yell. Yet a careful investigation of this interesting decade, a close look at its documents and artifacts, its gaudy mementos and odd paraphernalia, leads pretty surely to that conclusion.

You would be smaller and sicklier but also more sanguine. You would probably be more superstitious and more ignorant. It is certain that you would be smaller. Such men's clothing as has survived the attic and the moth looks shrunken to us. So does the women's: the Smithsonian Institution has an exhibit of gowns worn by presidents' wives, and the further they go from our time the smaller the gowns get. You would be sicklier since disease would be stalking you often. The deadliest of ills you would be exposed to would be tuberculosis, diphtheria, and typhoid. If you became a parent in the 1850s in Massachusetts (the only state to keep life-expectancy records then), your baby had a life expectancy of only about forty years.

Still, you would feel more sanguine than you would today. Though few of us learn to take disease or death for granted, you would learn to live with them as we have learned to live with the hydrogen bomb. In fact you would expect your children to catch certain diseases and be troubled if they did not, knowing vaguely that it would be worse to catch them later. You would feel more secure in the present and more optimistic about the future, because the history both of your country and your people had been one of spectacular progress. The only obstacle to continued progress (though a formidable one: slavery) you ignored if you lived in the North and refused to consider an obstacle if you lived in the South.

You would feel more secure because you would have more absolutes than you do now. You would trust in the great social institutions of church, family, school, and country. You would believe unwaveringly in God. You would have faith in the universe which He created and continued benignly to supervise. You would be certain that the family stood solid as rock. Your Americanism would be unalloyed; you would speak sincerely about "the rising glory of America." You would be more superstitious because you would probably still carry with you a baggage of Old-World belief to add to the New. You would be more ignorant because you would be less schooled. Though we all know that schooling does not necessarily abolish ignorance, the fact is that in 1850 slightly less than half of the school-age population went to school.

Everything considered, you would probably be happier if you lived in the 1850s. All this, that is, if you were an average American, an average white American. If you were black you could never escape the brutal, miserable fact that some white man owned you, though your owner would be apt to say loudly that you were better off than you would have been back in Africa.

And yet, slavery aside, if you were white you would not be violently different from what you are today. For us time has modified the values of the antebellum American but not reversed them. We still support the major institutions which he supported: the family, the church, the school, the elected government. We remain enterprising, outgoing; personally we keep some of our confidence. The difference we display, even among college students, is one of degree. Though we believe in the family, we break it up by divorce at a rate that would have stunned the American of the 1850s. In California, which shows us the future in various ways, there is now at least one divorce for every two marriages. Though we feel that organized religion is a good thing and build brave new temples, we have probably become, at best, tepid in our devotion to what Madison Avenue terms "the church of our choice" and readier to send our children to Sunday school than to attend services ourselves.

While the family and the church have become less meaningful the school has taken on far greater importance. It meant much to the antebellum American but he did not expect it to do the things we expect of it today. He did not expect it to work secular miracles. We have asked that the school do for our children and for us the things that we ourselves cannot do. We have demanded that it make us all better, brighter, and happier. No wonder that the school stays in crisis and the university, the capstone of education, is being blown apart.

We are calling on the government, like the school, to do more all the time. Ours is now a semisocialist state and promises to become more so with

every decade. The importance of the vote we cast, for magistrates or measures, is increasingly crucial. Or so most of us believe. A minority among us
has decided that the ballot is a farce. This minority not only refuses to have
any part in our governmental process but aims at demolishing it.

Yet the marks of the American character have not been erased. We still
show that we are the descendants of the people of the 1850s. We have inherited their conviction that work is good in itself as well as vital for one's
self-respect. We still arrive at the job on time; we still keep our engagements.
We bring up our young to be orderly, in private and in public, though more
of them revolt than ever before and throw order back in our faces. We still
believe that we can master our circumstances, that with enough energy we
can accomplish what we want. We still believe in success.

We still maintain a distinctively American life-style. When we travel
overseas we give ourselves away. It is not only a matter of a gaudy shirt or
the shiny luggage, of various sorts, that we haul around. On the surface it is
a matter of posture, of gesture, of expression. For example, we look restless;
we move fast. Underneath, it is a matter of assumptions that we do not even
realize we have made, such as that progress is possible and we can bring it
about. We still like to boast a bit about the "American Way" in spite of our
mounting problems. The boasting compensates, perhaps, for an insecurity
that the antebellum American could hardly imagine.

He took great pride in the United States and helped to make its mythology. He redescribed the exploits and characteristics of the culture heroes
of his era and told us something about himself in doing so. For him there
were many more heroes than for us. Ours are apt to be few and offbeat: the
high-living entertainer, the movie star, the famous football quarterback. His
were customarily statesmen, often with a military background. In our time
only General Eisenhower has come close to fitting that description for the
American public. In the 1850s the hero of heroes was still George Washington. It is hard for us to comprehend how much he meant. You could still buy
lithographs then, to hang on your dining-room wall, of Washington's grave
at Mt. Vernon or of the General staring woodenly at you. Abraham Lincoln
was only an ambitious politician when the decade ended, though today he is
the chief hero that history has preserved for us. His absence was unfelt since
there was a host of other heroes, though none with the universal appeal of
Washington. Benjamin Franklin represented the ideal of American enterprise and frugality; he stood out as a statesman too. Thomas Jefferson, though
tinged with godless radicalism, still kept a place in the hearts of many; in
fact he would be more admired as time went on, rather than less. So would

Andrew Jackson, the most recent idol of the masses. Anathema to the conservatives, he remained the people's darling. He was well remembered, since he had died only five years before the decade opened.

There were minor heroes as well as major ones, and at home and in school the antebellum child was told about their deeds. There was Nathan Hale, for instance, who regretted when about to be put to death by the British that he had only one life to give his country. There was the dashing sea-captain John Paul Jones. There was Zachary Taylor; there were others even less heard of today. And there were a few villains, led by the idiotic George III and the treacherous Benedict Arnold.

The heroes of antebellum America were honest, brave, forthright. And they were unpretentious men. The average American believed that they differed from him only in degree—they were never set apart through some divine right. They helped him to establish his identity, through their unostentatious private lives as well as through their public ones. Even as late as the 1850s he was still forming an impression of himself and then revealing it to others. "What is an American?" the French essayist Crèvecoeur had asked. For years foreign visitors as well as native American spokesmen were busy announcing the answer. Of the foreign observers in the 1850s the best was probably Count Adam de Gurowski, once of Poland and thereafter of several other countries, who settled in the United States and wrote about it in his book, *America and Europe,* of 1857.

To Gurowski, who liked him, the American was thoroughly interesting. He analyzed the impression the American made in a chapter called "Characteristics." As a preliminary he says that "the character of the people and the institutions have acted reciprocally on their development." In fact he sees no other nation with so close an identification between its institutions and its people. The American character that has emerged is marked above all by patriotism and love of national liberty. Its other qualities include a "thirst for knowledge," an excitement over the new (basically the result of a "nervous irritability" produced by our bad climate), a devotion to making money (which Gurowski excuses since only a prosperous nation can enjoy self-government), generosity to others, and an impatience toward criticism ("The Americans are well aware of their deficiencies, but they feel the sting of injustice done to them" by scornful foreigners). The American to Gurowski is a rough diamond but he is a diamond all the same.

He could not help attracting Gurowski's attention—and the attention of the world in general. Moreover, the midcentury American appeared especially interesting. He lived in a country which was drawing 277,000 immigrants on the average each year during the decade, a country where gold could be panned by the bagful in California and where it was already alleged to pave the streets of New York. He lived in a country of unbounded opportunity of many sorts. And he lived in a country which, while the world stared with morbid fascination, was gravitating toward a fratricidal war over Negro slavery.

Whatever the American did in the 1850s was becoming of some interest to the world: how he earned his living, how he made his home and raised his family, how he worshipped, how he educated himself, how he enjoyed himself. Some information came from our foreign visitors, none more accurate than Gurowski's. Some information came from the American writers and observers of the time. And yet even today we know little enough about the American of the 1850s, certainly less than we should. Most historians have concentrated on the politics of the decade, particularly the slavery question; but almost no one has devoted himself to the American's daily life. It can be argued that the real America was a workaday America, yet historians rarely examine it.

This is perhaps the more reason why we should try to discover the popular culture of the 1850s. The main obstacle lies in the difficulty of finding the materials but it is not insuperable. I talked about the matter in the introduction to my book *American Life in the 1840s:* "Much of life was taken for granted and never got into print. Much that did see print was later thrown away as being of no significance. Yet the task is not impossible. The books, periodicals, and pictures of those days remain, here and there, in the great research libraries. Drawing on them we can tell a good deal about American life. True, we cannot tell enough to assure ourselves that the portrait is always accurate, the reflection full and faithful. For we still have, by definition, only those books and pictures that survive. They are the books intended for the largest reading public, a public mainly middle-class and upper lower-class. The poor received little attention and left little trace behind them. The Irishman in the Boston slums or the frontier wife in Arkansas failed, understandably, to buy any books and, equally important, seldom became the subject of them. The pictures are those intended for the same public—with one increasingly significant exception. The lithographs that Nathaniel Currier and his competitors had begun to publish were so cheap that almost anyone could buy them. You could often find one on the wall of a frontier cabin or a little house in town. The other limitations on our source materials are that they are more often related to an urban rather than a rural audience, though the farmer is far from overlooked; to an

Eastern rather than a Western audience; and to a Northern rather than a Southern one."

For the 1850s, even more than the 1840s, the greatest gap is the absence of contemporary published materials by Southern slaves about Southern slaves. An iron repression kept anything from being printed and so reflecting the popular culture. Aside from that, somewhat more material can be unearthed about the 1850s than about the 1840s. The increase in amount starts with the census: the censuses of 1850 and 1860 yield fuller information than any previous one. We also discover more data in print and picture than for the previous decade. Literacy rose; publishing prospered. The presses found more customers than ever before. Good times allowed the popular lithographers such as Currier & Ives or Sarony & Major to multiply their offerings and sell them well. The portrait of America, even everyday America, can be painted more clearly.

Of course some sorts of material are more helpful than others. The working principles used in preparing *American Life in the 1840s* were also applied in this volume and so should be summarized. We have again omitted fiction, on the ground that it represents a distortion of history. It is sometimes a brilliant, memorable distortion but it is a distortion nevertheless. Concentrating instead on nonfiction, we have gone as a rule to the works of the authorities of the 1850s, to authoritative midcentury accounts. Because we have been after a comprehensive picture of American life, we have turned more often to the general than to the particular. Besides drawing on a broad range of nonfiction we have levied on the popular art of the time, especially the inexpensive lithograph, for its social content.

The materials in this book, all popular during the decade to the best of our knowledge, were in most cases issued in the 1850s. A few emerged earlier but sailed into the 1850s on a wave of continuing popular reception—for example, Samuel Hall's book about teaching which was already standard by the time of its 1852 edition or the Currier lithograph against drunkenness which obviously antedated the 1850s. And we include one document, a major speech by Wendell Phillips, given in 1855 but not printed in full till 1863.

The richness and diversity of the materials that can still be found shows us a workaday America which is, to repeat, essentially like our own and yet markedly different in emphasis. One example more might be enough to illustrate the point. When it came to making a living in the 1850s, farming stood first. Today it has been outranked by industry, yet it remains a mainstay of American life. The farmer is still on our front pages. But see how the geographical emphasis, in particular, has shifted. During the 1850s the state of New York came first among all the states in the amount of farming land within its borders. It was followed, in order, by Virginia (including what now is West Virginia), Ohio, and Pennsylvania. In the value of livestock New York again was first, followed by Ohio, Pennsylvania, and Virginia. In the value of farm implements and machinery New York, Pennsylvania, Ohio, and Louisiana ranked in that order. Today Louisiana and Virginia are far down the list. Ohio and Pennsylvania, though still doing well, have dropped some distance from the top. And New York has completely surrendered its supremacy.

The 1850s American—whether farmer or millhand, housewife or clerk —will look to us like ourselves in a distorting mirror, odd yet recognizable. Sometimes he will seem strictly modern, for instance when Gurowski notes that he is permissive towards his children. Sometimes he will seem sadly antiquated, for instance when he salutes the flag as "Old Glory." But he existed and can be recovered, in good part, through the manifold print and pictures of the period. And, as we shall see, we can start the process of recovery with the help of Gurowski himself, in all the splendor of his florid, foreign syntax.

I. *The American Impression*

Chapter 1

The American Look

THE sagest student of American society in the 1850s was an exiled Polish count named Adam de Gurowski. He came to America only after a lurid career in Europe. There he had intrigued to bring Poland into the Russian Empire; in failing, he was sentenced to death by the Poles but was saved by Czar Nicholas I. He worked in St. Petersburg for a time in an obscure government job, then left it to wander over Europe. Wherever he went he talked violently and irritatingly, whether it was in Berlin, Heidelberg, Munich, Berne, or Paris. And yet there was usually something to what he said. As he traveled from one place to another, he made himself a student of comparative cultures. He both observed the life around him and read avidly about societies ancient and modern.

In 1849 he arrived in New York from France, hoping to see the New World and make a living as a teacher or lecturer. He settled in Cambridge, where he met the Harvard elite. When he discovered that he could not make a living in the Boston area, he returned to New York; there he managed to get a job as an editorial writer on Horace Greeley's lively *Tribune*. He made New York his headquarters during most of the 1850s. Laboring with furious energy he published four books during the decade. The most outstanding was *America and Europe,* issued in 1857.

The book is distinguished by its candor and insight. It is the work of a fearless eccentric who never hesitated to write the truth as he saw it. He was as independent in his actions as in his opinions: what others thought of him meant little. Did the American sun hurt his eyes? He not only took to wearing large blue glasses but also wore a veil attached to the brim of his hat. No wonder that Americans stared at this bulky, bush-bearded man dressed in foreign clothes and striding along with his veil blown by the breeze.

In his book one of the best chapters bears the drab title "Customs, Manners, Habits, Etc." It is reprinted in large part below. To his study of the impression America creates, Gurowski brings his broad European background. It lets him make comparisons and set America in a context in a way that no other traveler had been able to manage. The result can sometimes surprise us, for example when he announces, as early as the 1850s, that we raise our children permissively and that our society is dominated by the young. He examines the effects judiciously, seeing both good and bad in them. And he has a sure sense of what is important in our culture. In the selection given here he begins with his observations about business—and nothing could be more central than that.

Source: Adam G. de Gurowski, *America and Europe* (New York, 1857), pp. 370–83.

CUSTOMS, MANNERS, HABITS, ETC.

Artisans, shopkeepers, tradesmen, merchants, bankers, in general all business men, in Europe as in America, must rely alike upon skill, shrewdness, acuteness, and aptitude for their pursuits. But as Europe is the centre of commercial, banking and industrial activity, production, and expansion, the commercial combinations are more wide-embracing and complicated there than in America. This alone obliges the European bankers, the chiefs of industry, and commercial men, to devote their intellect more intensely to various and accumulated operations. Besides, in Europe the crowd is dense, every spot is occupied, and he who falls is downtrodden, and usually has no opportunity to rise again and to gather new forces. On the continent, the failure of a commercial house generally disgraces the name of the party, his family, his children, and is often followed by suicide. Thus the existence of a man engaged in a regular honest business, is a struggle for honor, for life and

death. Here, on the contrary, an individual, unsuccessful in any branch or line, rises as quickly as he fell; dusts himself off, and rushes again into the same or another enterprise, without any great injury to his name or credit. An American changes place, and even occupation, pursuit, trade, running from one extreme to another, with a rapidity and ease neither thought of nor possible in crowded Europe. For these reasons, European merchants, bankers, and business men ought apparently to be more overworked, and have fewer hours to devote to social intercourse and even amusements, than the Americans. But the contrary is the case. In European capitals, in large and small cities, that class of men participates in all large and small, in public and private amusements and gatherings, for which the Americans generally either have no taste or no time. And nevertheless, the American seems to be always in a hurry and excited; at his meals, in his study, and at his counter. For example, in the morning hours, when the New York business population, old and young—and all is business in New York—pours out into the main artery, in Broadway, and descends hurriedly "down town," nothing in the world could stop or divert the torrent. Even if Sebastopol had been in their way, those men would have run over it at one rush.

The unsteadiness, however, which prevails in all American conditions and pursuits, renders it very difficult and thorny to the American business men to attend to the superintendence and direction of details in the management of their various interests. Although the business of the European is more complicated and more extensive, it can be more easily organized, brought into a methodical and regular activity, and thus be more easily superintended. In Europe the subordinate clerks have not as many various and free openings before them as in America; and thus they remain in their condition often for life; they acquire the necessary routine of each special house; win the confidence of the employers, and become faithful and trusty workers. Often in Europe the existence of a clerk and subordinate is intimately interwoven with the existence, the honor, the welfare of the house; he becomes a member of the body, a bone of its bones. In America men change continually as their prospects brighten, and thus the chiefs of commercial houses must continually and laboriously train new subjects, and exercise a more strict vigilance upon them and their daily work. Such a continual effort must be more exhausting, than are the intense and wide-reaching but methodical and calmly conducted, operations of European mercantile and bank-

ing houses. This daily fatigue and exhaustion may account for the fact, that generally very few men of mature age are to be seen in social circles and places of amusement.

Artisans, operatives, workingmen in overpeopled Europe, have far smaller gains and wages than the same classes in America. To make their living, they must therefore work longer and harder. The small workshops open earlier, and the operatives are more hours at their task in Europe than in America, and so are generally mechanics at out-door work. The various tools used by Americans being, however, more perfect and handy than those used by the majority of Europeans, the former no doubt accomplish more work in a given time than the latter. A European village, farm, and field are likewise already animated while the American one still slumbers; and generally only the darkness of night stops the toil of a European farmer, field-laborer, or journeyman.

Economy in general prevails not among Americans to the same extent, as it does among those various European classes, who are obliged to live by their labor, of whatever nature,—the superior social crust, formed of various elements, aristocratic as well as bourgeois, alone excepted. In America, labor is almost always productive—matter, nature is exuberant, and the general rise of every object so continual that the value of land, of products, etc., double quickly, almost as by their innate movement. No one seems to think about the necessity of saving, or of husbanding material resources. The Americans economize forces by their labor-saving machineries, which have been contrived by necessity,— but in handling the primitive matter and produce, they waste it with a lavishness unknown to Europeans, who are short of space, overburdened, compressed by vicious, social organization, and crowded upon one another.

The dwelling houses of the masses of Americans, their food—at least the provisions for it are better and more plentiful—and their external appearance in dress, is also more decent and neat than that of Europeans. Palaces, refinement, splendor, finish, elegance, luxury, taste, and genuine fashion are at home in Europe, and remain there unrivalled. But they are the lot, the patrimony only of certain classes. The average of Americans are better housed and fed, are far better and more substantially dressed than the average of Europeans. Homespun has also disappeared, and the consumption of various articles by twenty odd million Americans surpasses that of one hundred millions of Europeans. Peasants, villagers, almost all the laboring populations in Europe are generally poorly and cheaply clad; suits of clothes among them are hereditary, and women often principally wear those of their grandmothers. If America is deprived of the picturesque costumes to be found among European nations, she has far less tatters—and generally only imported beggars. The European populations enjoy, however, in one respect an incontestable superiority. The disgusting habit of tobacco chewing, which is so common in all social positions in America, and its so repugnant results, are almost unknown in Europe, chewing being limited, with rare exceptions, only to sailors and to the lowest and poorest inhabitants of maritime cities.

The love of show and of shining, of keeping up external appearances, and of thus winning consideration, is carried by the Americans to a degree unusual in Europe, and above all on the continent. *The coat makes the man,* is proverbial here. The love of external show, a social weed generating many evils, and in its various ramifications destructive of easy, unpretentious, sociable life, seems to spread more luxuriantly in the city mansions of the wealthy than in the cottages of the people. Among the masses, it has partly its source in a misapprehension and perversion of the notion of democratic equality, and, in its more intense development among the superior crust, it is one of the signs of a disease, eaten deeply into all degrees of English society, and inherited partly by Americans. Snobbism, one of whose numerous symptoms is to attach more value to outward distinctions than to the inner worth of an individual, and to reflect a borrowed lustre; snobbism, in its fulness and completeness, is nearly unknown to any class of continental societies, and no other language has an equivalent for it. Snobbism, however, generally loses its hold on the great current of the American people; those only are strongly affected by it, who attempt or think to rise conventionally above the mass.

The always hurrying, excited, busily occupied Americans have no time to imitate and to learn, from those who are regarded as standards, the daily use of those most minute details and rites of courtesy, whose scrupulous observation and exchange cement social intercourse, and smooth the asperities arising from the division of European society into classes, annulling these divisions with the level of politeness. The thoroughbred European aristocrat is generally the most scrupulous in observing towards his equals, and still more towards his inferiors in a social point of view, those highest degrees of masonry of good-breeding, in which few seem to be initiated here, or to the fulfilment of which either time or habit is wanting. In other respects, when the Americans are in a normal state, as is the majority of all social positions of the people, good-breeding prevails, and hearty, intentional politeness marks their address and intercourse. Intentional coarseness and rudeness are rare and exceptional among the masses; and their easy, off-hand, straight-forward manners are neither ill-bred, derogatory, nor offensive. Democracy teaches self-respect to everybody, in respecting others. The straight-forward address of the man of the West, as well as the often spoken of curiosity, inquisitiveness, of the American people, of the Yankee in particular, are neither offensive nor rudely intrusive. Only snobs, filled with superciliousness and affectation, shudder at them. But disgusting is the mixture of assumption, constraint, stiffness, affectation, fidgetiness, which by many are put on as good-breeding, or as refined demeanor, making them in turn rude or obsequious, as if momentary and feverish obsequiousness were courtesy or good-breeding. The inquisitiveness of the people at large is often a childish, naïve curiosity, striving for information. The Yankee always tries to increase his stock of knowledge; and, after all, even the cunning mixed with it is rather amusing than otherwise. Moreover, man is normally communicative and easy; closeness, secrecy, are an artificial state. They are a deviation from our nature, imposed by necessities, by a perverted social organization, but they are not innate. The people at large, practising and observing politeness in their own way, seem not to wear a heavy harness, while often for those who believe that they constitute a superior and distinct class,

politeness is not an innate or daily habit; but they put it on as a Sunday dress, or tight boots, becoming stiff, uneasy, and hurrying to throw off with joy the uncomfortable gear. The man of the South, possessing generally many amiable social qualities, is on the average more easy, elastic, urbane, and scrupulously observant of conventional relations, than is often the man of the Northern States.

Now, as of old, hospitality constitutes one of the noblest features of human society. In America, as every where, it has various characteristics and modes. Much of it is spurious, and much genuine. Houses thrown open, or dinners served up in rich private halls, with the purpose to overpower the visitor with costly furniture, plate, or wines, to earn his applause after such display, and have thus one's own vanity gratified, constitutes not hospitality. Practised in this way, it loses aroma and the convivial character, being marred by a kind of mercantile calculation. It is no more hospitality, but a speculation, a debt paid or contracted purposely, towards those who are in a position to repay it here or eventually in Europe. So the conspicuous social circles generally *pay* visits, while in Europe every body *makes* them. The genuine European aristocracy, as well as the wealthy classes, mixing with it, and largely practising hospitality, do not make it depend upon debt and credit; the favor, the honor, the pleasure bestowed, is mutual between the host and the guests. Hospitality and social intercourse generally spread a real charm when disinterested. Exchange of ideas, genial intercourse, stand higher than a simple exchange of dinners.

Unassuming, hearty hospitality more easily warms the roofs of the rich, who do not pretend to whirl in the vortex of society, and it is largely observed among the various quiet, industrious, professional, laborious classes, as well as in cities and villages. American characteristic hospitality, as practised by single families and individuals, as well as by entire communities or associations, administering to the individual sufferings and wants of thousands and thousands brought to this country,—this hospitality equals, if it does not surpass, what in this way is accomplished by any other nation.

In cities as well as in the country, in streets as in the fields, in mansions as in cottages, in large or small gatherings, the Americans show a different aspect and physiognomy from Europeans. Rather dusky than radiant, but rendered nervous by the struggle to enjoy naturally the moment, and by the fear of hurting imaginary propriety, they give the impression that they either do not care or do not understand how to win from life the cheerful, congenial, exhilarating side. At such moments the pang of severe duty seems to furrow their brow, rarely and only occasionally irradiated with impulsive joyousness. The European masses, bending under heavy burdens, are more impulsive to merriment, than the far happier and more prosperous Americans. Glee smiles from under misery, and the Europeans are always ready to transform the minutes of respite into a gay repose. Song and dance are the friendly fairies of their toilsome existence. From North to South, from the Atlantic to the borders of Asia—when extreme misery has not dried out the last drops of vitality—the workshops of the operatives, the suburban streets and gardens, the farms and fields, at dawn and twilight, re-echo with national or love songs, peculiar to each country. As neither the lark nor the nightingale, so almost never human song resounds in American fields, gardens, or groves. Cheerfulness is a spontaneous impulse, is catching with Europeans of all classes. Americans—on the average—seem not to possess the rich gift of extemporizing pleasures. Their enjoyments must be prepared, deliberated, but do not flow from the drift of the moment. Dance is for them a study, instead of being a smiling attraction, an unconscious rapture. It reflects a mental sultriness, has the appearance of a nervous excitement, of a laborious muscular effort and task. Often likewise easy, cosy talk in their gatherings is superseded by speeches, by exertions to produce an effect, to bring out themselves rather than to enliven, to charm their companions. The art or gift of conversation, so general in Europe, is not yet domesticated in America.

Americans stand out the best in the simple domesticity of family life. It is the only normal condition growing out of their earliest traditions and habits; it is their uninterrupted inheritance. The domestic hearth, the family joys and hardships must have formed almost the exclusive stimulus of existence, for the first settlers; therein they concentrated all their affections and cares. Out-door variegated attractions, comparatively recent here, and previously accidental, from time immemorial almost are innate to European life. Religious convictions, local impossibility, the limited means of the colonies, prevented them at the outset and for a long time afterwards from recurring to public joyful gatherings, from creating the like various pastimes and forming the habit and possessing out-door sociable attractions. The day spent in hard labor or in professional duties, was cheerfully ended in the family circle. Even now, notwithstanding the rapidly increasing wealth and expansion in large cities, out-door pleasures seem rather exotic to the American life. At any rate far more so in America than in Europe, the family hearth is about the only preventive against gross and often degrading recreations; it alone assuages the tediousness and burdensomeness of existence even for the rich, who often find that it is almost easier to make a fortune than to know how to use and spend it.

American homes are warmed by parental love. The relations between parents and children, harmonizing in their outward manifestations, with certain conditions and modes special to the development of American society, being misunderstood or not thoroughly examined by several European writers and visitors, have created the erroneous opinion of the want of parental feeling. At the outside, however, the reverse is apparent; less filial affection, or at least a less demonstrative one from children towards parents, seems noticeable; less so than is customary in Europe. Family ties seem to be looser, because generally Americans bear small affection to the spot of their birth; young members leave it or change with indifference, and parents do not make undue sacrifices to keep their children around them. Events providentially enforced upon Americans this unconcern, otherwise the task of extending culture and civilization would not have been fulfilled. Fortunes and means of existence were small among the settlers, but the space, the modes to win a position by labor were unlimited, and thus children began early to work and earn for themselves. Thus early they became self-relying and inde-

pendent, and this independence continues to prevail in filial relations. Parents then, as now, worked hard and accumulated for their children. But the facility of early becoming artisans of their own destinies, of securing independence by labor, activity, and intelligence, in times and conditions when no other pastimes were possible, matured and emancipated children from parental authority and domestic discipline. For centuries and centuries in Europe, conditions, positions, occupations, pursuits, labors have been hereditary, families have been riveted to one spot; generation after generation living in the same precincts of a wall, in view of the same parish spire, under the same roof, in the same workshop, laboratory or study. Generation succeeded to generation, without breaking the family group, without loosening the parental discipline. American parents, allowing an almost unlimited choice to their children, spare nevertheless no hardships and pains to bring them up, and to educate them according to their conception of what is the best and the most useful for the mature duties of life. Parents love their children as dearly and intensely here as in Europe, but exercise less control, less authority. Further, in Europe parents part with a share of their property, in order to facilitate, in various ways, the establishment of their children; in America, where labor is the corner-stone of society, where originally the fortune of the parents was limited, but a boundless facility existed for every beginner to acquire one, parents could not endow their children. This wholesome habit being still common, is no evidence, however, of a want of parental love.

American parents are far more forbearing, nay meeker with their children than are those in Europe. What here results from freedom or a yielding disposition, to the European comprehension appears as irreverence. A slight or no constraint is imposed upon children in America; and as childhood—in virtue of a cardinal animal law—is eminently imitative, their good-breeding depends upon the bad or good examples which in various quarters are freely set before them. Children accustomed to the utmost familiarity and absence of constraint with their parents, behave in the same manner with other older persons, and this sometimes deprives the social intercourse of Americans of the tint of politeness, which is more habitual in Europe.

In America children generally lead and regulate their parents, in the choice of social intercourse, and in most of the relations and modes of life. Many are the reasons which account for this seeming anomaly. Nothing is traditionary here, as in Europe, and still less so are positions, luxury, refinement of habits and modes of existence in whole classes or single families; parents, therefore, who started in life with small means—and such a start has always been common—acquired fortune, but had no time to acquire external refinement, to study and to master the conventional knowledge of society. They feel the deficiency, and to make it up they surround their children with all external signs of prosperity or wealth, and wish them to possess that art which they want themselves. Through and in the children parents enjoy wealth and standing, becoming thus docile to their impulsions or advice. The simplicity, the frugality of the parents, contrasts often even disagreeably with the prodigality, the assumptions,

self-assertion, and conceit of the children. In European domestic life the children even of the highest aristocracy, are educated with more comparative simplicity than is the case in America. Parental authority extends over the grown up, and they always occupy the background in all relations of conventional intercourse with society. In America, parents, as well as persons of mature age, are seemingly overruled by the younger generation. European youth of both sexes, of all social positions, from the wealthiest to the poorest, from kings, aristocrats, down to the lowest plebeians, in all feelings, emotions, as well as in worldly concerns, remain children longer than they do in America. Here they mingle with society, with life, almost from the swaddling clothes. And so young unmarried girls give the tone to all those social gatherings, which in Europe are under the exclusive sway of married women, of matured men. The American custom and combination is more normal and natural in itself; and it corresponds to that bourgeois construction of society, which lies at the bottom of the American social life. Of old, among the European bourgeoisie and the laboring classes, convivial gatherings had pre-eminently in view to amuse young people, to bring them together, to facilitate marriages. Those who have already made their choice and settled for life, abandon the gay foreground of the scene, to attend to more serious duties. Such was likewise the social custom of the colonists, and such is that of their descendants. In abstract comprehension, dissipation and even the innocent admiration commonly paid to married women, and their forming the pivot of social whirling, are as many dissolving ferments of the actual state of society, wherein the unmarried girl is the natural centre of attraction, and one of its elementary and cementing forces. Gatherings organized in this manner lose, however, the charm depending upon the contact of various ages; and youth, uncontrolled and paramount, becomes regardless of the pleasure of others, pushing aside, and often, without the least restraint, whatever stands in its way. Society in America has thus a physiognomy of freshness, together with a tint of harshness—being in turn attractive and repulsive.

Even in the serious decisions of life, children in America enjoy a fulness of independence, not customary in Europe. They make freely the choice of their intimacies, then of their church, of their politics, their husbands and wives. On the average far more marriages are contracted in America without the consent of parents, than in any of the European social classes. Aside from the prevailing looseness of what in European customs constitutes the parental authority, the facility with which one can create here for himself a position, and secure the material means of existence, makes the choice less dependent on parental will or advice.

GOOD MANNERS FOUNDED ON HUMAN RIGHTS.

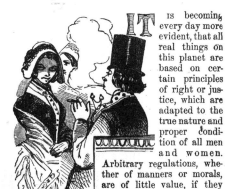

IT is becoming every day more evident, that all real things on this planet are based on certain principles of right or justice, which are adapted to the true nature and proper condition of all men and women. Arbitrary regulations, whether of manners or morals, are of little value, if they are not in accordance with these universal laws. For every possible requirement there must be some good reason. A law that is not founded in the natural principles of justice, is void from the beginning ; or becomes of no effect, or obsolete, as soon as the emergency has passed for which it was ordained.

This and other cartoons and caricatures used as tail pieces are from The Illustrated Manners Book. *The work of an anonymous author, it was issued in New York in 1855.*

Chapter 2

The American Mirror

IN the observations of Adam Gurowski we saw, perhaps better than in any other visitor's account, how the America of the 1850s looked to outsiders. But it is also important, if far more perplexing, to see how America looked to itself. All generalizations about it have their exceptions but this does not mean that it is profitless to talk about Americans in general. Some characteristics emerge fairly clearly. They can be seen in the group of visual documents which follow.

The lithograph "Torchlight Procession around the World" expresses America's youthful, boisterous pride in what it has done and is doing. It leads the world in communication, and the main message it has to communicate is Liberty. The primitive peoples all over the globe hear the message and at the same time help to spread it. England hears as well. This is an America already proud of its technical achievements: the inventor and the enterpriser are already respected. This is also an America proud of its young people and complacent about the flamboyance of its democracy. The torchlight procession and the firemen furnish just the right metaphors for these characteristics.

The lithograph "American Independence" is pastoral in tone and feeling. But there is noise in it: the Fourth of July is being celebrated with a bang. This lithograph, gentle and prettified though it is, reminds us that the Americans are a free people with a proud heritage. The lithograph also shows us the American family as Americans liked to picture it: here we watch a loving, closeknit group.

The "Torchlight Procession" lithograph was emphatic in its democracy. But there was also a sense of respect for leadership that marked the American character of the 1850s. Not that the members of the elite failed to suffer their share of sneers and jibes; they did but they were also envied. And in general, whether they were self-made men or rich by inheritance,

12

they were accorded a grudging respect. The same thing held for our political leaders. In the taverns or in the town halls they were often categorized as either fools or knaves. Nevertheless, the politician was important and he was listened to. Most important of all was the president of the United States. The lithograph entitled "The Presidents of the United States" is an index to how much he was respected, if not always for himself then for his office. Here we see all the past presidents, the leaders of the republic. The lithograph was put out by Kelloggs and Comstock in the confident assurance that the public would buy it, and it did.

In "Things as they were, and Things as they are" we see the other side of the coin. True, America has shown the world its industry and energy. It is a nation that moves fast, eager for the newest in news and in many other things. Yet it recognizes that it has surrendered its tranquillity. The lithograph testifies to a yearning for idyllic peace, for the past that never was.

The lithograph "Historical Monument of our Country" testifies too to the power of the past but in a different way. It reveals our urge to put ourselves into perspective in time and place. The lithograph shows our affiliations both with the past and with the rest of the world. It is a European past and a European world, of course. Assertive though we are, we feel the need for the security that the long view of history can afford us.

Source: *Torchlight Procession around the World.* "Author and publisher": A. Weingartner, 1858.
The Harry T. Peters "America on Stone" Lithography Collection,
The Smithsonian Institution

Few lithographs of the 1850s give a better picture of the Americans' view of themselves. Every inch of this one has something to say. Suppose we start with the dedication, which has a double meaning. In a general sense the lithograph is dedicated simply to a youthful, exuberant nation. But in a specific sense it is dedicated to a drive for literary independence. To the reader of the 1850s the phrase "Young America" was recognizable at once. It was a journalistic tag for a group of radical young literary critics, mainly Democratic, who had called loudly for an American, as opposed to a British, literature. Their leading propaganda journal they christened the *Democratic Review* and in it they sounded the trumpet for a "people's literature." They aimed to take advantage of the spread of literacy and on the whole they succeeded. They managed to frighten the Boston conservatives thoroughly in the process.

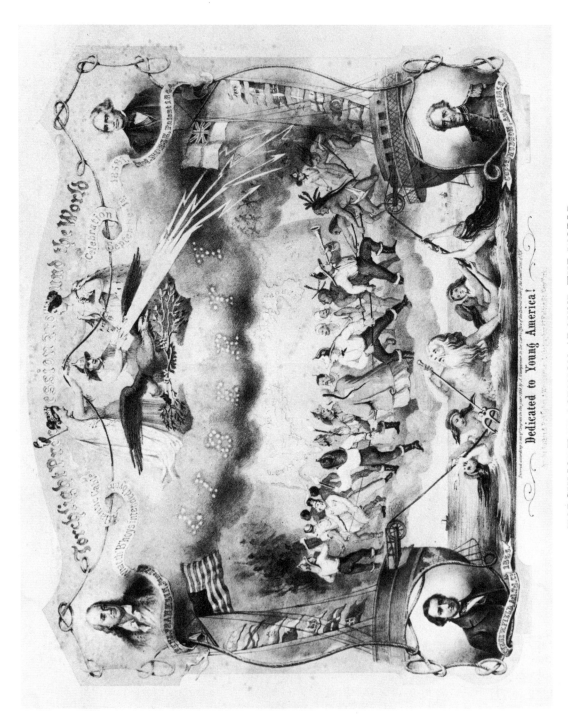

TORCHLIGHT PROCESSION AROUND THE WORLD

Most of the leaders of "Young America" are as forgotten now as the leaders of our "hippies" will be in another few years. For example: Evert Duyckinck, of the misspellable name. But their patron saint was one of our first great writers, a man who called as ardently if not as loudly for a native American literature as they did. This was Ralph Waldo Emerson, a prophet of newness who was detested by New England conservatism. But by the middle 1850s Emerson was growing respectable and Young America was winning its battle. American literary independence was being widely hailed; this lithograph testifies to the fact.

American liberty is the theme of the lithograph. Liberty shines in the sky and is being exported around the globe. The immediate occasion is the laying of the Atlantic cable between the Old World and the New, between England and America. The cable will transmit the message of freedom to the Old World; there is no indication of what message the Old World will transmit to the New. The looped cable forms the frame of the crowded picture. At the top of the picture the goddess Liberty holds up the cable with the help of an impassive Queen Victoria, while just below them the United States, as a "fire laddie," sends a bolt of electricity in the direction of England.

The choice of the fire laddie there and in the center of the lithograph is significant. The volunteer fire companies of the mid-nineteenth century somehow surrounded themselves with an aura. They were renowned both for courage and contentiousness. They liked to fight not only fires but other firemen, city "swells," and anyone else who offered himself. The public regarded their belligerence indulgently. In the Eastern seaboard cities many of them were Irish and therefore considered quarrelsome. Sometimes they were called the "b'hoys" in an Irish brogue, though the term was also used at times for city toughs in general. Here the b'hoys are being helped to lay the cable by the heathens of the world; the Europeans are curiously absent.

The caption describes the laying of the cable in terms of one of the favorite American folk festivals, the torchlight procession. Though usually political it was not always so. The procession lent color and warmth to an America that needed surcease, even then, from the business of making a living. It was not the best metaphor for the laying of the cable but it was a useful gimmick for the artist.

We also have Neptune gazing up in astonishment at the procession and, at the corners, four faces looking thoughtfully at us. Franklin's had to be there because he had long established himself as the patron saint of American ingenuity and enterprise. He had, in the American view, invented the electricity which would course through the cable. And he had demonstrated the kind of enterprise which would make such a bold project commercially sound. Across from him we see Samuel F. B. Morse, inventor of the magnetic telegraph. Below him is W. L. Hudson, the captain of our frigate *Niagara,* which was helping to lay the cable. Across from him is the American promoter of the cable and head of the Atlantic Telegraph Company, Cyrus Fields.

Perhaps there is one other thing we ought to mention. It is the American optimism evidenced by the picture. For the Atlantic cable had not yet been completed. The legend reads "Celebration

September 1st 1858?" The fact is that the cable was completed in August 1858, broke down two months later, and was not a permanent success till 1866. But we Americans knew all the time that it would work.

Source: *American Independence*. Lithographed by L. H. Bradford and published by C. H. Brainard, 1859.
The Harry T. Peters "America on Stone" Lithography Collection, The Smithsonian Institution

This homey scene depicts the chief American festival, the Fourth of July. Its exploding gunpowder, in firecrackers or toy cannons, symbolized the shot heard round the world. For us it is hard to realize the depth of American pride and patriotism in the 1850s. The Fourth was a day when our nation congratulated itself. There were parades of sweating citizens, fraternal orders, and militia. The fire laddies were apt to be marching too. Then there were speeches in the courthouse square, usually marked by a screaming-eagle rhetoric now as old fashioned as a stovepipe hat. And then there were refreshments: much food, much lemonade, and sometimes surreptitious gin or bourbon.

At home the flag went up and fireworks resounded throughout the day. The family gathered while the boys shattered eardrums. In "American Independence" all the details of the stereotype of the time are shown. The family is a three-generation one, including the grandfather. If the lithograph had been made a generation before, incidentally, he would have been shown in his Revolutionary War uniform. Everyone looks well dressed. The house is a two-story one, with a porch framed with the traditional vines.

The artist has had some professional training and knows popular taste. He prettifies every face and fuzzes each detail. He shows skill in the structure of the lithograph. We look automatically at the boy in the center of the picture and then follow the diagonals of his body down to the little cannon. The boy in the foreground wears dark clothing to contrast with the light blouse and pants of the boy with the cannon, and he also leans forward to balance the boy who leans back. The boy on the far left frames the picture with his upright flag. Its verticals are repeated in his figure and in the corner of the wall behind him. The composition is framed on the far right by the column of vines behind the father.

In general the chiaroscuro is elementary but effective. The darks alternate rhythmically with the lights, and our eye falls naturally where the artist wants it to. A century later this artist, with the same talent but more training, might have been painting the saccharine covers of the *Saturday Evening Post*.

AMERICAN INDEPENDENCE

17

Source: *The Presidents of the United States.* Issued by Kelloggs and Comstock, 1850.
The Harry T. Peters "America on Stone" Lithography Collection,
The Smithsonian Institution

America was still debating whether it should view itself as a democracy or a republic. On the one hand, it was becoming more democratic—except in the slave plantations of the South. The scope of public schooling was being steadily widened. The American economy was expanding at an unheard-of rate. For most people times were good and even the Panic of 1857 acted only as a temporary impediment. The franchise was being extended. In short the average man was doing better all the time. He showed the fact in the breeziness with which he regarded his political leaders, often giving them irreverent if sometimes affectionate nicknames. Martin Van Buren was called "The Fox of Kinderhook," for example; Zachary Taylor, "Old Rough and Ready."

On the other hand, America also saw itself in some ways as a republic. After all, it delegated a good many of its powers to an elected elite. It preserved the Electoral College, as elitist an institution as a democracy could imagine. It had a growing aristocracy of wealth. And, as Tocqueville observed in his *Democracy in America,* it had a professional elite in the lawyers and judges of the nation. The American conservatives, especially, liked to think that the model for the country was the Roman Republic, and the creation of the Senate of the United States was an example in point. So were the classical columns which adorned many a courthouse and government building: they were intended to remind us of Rome. So were the columns in the lithograph "The Presidents of the United States," one column being appropriately topped by Liberty and the other by Justice.

Moreover, though we might nickname our presidents and even track dirt on the White House carpeting, we felt a genuine respect for them. No other president received the veneration accorded George Washington but that was understandable. Yet even those who suffered defeat when trying for a second term were not forgotten. Even the nonentities were honored for the sake of the office they held. And the notable presidents, such as Jefferson and Monroe, were put in the newly improvised American pantheon.

There is no better way of seeing the changes a century has brought than by realizing that this kind of lithograph was highly popular in the 1850s. Today nothing like it can be found. The twentieth century has seen some of the best as well as some of the worst of American presidents, and yet anyone who put a picture of our last twelve presidents on his wall would be wondered at. Doubtless they do not even hang in a schoolroom corner.

However, here are the chief magistrates of an earlier era, looking the way the artist thought that presidents ought to look: solemn if not severe, thoughtful if not stern.

THE PRESIDENTS OF THE UNITED STATES

Source: *Things as they were, and Things as they are.* Drawn and lithographed by John P. Oertel; printed by Nagel and Weingartner, 1853.
Reproduced from the Collections of the Library of Congress

Though the Americans conceived of themselves as a brisk, no-nonsense breed, they had occasional misgivings about their condition. The misgivings were a sign of maturity and did not come to the surface, except here and there, till about the middle of the nineteenth century. They are symbolized in Oertel's lithograph.

The message is crystal clear. The old days were immeasurably better than the new, and the villain who destroyed them for us was Johann Gutenberg. He stands, a stately form, on the pedestal which separates the old from the new in the lithograph. His figure and the top of his pedestal are in the light, but if we look down into the shadow we see that the pedestal rests on a shaky foundation: a snail and the head of a vicious-looking American eagle.

Things as they were are epitomized in the seated monk writing quietly in his cell. A crucifix hangs on the wall and beneath it is a font with a bird perched peacefully on its brim. Outside the monastery window a pleasant prospect rises of trees, houses, a church, and—on the hilltop—a misty castle. On the other hand, the weapons of feudalism frame the picture at the left.

The weapons are balanced on the far right by the liberty cap on the flag pole; and liberty is today's choicest blessing. But the other elements in the righthand half of the lithograph have little of the blessed about them. The yelling newsboy is the center of interest. A sturdy ragamuffin, he runs out of the picture waving the latest Extra hot off the press. Behind him sits the newspaper editor holding the latest tape of news in his hand from the printing-telegraph machine. Above his desk is an artificial light and he turns from it to look out his window on the hulking factory with its belch of smoke. Copy hangs on a hook above the desk also, while below it is a wastebasket stuffed full of crumpled sheets. Above him and to his right stands a telegraph pole with its train of wires; ships of commerce are framed below the wires. At the base of the lithograph the speeding railroad train is offset by the galloping courier on the monk's side of the picture.

Oertel's technique is better than competent. His lithograph lacks the strong lines that reproduce well, but the composition is simplicity itself and bound to hold the eye. The masses are evenly distributed and in spite of the symmetry the picture has movement. The eye travels naturally from the left to the right. The monk sits facing the right and the newsboy is hurrying out at the right. The movement is appropriately clockwise. And there is a teaser in the lithograph: the man of "Things as they are" has his head turned away from us; we wonder what he looks like.

As Henry Thoreau was saying, though no one appeared to listen, "Read not the Times. Read the Eternities."

THINGS AS THEY WERE, AND THINGS AS THEY ARE

21

Source: *Historical Monument of our Country*. Painted and engraved by I. M. Enzing-Miller, 1858.
Reproduced from the Collections of the Library of Congress

Here is one of the splendid panoramas that Americans loved. It was first, and folksily, called "Family Monument" but it was far too elaborate for any family metaphor, and far too splendid, so the title was changed. The picture constitutes an American effort at identity.

Because the view is historical we can understand the slighting of the present and recent past. Nevertheless, one or two of the things the panorama omits are as significant as those it includes. American business, bustling and thriving throughout the country of the 1850s, makes a scant appearance. Industry and transportation are symbolized only in a tiny building and a puffing train in the far distance at the left of the picture. However, the pioneer is present, pitching his tent while his oxen bed down: apparently the West is being won.

Naturally much of the search for an American identity meant a return to the past. We needed to know our roots, and so this lithograph performed a profitable service. It showed us what we had been, thereby helping us to comprehend what we were now. As we look from left to right we see Columbus (the year "1492" is drawn behind him) claiming our land for Spain. In his train follow conquistadores and Catholic missionaries. They watch him plant the flag as do the worried Indians next to it. In the lower lefthand corner a manacled black slave, eyes raised heavenward, sits in a boat of Spaniards.

In the center of the picture a colonial proprietor gestures to his husbandmen. In the lower righthand corner a group of courtly figures discuss some grapes. Above them the British are conquering North America, if at the expense of their fallen general, James Wolfe. But in another part of the lithograph the British are not doing very well. Their lion lies dead, tongue lolling, and the unicorn has been pounced upon by the fierce American eagle.

Up above them a pyramid rises, adorned with a rich frieze of figures. Washington stands atop the pyramid with succeeding presidents trailing respectfully behind him. He rests a hand on the Constitution. Beyond him sits a classical female holding the Declaration of Independence. Her sister floats above her with a sword, balancing the figure of Liberty on the other side.

The composition is also pyramidal. Most of the light focuses on the central pyramid; the rest is thrown on the figures at the center of the lithograph. The management of light and shade is patchy but effective, so the canvas is crowded but not unpleasantly so. Whoever bought the lithograph could be assured of hours and days of gazing before he became aware of all that it contained. Not the least of the artistic merits of the lithograph is its movement. Nearly everybody is doing something. This is a busy picture in more ways than one. Its technique lies in the European tradition; the newly emerging American art has left little mark on it.

HISTORICAL MONUMENT OF OUR COUNTRY

II. *Making a Living*

Chapter 3

The New-Fangled Machine

As America's rate of change speeded up in the 1850s, the pacesetter was industry. There had been factories, machines, and industrial inventions before but never as many. The machines, culturally, were the most significant. Even in those days the American was attracted by the machine. It held a genuine fascination for him, so far as we can tell; in addition to appreciating its products, he enjoyed seeing how it worked.

The most loudly heralded showcase for the machine was the great Crystal Palace Exhibition in New York City during 1853 and 1854. In it were gathered many of the latest and best products of art and industry, with new machines and recent inventions prominent among them. It was essentially an American show, though some of the exhibits came from across the Atlantic. Ever alert for news, Horace Greeley's New York *Tribune* reported on the exhibition in a series of pieces which Greeley revised and edited thereafter in book form as *Art and Industry*. In order to sell every possible copy, it was issued promptly during the exhibition's first year. The book bears the characteristic marks of Greeley's hand. The prose is often pungent as it weighs the merits—and demerits—of the assembled exhibits and tells the story of the exhibition itself. Greeley is perfectly capable of publishing one chapter entitled "The Banquet" (about the initial ceremonies) and then following it with another headed "Strictures on the Banquet."

Greeley devoted an important chapter to the latest machines. A decade before this he would have had much less to write about; a decade after this no single chapter could have contained all the notable examples of our industrial ingenuity. "Machinery and Inventions" is reprinted in part below. For any reader today who knows what happens under the hood of his automobile, the chapter is rich in historical interest. But even the humanist can get through it, thanks to Greeley's lively, often caustic commentary.

The chapter has several social implications. We can see for instance that America, today besotted by personal cleanliness, was even then at work making washing machines. We can find planing machines that will put the old-fashioned skilled artisan out of work, leaving a mere tyro in his place. It will be our civilization's loss. As Greeley observes with regret, "A man who could slap together a dozen or two four-panel doors a day is a very different man from the old steady workman, who prided himself on splitting the gauge-line with his joint-plane the whole length of a sixteen-foot board." On the other hand, machines are here; they might as well be used. We can see the implications for American agriculture in the new corn shellers, the new grist mills. Greeley says of one of the latter, "Its cost is too high to render it purchasable by farmers on a moderate scale, but the great grain-growers of the West may have it as well as millers." There is no doubt that a new day is coming. Consequently, Greeley urges his readers, "Let no one spend even an evening in the Palace without traversing the department of Machinery."

Source: *Art and Industry,* from the New York *Tribune,* revised and edited by Horace Greeley
(New York, 1853), pp. 296, 298, 299, 302–8.

MACHINERY AND INVENTIONS

A volume would scarcely suffice for a full description of all the inventions and labor-saving machinery in the Crystal Palace; while to reconcile their conflicting claims to originality and efficiency, would over-tax the powers of any writer. We can only speak of the most notable, as a necessarily hurried examination of each has enabled us to do, giving our impressions, without claiming for them any other merits than sincerity and impartiality. Once for all, be it understood, that we do not aspire to guide the judgment of buyers or operators; they will of course examine for themselves, expecting of us only indications that this or that article seems worthy (or otherwise) of their consideration. . . .

Washing.—We had nearly lost our faith in Washing-Machines, except on the largest scale; but there is a rough-looking customer lately brought into the Exhibition, which revives it. It consists mainly of a cylindrical base or boiler, holding some ten to twenty gallons, into which the clothes are put *without* soaping; the soap is put in with them, and hot water and steam are introduced from a box or boiler below, so that whatever space in the cylinder is not filled with clothes is about half full of boiling suds and half of steam. Then the cylinder is made slowly to revolve, so that the clothes are alternately immersed in steam and in boiling suds, until the alkali of the soap has dissolved or neutralized all the grease, and the clothes are "without spot or blemish." The time required for this is from five to ten minutes, according to the tenacity of the grease, though we were informed by some of the workmen in the Palace that their oily overalls had been thoroughly purified by it in five minutes. The machine costs fifty dollars without, or seventy-five dollars with a boiler above for rinsing, and requires very little room. We think it might make the fortune of the patentee or owner, provided he knows enough to advertise it sufficiently.

Printing Uneven Surfaces.—"Burnap's Veneering Press, especially adapted to Veneering Uneven Surfaces and laying large Veneers at a single operation," strikes us as ingenious and valuable in its way; but our main interest in it centres in the light it sheds on the problem of printing irregular forms or uneven surfaces. We heard, some months since, of an invention in Austria whereby such surfaces were successfully printed, but have seen nothing that exhibited the *rationale* of the operation before this, which works by hydraulic pressure and adapts a flexible, elastic surface or *tympan* to the rigid, irregular surface opposed to it, and of which an impression is required. The principle seems susceptible of wide application. . . .

Stave-Dressing, Planing, &c.—Four machines for Stave-dressing are on exhibition. Gwynne & Sheffield's is a well-finished machine, capable of dressing for the truss-hoop ninety staves a minute. The machine drives three knives, one to each edge and one to cut the face of the stave. The wood, after being thoroughly

steamed, is offered in a block, the upper edge-knife strikes it, trims a half-inch, then descends the main blow separating the stave, then the lower knife trims the lower edge. For flour and fruit barrels, these (maple) staves will make good work after seasoning. They are "shaky," however, in consequence of being peeled off like a shaving from the block. Had the block been dry they would have split; the steaming alone saves them.

The Barrel-making machinery of C. B. Hutchinson & Co., Syracuse, begins with a cutter, which cuts (from bolts or blocks) the staves to the proper curvature, so hollowed and rounded that no further dressing is needed—of course, with a great saving of material as compared with the old, manual process. Different machines cut from one thousand to two thousand staves per hour, according to size and thickness. To these succeed a Jointer, a Crozier, a Heading-cutter, and a Head-turner—each doing its work rapidly and accurately—the last turning out eight hundred barrel-heads per day, and requiring but one horsepower to propel it.

The third set of machinery is that of Wm. Trapp & Co., Elmira, N. Y., consisting of similar contrivances to those just mentioned, and said to produce three hundred barrels per day, from a single set of machinery. The barrel or keg made by this process seems decidedly superior in tightness and finish to one made with like care by hand; while the operator does nothing but hand on the blocks and pass the staves, &c., from one machine to another, until the barrel is ready for setting up and hooping. We cannot doubt that, where casks are wanted that will hold fast the most insinuating liquids, it will be found expedient to have them made entirely by one or other of these sets of machinery.

Near the beam-engine, at the extreme north of the Arcade, is a third Stave-dresser, for tight work, which appears well. It is simply a planing machine so arranged as to plane out a barrel-stave complete, just as floor-boards have been dressed for the last ten or twelve years. Hawkins is the inventor's name. This planing-machine, on the principle of revolving cutters, is a dangerous one to use. India rubber and planing-machines breed law-suits as fast as they do money.

Woodworth's planing machine is here in all its glory, and also a molding-mill to dress out a very common pattern. This is the best known of all the machines of the kind in the country. Its interests are familiar, *ad nauseam,* to all the United States Courts; its claims have been heard in Congress. It does excellent work and pays well.

Beardslee's Patent Planing Machine is a device which has nothing at all in common with Woodworth's. It consists of eight broad knives or plane-bitts, set up vertically in solid cast-iron stocks, and so adjusted that the board is driven along their face, and each takes a shaving as broad as the board; each knife is set to a finer cut than the preceding one, till the last shaving is as thin and soft as silk. The machine has an attachment by which both sides of a board are planed at once. The inventor applies the same plan to tongueing and grooving. This is the most efficient machine as yet invented. It planes boards as fast as one man can handle them, say one hundred and thirty to one hundred and forty linear feet of length per minute. Its faults are most manifest upon knotty stuff. The knives require a careful and a skilful workman to set them. The working model of this machine on exhibition

is a pattern for all inventors who wish their inventions judged of by a model. This model, and one of a power-loom, are the only two properly finished models in the Exhibition.

Barlow's Patent Planing Machine differs from Beardslee's, in giving a reciprocating or drawing motion to some of the vertical knives or bitts. Minor differences we will not note.

These labor-saving machines have worked a revolution in the carpenter's trade. It is very rare now that a carpenter sets out to dress out boards by the hundred feet. The planes are well-nigh disused. What with planing, molding, mortising and tenoning machines, little is left to the carpenter but to put together the work. A regular old-fashioned carpenter is getting to be a curiosity. A man who can slap together a dozen or two four-panel doors a day is a very different man from the old steady workman, who prided himself on splitting the gaugeline with his joint-plane the whole length of a sixteen-foot board.

Charles W. Bemis exhibits a very beautiful arrangement of the String and Circular Saw. The String Saw is carried by a working-beam, which ends in an arc of a circle, over which an elastic steel strap is conformed at every stroke. The saw is stretched between two such beams, and thus dispenses with the "gate" and "guides," and moves very lightly upon centres, instead of slides. The shortness and perplexity of the curves cut by this simple tool, are a steady wonder to visitors. The Circular Saw is peculiar only in its gearing. A boy of twelve can turn the crank so as to rip a three-quarter inch pine-board with great ease. These are cheap machines. Every carpenter should look at them; they will save him time and labor.

Sherwood's Prismatic Lathe, is an engine for dressing out ballusters, bedposts, newels, &c., into prismatic shapes. The superior richness of a prismatic post over a circular one of the same pattern, is really surprising. The machine is very simple. The post is held fast on centres, while a series of cutters ranged along a shaft, revolve with great rapidity, and dress off one side. The post is then turned one-sixth or one-eighth of a revolution, and a second side is cut. Each pattern must have a set of knives or cutters, and these are so costly, that, except in cities, the machine will not pay, through lack of work to keep it running.

Thomas S. Minniss exhibits a model of anti-friction bearings for heavy shafts. His device is to float the revolving body upon water, oil, or mercury, according to the necessities of the case. Of course his shafts will move smooth as oil and free as water. Very possibly it is a good device, though we apprehend that its novelty will deter men from its use. It is a good invention—look at it.

With regard to Steam Engines, we may say that no visitor is competent to criticise a novel steam-engine simply by looking at it. The rotaries are numerous and ingenious. We hope there is a good and economical one among them all, but we doubt it. Nevertheless, a direct-action rotary steam-engine is a desideratum—and, for that matter, so is perpetual motion. The three engines at work may be spoken of very briefly as follows: The Southern Belle, running without any labor, is true to the name *belle*—very showy, and (at present) very useless. No shop would ever dream of making or buying such an engine for use. It would keep one man busy the whole time to keep it bright and clean.

The Lawrence Engine—two cylinder —is neat, unostentatious, and workmanlike. There is nothing novel, however, in its structure.

The Beam Engine, from Providence, by Corliss & Nightingale, exhibits a new application of the governor. Instead of applying it to the usual regulator-valve, in this engine the governor is very ingeniously made to adjust the "cut-off," so as to regulate each cylinder-full of steam, stroke by stroke. The workmanship and the ingenuity displayed in this machine, are above all praise. As to its practical utility, only experience can decide.

Dick's Iron Shears, made at Hadley's Falls, (Holyoke) Mass., is a massive engine, decidedly in advance of all the boiler-makers' shears we have seen, in the length of cut, the ease of handling the iron sheet, and the accuracy with which the scribed line can be followed. Plate-iron a half-inch thick can be trimmed as closely as a lady cuts a cap or collar-pattern. There is a rival machine from Erie, Pa., which may be equally good in principle, but does not appear to possess equal power.

Mechanics will do well to examine a Screwing Machine, as the maker has chosen to call it—an engine for threading iron bolts and nuts of all sizes, from a half to two inches in diameter. It is difficult to cut a thread upon a bolt without crushing or damaging, to some extent, its true cylindric shape. The "spurs" and "dies," with the device for applying them, are worthy of study. The same exhibitor offers a Shaping Machine, for turning curves, beads, &c., by a fixed head and slide-rest motion, which is a very thorough and workman-like tool. A box of standard-measure gauges for bolts and drills, consisting of twenty-seven hardened steel rings, and as many steel cylinders, varying in diameter from three inches down to one-eighth of an inch, is a valuable addition to any large machine-shop. The accuracy of these tests is such that they detect a difference of magnitude less than the thinnest tissue-paper. Joseph Whitworth, Manchester, England, is the maker.

A new Portable Grist-Mill—new to us — (John T. Noye, Buffalo, N. Y.) seems very neat as well as most efficient. Its advantages are compactness, portability, freedom from heating and efficiency. It is abundantly certified to grind, with stones (French burr) three feet in diameter, eighteen bushels of wheat, or twelve barrels of water-lime, per hour. Its cost is too high to render it purchasable by farmers on a moderate scale, but the great grain-growers of the West may have it as well as millers. There are cheaper mills exhibited, which any farmer may buy; and we think the day cannot be remote when each considerable feeder of grain will grind it on his own premises.

"Holden's Patent Sheer-Cut Draft" (Moore Holden, Lawrenceburg, Ia.) is an undoubted improvement on the old method of dressing mill-stones, though there may be new devices which rival it. Millers should know.

"Storer's Corn-Kiln," to dry grain so as to secure it against the danger of heating and spoiling, is a New-Jersey invention. The cost of drying by it is said to be less than half a cent a bushel. It dries starch, paint, meal, &c., as well as grain.

How many Corn-Shellers there may be in the Palace, we cannot say: the last we noticed is that of William Reading, Flemington, N. J., certified by Hon. J. M. Clayton to shell one thousand bushels per day with a force of three men and four horses, and claimed by its patentee to be capable of shelling one hundred and fifty to two hundred bushels per hour. The ears are shovelled into its hopper with a scoop, or poured in from a basket, and the cobs are delivered apart from the grain. It was patented in July of last year, and one house sold two hundred and seventeen between November and April last.

Several Cotton-Gins are now on exhibition, but that of E. Carver & Co., Bridgewater, Mass., attracts most attention, being actually employed at times in ginning the great Southern staple, whereof the ginned fibre escaping from the machinery, is arrested and confined within a mammoth glass case or sentry-box of windows. The basis is of course Whitney's immortal invention, but Mr. Carver avoids the choking or clogging of the spaces between the grates and the tearing of the fibre thence resulting as well as the tendency to overheating and destruction by spontaneous combustion. There can be no doubt of the practical utility of Mr. C.'s grate and cylinder-brush,—the latter producing a strong centrifugal current ejecting the ginned cotton to any required distance and preventing that dropping upon and winding around the shaft, or collecting between the ends and ceiling of the gin, which was formerly a serious defect and a source of perpetual danger from fire.

There is one novel invention of which we may have already spoken, but which is so placed as to attract no attention commensurate with its merits. We allude to that for Veneering Uneven Surfaces by means of hydraulic pressure—which will reward the careful study of inventors. We see in it the germ and suggestion of other uses, perhaps more important than that to which it is primarily applied. In printing, modelling, literal copying from nature, art or antiquity, it may be made extensively useful.

In the small court assigned to specimens of Typography, Books, Binding, &c., may be seen some primitive results of a new invention in Graphics—an extension of Printing into the domain hitherto held by Engraving, Lithography, &c., which is destined to work a revolution in Color and Fancy Printing, if no other. Mr. Donlevy (the inventor) produces, by the use of Plastic and Stereotyping, typographic effects superior in accuracy and force to those hitherto attained through either Lithography or Wood Engraving, and at far less cost.

A machine for making *cots,* or little leathern rolls used in spinning (and of which twenty thousand per day, hitherto made by hands, are worn out in Massachusetts alone,) is one of the most ingenious contributions of Connecticut to the Fair. Those who are familiar with Whittemore's machine for cutting, bending, and setting card teeth, or the machine for making chain of brass or other wire, invented at Derby, Conn., will readily anticipate its best points. The leather is drawn into the machine in the shape of a strap or belt, is cut off at the proper length diagonally, so as to form the best edges for gumming, is then rolled or doubled over so that the two edges, being gummed in the operation, exactly meet; when they are pressed firmly together and the now perfected

cot dropped through the machine and another length drawn in, to undergo the same process. The inventor's name has escaped us, but it will not be soon forgotten.

A Weighing and Packing Machine, for packers of Tea, Coffee, Pepper, Spices, &c., &c., is exhibited by Slater & Steele, Jersey City, which seems excellent in its sphere, though that sphere is a narrow one. The material is fed from a hopper over head, is weighed in its descent from the hopper and discharged in pounds, half-pounds, or otherwise as may be required, into a funnel resting in a square box, into which a paper has already been conveyed by the machine. The box forms one link in an endless chain of boxes revolving around a platform, and moving on a few inches, receives through the tunnel a square stamp just fitted to it, and thence passes to another and another, until the fourth delivers it pressed into a solid mass and enveloped. Mr. G. D. Jones is said to be the patentee.

A Tobacco Pressing Machine is exhibited, costing eight hundred dollars or so, and said to press Tobacco from loose rolls into plugs as fast as twenty men have hitherto been able to do it. We should judge that one of these machines could press as much Tobacco in a day as all mankind ought to chew from this hour to the final conflagration of the world.

Chapter 4

The Good Earth

IF YOU were employed when the 1850s opened, you probably made your living on a farm. The census of 1850 counted 7,700,000 workers in all and of those 4,900,000 labored on the land. The census of 1860 counted 10,500,000 workers and of those 6,200,000 were engaged in farming. That meant that though American industry was beginning its exciting march, American agriculture still stood first. It remained our prime national resource.

It was fortified by a whole cluster of feelings that linger even today. We maintain a mystique about agriculture, a mystique which guarantees the farmer our respect as well as our subsidies. What if he has manure on his shoes? We feel that there is something innately good about his farm, something we cannot find on asphalt pavements or in clattering factories. Our attitude has altered little, regardless of the changes a century has seen in farming itself.

During the 1850s farming in most of the country was increasingly marked by a diversity of crops and a search for improved methods. In the South, however, it was marked by an emphasis on a very few crops, cotton above all, and the tenacious use of slave labor. New England continued to provide a good deal of the agricultural leadership, though some of its more enterprising farmers were moving to the rich lands of the Midwest where they would use the new machines Horace Greeley had described.

The median for American farming of the 1850s might be struck in a decent New England farm owned by a sensible farmer. In the North it would be halfway between the marginal Maine farm which yielded its scrabbling owner a bare existence and the outspread acres of a Western wheat farm. In the South it would be halfway between the wretched tenant farm and the opulent plantation.

The place to find the midpoint might be in the Connecticut Valley, still one of the productive farming areas, as we can see from the pages of the *Connecticut Valley Farmer*. In the autum of 1854, when most harvests were in and farmers had some time to read, this lively periodical published an extended essay called "The Economy of Agriculture." The author was a thoughtful Yankee doctor, Davis Rice. His essay shows the mystique about farming mentioned before but is salted with shrewd advice. He knows what he is talking about.

Source: Davis Rice, "The Economy of Agriculture"

Connecticut Valley Farmer, 2 (November 1854), 97; (December), 113; N.S. 1 (January 1855), 3; (February), 18; (March), 35; (April), 50.

THE ECONOMY OF AGRICULTURE

The pursuit of agriculture at the present day, is regarded and acknowledged as among the most honorable and useful of all callings. It is the grand source to which we all turn for the sustenance of the body. It is an honorable pursuit, and should therefore be carried on with boldness and energy. It is an useful and highly productive occupation and one to which the principle of economy can with great profit be applied.

Economy in agriculture is as essential as it is in the domestic affairs of the kitchen—as important as in any other affair of life.

I propose to point out some of the branches of the calling, where economy ought to be regarded and applied. In the first place, we will consider the *farm*, as it very often exists, and as it always should be. Many imagine, that in order to be thriving and prolific farmers, they must possess a great number of acres. This is a sad mistake; an entirely wrong conclusion. It is the bane of profitable farming, and the idea that a large estate, a great number of acres, is an essential to proficiency and profit is a serious error. Do not seek to own a great number of

acres, especially if the soil lacks fertility. Such an inheritance, such an estate, brings with it innumerable evils. If the soil is deep, and rich, a moderate sized farm is enough, both for pleasure and profit. On the other hand, if it be sterile, most certainly a small farm is most to be desired, for long and tedious will be the process of reclamation. I say again, a large farm brings with it many evils. It must be fenced around, and be divided by fences into lots. In the endeavor to make and keep in repair so much fence, none of it is substantial and permanent, and the consequences are your cattle are continually getting into your neighbors' lots, and your neighbors' cattle are not slow in returning the compliment, and the time that you are obliged to spend in building new fence and repairing that which is decaying and tumbling down, and causing so much perplexity, might be more profitably employed. Again, your pastures are growing over with shrubbery, ferns and thistles, and your mowing lots abound in white top and daisies. You must mow over ten acres of land, to obtain as much hay as you would from two, properly attended, and what you get is actually of a much poorer quality. The surface of the home lot is uneven and covered with rocks and knolls, for with so many acres to look after, you cannot find time to level down the rough places, nor to gather out the rocks. The truth is, nothing can be profitably or properly done, and your labor much of it is absolutely lost.

Beware of too many acres. Sixty acres of land, rightly divided and managed, are enough for a good paying farm; enough to support a family of half a dozen, and yield a profit besides. A farm of such dimensions, well tilled, and managed with care and discretion, will prove of more actual value, than one containing two hundred acres, in my humble opinion.

A moderate sized farm can be well and substantially fenced; the pastures kept clear from brush and noxious weeds, and such applications be made to them as will produce sweet and luxuriant feed. The mowland can be cleared of rocks and stumps, and the knolls and rough places, all leveled down. It can be well attended to, made to produce great crops of the right kind of grass. The hillsides will be pictures of luxuriance and beauty, and the meadows will "bud and blossom like the rose." Be careful then farmers how you own too many acres. I shall assume the right of declaring, that a large farm, a farm made up of a great number of acres, with all the consequent ills, is neither a profitable nor economical possession.

Again, do not have a superabundance of buildings, nor build unnecessary ones. It is important to have houses and barns and convenient outbuilding, but not an over plus; nor those that are not absolutely wanted. The farm-house should not be too large, nor irregularly or in-

conveniently constructed as it often is, but should be built with strict regard to comfort, utility, neatness and permanence. An uncouth air-castle, half finished, on a pretty farm, is an uncomfortable spectacle, to say nothing of its inconvenience and attendant pecuniary loss. The farm buildings should be made of good and suitable materials, due reference being paid to expense, convenience and comfort, and the adaptation of means to ends, so as to get the greatest possible benefit, in every aspect, with the smallest cost. I do not intend to particularize a great deal, but to treat all subjects that I may consider on general principles. Too much roofing is an extravagance, and savors of bad calculation. Shingles are expensive, and roofs must be often renewed, and it is an easy matter to build at first, so as to avoid all unnecessary expense from this source. Study well the application of the principle of economy in your buildings, for the cost of maintaining and enduring an overplus of badly constructed houses, barns, sheds, and outhouses, is a heavy tax upon the patience and purse of the considerate farmer.

Always have a brick or stone ash house, entirely disconnected with your other buildings, in some convenient place on the premises. You may by these means save your property from being destroyed by fire. . . .

Division of Farms—Manures—Composts—Application of Do.—The division of a farm into lots, suitable for mowing, pasturing and tillage, requires a very nice and accurate judgment, for they should be so arranged, that each in its place may be to the owner the most highly advantagous and productive. The mow lot ought to be the most accessible, level, and fertile portion of the farm, most commonly made of the lowlands, deep, and rich in soil. The highlands are usually more suitable for grazing, orcharding, and some varieties of grain. The mow lot should be even in surface, —well drained if too moist, and if too dry, and circumstances permit, irrigated; and should be kept in a highly productive condition by the frequent application of suitable manures, so that the greatest amount of profit may be realized, with the least outlay of labor and expense. The pastures should be kept entirely free from bushes, shrubbery, brakes and thistles, by going over them yearly with the scythe and ax. A few shade trees may be left for the cattle to lie under during the hot days of summer and autumn. Suitable manures and phosphate of lime, should be applied at intervals to keep the feed fresh, luxuriant and healthful. (See treatises on manures.)

By the foregoing remarks it will be seen that a very important principle in the economy of farming is, the suitable division of the farm into lots for mowing, pasturing and tillage; and the adaptation of the proper soil, to the right crop, so as to obtain the greatest profit. For suitable instructions on these points, I refer the reader to the numerous works on agriculture with which our book stores at the present day abound.

Another point to which I wish to draw the attention of agriculturists is, the economy of making and saving manures.

In the barn-yard and in the hog-yard, a great deal is lost by mismanagement and neglect. A barn-yard should not be too large, and should be rightly proportioned as to the quantity of stock. It should be so situated in connection with the mow lot, that if it be on a hill side,

all the wash may flow over the largest surface possible. If on level ground where there can be little if any flow from the yard, it should be made dishing —a little the lowest in the center, and after large and powerful rains, when the wash of the yard collects in pools, a sufficiency of muck, turf from the roadside, or chip-yard scrapings, should be thrown in to absorb it, that nothing may be lost. Barns ought to be made with cellars underneath them if possible, so that the stable manure may be housed and all its strength and virtues preserved. . . .

Grass—Grain.—Another subject, which I desire to notice, is the making and feeding out of hay, and other kinds of fodder. Herds-grass should be cut in just the proper time, which I consider to be when the blossoms are about half off. If cut sooner, a part of the nutricious properties will not have formed, and if later, they will have become dried out in part and lost. It should be well dried before being carried into the barn. If put in too green, or if allowed heat in the haycock, it receives a great injury, and is depreciated in value. Fermentation takes place, it becomes mouldy and musty, and its nutritive properties are in part destroyed. There is no method of treating a green load of hay, so as to make it come out as valuable, as if well and properly dried. Putting on salt, and mixing in with it, when put into the mow, a quantity of dry hay, may in part prevent the evil, but it will not entirely cure it. The best, and only proper way is, to make hay well, before putting it into the barn. Hay, if not too green, should be put into small cocks at night, for the dew injures it very materially. Clover ought to be cut just as the blossoms begin to get brown. If left until too ripe, there is a great loss by the falling off of the heads. It does not require quite so much drying as other grasses, being coarser and lying up looser on the mow. I do not consider it a very economical crop to raise, where herds-grass can be grown equally as well. Horses and sheep will eat a part of it, but it is very apt to make horses cough,—a fact which is worthy of notice. The second crop or rowen, on most lands is short, only partially matured, and being cut late in the season, is very difficult to cure. It makes very good fodder for cows and young stock, if cured without mould. If carried into the barn too green, on account of an impossibility of drying it, mix it with well cured meadow hay,—a layer of the rowen, and a layer of the meadow hay alternately. In this way both varieties will be improved, and if shaken together when fed out, will be nearly if not entirely eaten with a relish. Hay and all other kinds of fodder ought to be fed out to animals with great discretion, at such times and in such a manner as to prevent waste, and so as to get the greatest benefit from it. The coarser kinds of fodder should be used in the coldest weather, when animals have the keenest appetites. They will eat greedily on very cold days, that which they will not touch on very warm days. Oat straw, corn stalks and husks, meadow hay, &c., should be thrown to animals in severe weather, and the better varieties on warm days, and during the part of spring when cattle invariably are particular about their food. Do not feed too much at a time, but feed often, and in this way nothing will be wasted by getting under foot, and by being trod upon, but all will be consumed.

Refuse matter that accumulates in the manger may be used for bedding. In this way it will get incorporated with the manure, and become useful. It should not be thrown in masses about the yard for the wind to blow away, and where it can do no good, but should be put under the cattle's feet where it will become attenuated and incorporated with substances that will make it valuable. Cattle should usually be kept in the yard constantly, and not suffered to run about in the highway, and lots around the barn. They receive no benefit if allowed to do so, and a great part of the manure is lost. Horses should be fed on herdsgrass, it being by far the most proper and natural food of the hay kind for that animal. Clover, although they will eat it readily, is almost certain to produce a cough,

If kept partially on grass, oats, or a provender composed of corn on the cob, and oats ground together, is the safest, or one of the best mixtures to feed. If clear corn meal is used, it should be mixed always, with a quantity of hay cut fine, with a straw-cutter. Broom-seed is a miserably poor grain for a horse, whether fed alone, or mixed with any other substance, as it often produces disease of the kidneys, and destroys life. It is a very bad article, and ought not to be fed to horses when other grains can be procured. The harvest time is a period when the farmer should regard strictly the principle of economy in all that he does. Grains should be cut before too ripe, and dry, lest much be lost in the process of cutting, binding, stacking and carting. It should not be stacked, or put into the mow too green, or after having been moistened by the rain, lest the kernel swell and grow, and the quality of the grain become greatly injured thereby. As soon as practicable, it should be beaten out and stored away.

Harvesting.—The Orchard.—The Garden.—A great deal is lost, in not threshing out grain in season, by the depredations of rats and mice, and the quality of what remains is by no means improved on account of the additions made by those noxious animals. Potatoes should not be dug until thoroughly ripened, for an unripe potato is a miserable thing. They should be dug in fair dry weather, and suffered to lie in the sun long enough to prevent the adhesion of earth. If put into the cellar damp and clogged with moist earth, they will be quite certain to rot. It is good economy to sort potatoes at the time of digging, for it cannot well be done after having been stored away in the cellar. The small and misshapen ones will answer for feeding out, and the best varieties and lots will not only be rendered more saleable, but will be in a condition ready for use, either to sell, eat, or plant.

I now approach a subject which I consider of vital importance and·most decidedly an economical possession, viz., the apple orchard. No family thinks of getting along without apples. They enter into many culinary dishes of the pantry, and are in constant demand as a pleasant, palatable and healthful fruit. It costs no small sum to purchase them for a family, for a single year. I have tried the experiment and know that the apple bill is no small affair. If you have no orchard on your premises, spare no time in setting out one, at your earliest opportunity. If you are young, or middle-aged, you may live in all human probability to enjoy the fruits of your labor. If you are aged, your farm will be improved in value and appearance, and your children will have the inheritance, the boon of your excellent forethought. If you have an orchard already, bestow labor upon it and it will reward you abundantly for your care. Keep it properly trimmed and

clear of dead and decaying and superfluous branches, and the moss from collecting on the trunks of aged trees. It is a bad and destructive practice to plow among apple trees, for by so doing the roots are bruised and broken and the tree deprived of its organs of life, and growth. Old trees that bear good varieties of apples, should be carefully attended to, being kept well pruned and treated with an application of wood ashes (after removing the turf for two or three feet), to be applied about the trunk. The turf should be replaced with the grassy side down over the ashes. Old trees cared for in this manner will renew their age, and in some instances quadruple their usual quantity of fruit, which, at the same time, will be greatly improved in quality and flavor. In harvesting apples, they should never be shaken off from the trees, but plucked off with the hands, and placed carefully into baskets. Shaking them from the tree bruises them, and causes them to decay early in the season. Great care should be taken in transferring from one receptacle to another, lest they get injured by bruising. Winter fruit should not be put into the cellar so long as it can be kept out without freezing. If put in early they will sweat, heat, and decay. They may be put into barrels or boxes, and suffered to stand in an open, cool, airy, out-house, until it is time to carry them into the cellar. I respectfully ask the attention of lovers of fruit, to the above suggestions.

Again. Every person should cultivate a garden. It should be ample and well attended to. I lay it down as an axiom, that a garden properly managed, will produce more towards the maintenance, luxury, and comfort of a family, with the same amount of labor and expense, than almost any other thing I can name.

Early potatoes, green peas, lettuce, beans, cucumbers, melons, sweet corn, beets, onions, turnips, squashes, &c., &c., are no mean return for the pleasant and healthful exercise and labor bestowed in raising them. I am aware that some farmers have no taste for gardening, and seldom if ever raise many vegetables, choosing to purchase them or go without. This is bad economy, or rather just no economy at all, as you please. A garden can be made and attended upon, at such leisure times as would be devoted to nothing else, and the whole be made a matter of pleasure and recreation. A garden well laid out and teeming with luxurious vegetation, is a pleasant sight to behold, and as I view the matter a very pleasant thing to possess. Pleasant to look upon, pleasant to cultivate, an ornament to the premises, abounding in wealth to the possessor and a fortunate and economical source of delicious and luxurious dainties and substantials for the table.

If you do not understand gardening, begin to learn it now; it is never too late. If you have no garden, make one by all means, and you will never regret it; and you will soon learn the great economy of such a desirable, ornamental, and fruitful possession.

Swine and Poultry.—A few remarks on the most economical method of selecting and keeping Swine, may not be unprofitable or out of place.

First, be sure to get animals of a good breed, those that are well proportioned, and will fatten easily. The old fashioned, long nosed, long eared, bony, lank variety, are poor property. They will eat all and everything put before them, and squeal for more, but will never get fat. Swine should have large airy and ample pens in summer, and a warm place to nest and sleep in the winter. Your swine will not fatten if suffered to lie in the mud exposed to snow, sleet, rain and foul weather. A hog has nerves and sensations, as well as other animals, and thrives as much better by kind attention and care. They should not be over-fed. But in his animal organization, he is as susceptible to disease as any other creature, and should be as considerately treated. They are often made sick by being fed too much at a time, especially with corn in a green state, and with corn meal. All kinds of grain should be ground before being given as food. A mixture of corn, oat, and barley meal, is far better than either alone, for this animal, and more safe to feed out. Throw into your pen a pan full of charcoal and ashes occasionally. The alkali of the ashes, and the antiseptic and antacid properties of the coal, will do your swine good, and give them an appetite. Keep your hog-yard well supplied with turf, and rotten leaves from the forest, weeds and muck. It gives the animal a good chance for exercise, and affords a large quantity of excellent manure. If your hogs get sick by over-eating, give them a quantity of Epsom salts for physic. It acts promptly and is much better than sulphur. Dissolve them in a quantity of milk and they will partake of it readily. It is not economy to keep very fat hogs, a great while after very cold weather sets in, for all farmers are aware, that they will not make much headway after that time. But I will leave this part of my subject. I may not have advanced many original ideas, but it is not a bad plan to revive and bring to mind *old ones* occasionally, especially if they are good, and worthy of notice.

Is it economical to keep poultry? Farmers will answer this question very differently, and still they may all answer it rightly. It depends altogether upon circumstances. If you do not take proper care of them, but let them run into your fields and gardens, and into your grainloft and granary, scratching, trampling down, and devouring as they go, then there is no economy about it, but on the other hand destruction, and loss. It would be far better not to have any fowls.

On the other hand, keep a few fowls, —look after them,—shut them up during the spring months, keep them away from your grain-loft, and corn-barn, and out of your garden by a proper fence, or some other way, and it will be economy to keep them.

One more idea, and I will close this humble exposition of economy applied to matters of husbandry, hoping that the effort may induce others to bring out the subject in a clearer light. It is highly economical to possess an adequate agricultural library, not that scientific farming as laid down in the books, is to be entirely depended upon. By no means. Practical and scientific farming, are twin sisters. They go hand in hand, and ought not to be separated. You have acquired a great deal by experience. It is the *best* schoolmaster, but not the only one. There is not one acre of land under heaven, but what will produce more, under the cultivation of a practical hand, guided, by a scientific head. I lay this down as another axiom, and it will stand the severest test of criticism. Again, works on agriculture serve to divert the mind, and furnish material for reflection while the farmer is at work. It is pleasant to reflect how, and why a thing exists; how, and why this piece of land will produce one kind of crop, in greater abundance than another; how, and why this compost manure, is more desirable for this, that, or the other kind of grain. Agricultural works will explain all these queries, and unravel the whole mystery, affording a great variety and amount, of pleasing and profitable instruction. Physicians sometimes attempt to practice medicine, taught only in the school of experience. They may be very good practitioners, but would you not prefer one, if you were sick, that possessed a thorough knowledge of the *science*, combined with *experience?* Pettifoggers sometimes attempt to plead in our courts, but if you were engaged in a suit at law, that depended upon some nice legal interpretation, whether or not you were successful, would you not prefer for council, a wise and learned man? Then why, if you have a piece of land that will not produce from a lack of some important element, that may be supplied,—why not consider the matter in the broad light of science, and be in part guided by it, instead of relying entirely upon chance and the uncertain teachings of experience. I close by adding, procure an adequate supply of standard agricultural books, for your library,—read them on rainy days and long winter evenings, and they will prove a rich source of amusement, relaxation, and profitable instruction.

Chapter 5

The Clerk in the Counting-House

THE DAYS of barter were drawing to a close. In its place, buying and selling grew steadily as a vital part of American economic life. More merchants and clerks than ever were making a living in the country's economy. The census of 1850 showed 420,000 of them; by the end of the decade the number had risen to 780,000. An exceptional insight into their occupation can be gained from a course of lectures given by a Philadelphia minister, H. A. Boardman, and published in book form as *The Bible in the Counting-House*. It evidently struck a chord, for the first edition was printed early in 1853 and by the next year the fifth edition had appeared. The book dealt chiefly with the duties and responsibilities of those engaged in commerce. Boardman's approach was based on two things: the Bible and the Puritan tradition of business as godly and business prosperity as a divine blessing. In his seventh lecture, "Principals and Clerks," reprinted in part below, he describes the do's and don't's involved in being a good clerk.

Like any proper Philadelphian, Boardman quotes Benjamin Franklin and lauds the secular virtues he embodied. But he adds a shiny Christian gloss to them. And for the sake of contrast he paints for us not only the good clerk but the bad one. The good clerk is naturally very, very good, while the bad one is apt to be dissipated, lazy, gossipy. "He may alienate customers by the gruffness of his manner or his offensive volubility." He may be a spendthrift itching to "rent a suite of richly-furnished rooms, keep up an elegant wardrobe, decorate his person with costly jewelry, and indulge in expensive amusements." He may read "trashy novels." He may be a speculator. Above all, he may tap the till, stealing from his employer to satisfy himself. There is no doubt about it: one can see that the moral perils of trade are far greater than those of farming.

Source: H. A. Boardman, *The Bible in the Counting-House* (Philadelphia, 1853), pp. 233–41.

PRINCIPALS AND CLERKS

Every clerk should identify himself with the house he is engaged in. This is one of the most obvious principles appertaining to this relation. From the moment you enter the service of a firm, their interest must be yours. You sustain a relation to them, which you hold to no other house. While you are not to stoop to any immorality for the purpose of serving them, you are to guard their property and their reputation, as though they were your own; you are to avoid whatever may injure them, and do all in your power to contribute to their prosperity. If it is incumbent upon your principals to take a friendly interest in you, the correlative obligation rests upon you to promote, as you may be able, both their business and their personal comfort. It is not always the fault of the principals, that the tie which binds the tenantry of a commercial establishment together is of a mere mercenary character: the most liberal policy on their part may be thwarted by a set of perverse or selfish clerks.

It is only a modification of the principle just affirmed, to insist upon *the strictest fidelity in discharging all the duties proper to the position you occupy.* It cannot be necessary to repeat here the familiar adage, that "whatever is worth doing at all, should be done well." But let every clerk remember, that there is no department of the work entrusted to him, which is not embraced in the obligation, to serve his employers to the very best of his ability. There are many ways in which he may violate this rule, short of going to the safe and thrusting his hand into the money-drawer. He may fail in punctuality. He may so exhaust his energies with an evening's dissipation, as to be unfitted for the next day's duties. He may perform his work in a listless, drowsy manner, not only unjust to the house, but provoking to his fellow-clerks, since their toil will have to bear the brunt of his laziness. He may see goods suffering from exposure or other causes, without protecting them. He may alienate customers by the gruffness of his manner or his offensive volubility. He may disappoint others by failing to have their goods or their bills ready at the stipulated time. He may arrogate an unauthorized responsibility in the opening of new accounts, and thus involve the firm in vexatious and mortifying negotiations. He may neglect to forward goods as per agreement, without writing to apprize the owner of the reason. He may turn town-crier, and publish far and near those private matters concerning the business of the house, which every sentiment of honour should restrain him from breathing outside the ware-rooms. He may recommend for a clerkship some inefficient or unreliable crony, who wants a place, but does not deserve one.—These, and very many other things like these, which a clerk may do, are incompatible with fidelity, and in derogation of his employers' just claims upon him.

The essential quality for a young man

in this position, is that *sound moral principle* which is at once the best monitor to duty and the surest guarantee of confidence. I can picture to myself the daily routine of two clerks, one of whom is swayed by principle, and the other by policy. The latter is of that class the apostle had in view when he said—"not with eye-service, as men-pleasers." His performances are all summed up in the phrase, "eye-service." When his employers are present, he is extremely diligent. Behind their backs, he is a model of sloth and unfaithfulness. So it can be concealed from them, he cares not how late he comes to his work, how little of it he does, nor how much he slights it. Whatever time he bestows upon labour, is so much lost: he finds his *life* in lounging and trifling, in idle gossip and trashy novels.—His fellow is of a widely different type. The power which controls his movements, is not in the eye of his master, but in his own breast. It matters not with him, who is present, or who absent. His work is to be done, irrespective of all outward circumstances. The interpretation he puts upon his articles of agreement, makes him do for his employers as he would do for himself. Always at his post, he pursues his avocation with an unfaltering step. Impelled to diligence and constancy, not by the fear of a discharge, but by the consciousness of right, he enjoys a serenity of mind to which his companion is a stranger, and is as steadily advancing towards honour and usefulness, as the other is sinking into disgrace and contempt.—It cannot be too often reiterated in the ears of our young men, that *this* is the true path to success. "Wait not for great occasions before you begin to act; wherever your lot may be cast, the sphere of duty lies immediately around you. Fill it up with

an example of the kindness that attracts, the sincerity that can be seen through like crystal, the diligence that anticipates duty, the trustworthiness that defies suspicion, the openheartedness that opens other hearts, the manly character that commands esteem, the Christian character that arms its possessors with a power more than earthly. Defer not to a distant time the intention to begin." "One today is worth two to-morrows." Only treat duty as a sacred thing, and you will find that "in keeping *His* commandments there is great reward."

Among the minor causes of failure with young men in this relation, the subject of *tempers* and *manners* deserves a prominence which cannot be conceded to it in these brief discussions. That a clerkship is frequently a severe school of discipline for the temper, cannot be denied. But this is a part of the necessary training of a merchant. Let it encourage those who are subjected to the caprices of unreasonable employers, who are found fault with when they are guiltless of all wrong, scolded when they have done the best they could, and denied indulgences which others enjoy, that the self-control they are acquiring under this rough tutelage, may be of more value to them hereafter than all the smiles their masters could lavish upon them. And beware of cherishing tempers which might give just occasion for reproof. It is not enough that you be honest and industrious and intelligent. A clerk may be all this, and yet neutralize the impression of his good qualities by a levity which makes him seem a mere trifler. Or he may repel people by his sulkiness or his irritability. He may be foolishly sensitive to affronts. He may be a slave to envy and jealousy. He may be utterly deficient in that good feeling which would make him willing to lend a helping hand to his fellows in time of need. He may be too proud for his station, and deem it an indignity to perform offices which better and wiser men than himself have often performed without scruple. "A man's pride shall bring him low, but honour shall uphold the humble in spirit." Let me quote on this point, a paragraph from a very pleasant letter of Dr. Franklin's (written in his seventy-ninth year) to Dr. Mather of Boston: —

It is now more than sixty years since I left Boston; but I remember well both your father and grandfather, having heard them both in the pulpit, and seen them in their houses. The last time I saw your father was in the beginning of 1724. He received me into his Library, and on my taking leave, showed me a shorter way out of the house through a narrow passage, which was crossed by a beam over-head. We were still talking as I withdrew, he accompanying me behind, and I turning partly toward him, when he said hastily, "Stoop. Stoop." I did not understand him till I felt my head hit against the beam. He was a man that never missed any occasion of giving instruction; and upon this he said to me, "You are young, and have the world before you: stoop *as you go through it, and you will miss many hard thumps.*" The advice thus beat into my head, has frequently been of use to me, and I often think of it when I see pride mortified, and misfortunes brought upon people by their carrying their heads too high.

People of every avocation may profit by this lesson; and the clerk who is disposed to take it voluntarily, will fare better than he who waits to have it "beaten into his head" by some mortifying occurrence or positive loss. Rely upon it, if you do not know how to "stoop," you have a rugged path before you—very much such a path as a platoon of soldiers would find who should under-

take to march with military precision, carriage erect, eyes straight forward, and muskets a-shoulder, through a tangled and swampy forest. Sooner or later, you will have to "stoop"; and you will do it with more grace and more comfort if you practise the art now, than if you let your muscles acquire such a rigidity that when the inflexion becomes unavoidable, the performance will be certain to savour of the awkwardness of a rustic on his first introduction at court.

One of the common sources of danger and disaster with clerks, is, *extravagance in their mode of living.* The usual scale of mercantile salaries in our cities, is adjusted to the most economical habits. It is, therefore, a perilous thing for those who depend upon these salaries to become smitten with a passion for display. How is a young man to rent a suite of richly-furnished rooms, keep up an elegant wardrobe, decorate his person with costly jewelry, and indulge in expensive amusements, on a stipend of a few hundred dollars? It is natural that the employers of a young man who is seen to be attempting this, should have their eyes upon him. And if the experiment goes on, they will be curious to learn whence he derives his income. It may come from legitimate quarters: he may have collateral resources of which they are ignorant. Or it may come from their warehouse. The love of dress and company have mastered his integrity, and put him upon a system of peculation. Possibly, he has become a *speculator.* If he occupies a "confidential" position, and has free access to the finances of the firm, some intriguing operator may have enticed him into a course of stock-gambling. Once committed to this nefarious business, the checks of the house are dealt out freely to his partner in iniquity, and for a while, he has no lack of revenues to sustain his luxurious habits. Ordinarily, however, "the triumphing of the wicked is short": his dishonesties are brought to light, and he is either driven out of society in shame, or consigned to a penitentiary. If any are disposed to argue that in cases of this sort, unhappily become so common, the burden of guilt lies upon the receiver of the funds abstracted, I shall not quarrel with them. The man who will encourage a clerk in such a career, who will stimulate him to obtain by robbery the moneys requisite to carry on one speculation after another, is a hundred-fold more deserving of the State-prison than the wretch who breaks open your store and carries off your goods. The defects inseparable from human jurisprudence, make it difficult to convict this class of offenders; and so it happens that they are apt to go "unwhipt of justice."

But there can be no difference of opinion among honest men as to their moral turpitude. Still, this does not excuse the allies and instruments of their villainy. The clerk who allows himself to be drawn into a plot of this kind, richly deserves the reprehension which his treachery and fraud are sure to bring down upon him:—and he deserves it all the more, because his own extravagances are usually the remote spring of his derelictions.

Chapter 6

Advice to a Young Lawyer

IN antebellum America the professions occupied a highly respected place. The ministry, with its own special sanction, rated first in public esteem but the legal profession came a strong second. We recall Tocqueville observing in *Democracy in America* that though we had no hereditary aristocracy we had a professional one. It was made up of lawyers, with the judges near the top and the Supreme Court justices above them all. The law was then as now a highroad to public office. It had manifest claims to public esteem, not the least being that the law was a learned profession in a day when learning was rare. The path to eminence in law is described for us by Mrs. L. C. Tuthill. The author of several manuals on how to succeed (under the general title of *Success in Life*), she offered *Success in Life: the Lawyer* to the public in 1850. Her method was anecdotal. Selecting the most prominent lawyers of the past, she drew on their careers for stories and illustrations of her points. For especially cogent counsel she went back to William Wirt and headed one chapter, the chapter reprinted here, "William Wirt's Advice to a Young Lawyer."

Wirt's "young lawyer" was an actual person, as we can see when Wirt warns him against his undue hilarity and satirical wit. But Wirt was also speaking to young lawyers in general, advising them both about the law as a trade and as a mode of life. Like the Reverend Mr. Boardman when he was counseling his clerks, Wirt upholds the Puritan ethic. He believes in long, hard hours. "Live in your office" is his advice. He believes in honesty and modesty. But he also believes in the law as an occupation for gentlemen, so he sometimes sounds much more like Lord Chesterfield than like Mr. Boardman. The opening quotation from Wirt is pure Chesterfield: "Endeavor to cultivate that superior grace of manners which distinguishes the gentleman from the crowd around him. In your conversation avoid a rapid and indistinct utterance, and speak deliberately and articulately."

47

It is worth remembering that the 1850s was a transitional decade: many of the machines were new but some of the manners were old. Though this advice of Wirt's sounded a bit elaborate by the 1850s, it is significant that Mrs. Tuthill chose to quote it. The lawyers were still, in the main, gentry while the clerks were commoners. Wirt might advise his lawyers to file their papers neatly but these were their own papers.

Source: Mrs. L. C. Tuthill, *Success in Life: the Lawyer*
(New York, 1850), pp. 113–19.

WILLIAM WIRT'S ADVICE TO A YOUNG LAWYER

In 1806, Mr. Wirt removed to Richmond. The following excellent advice forms a part of a letter written about this period to a young lawyer, in whom Mr. Wirt felt great interest.

"Endeavor to cultivate that superior grace of manners which distinguishes the gentleman from the crowd around him. In your conversation avoid a rapid and indistinct utterance, and speak deliberately and articulately.

"Blend with the natural hilarity of your temper, that dignity of sentiment and demeanor, which alone can prevent the wit and humorist from sinking into a trifler, and can give him an effective attitude in society.

"Get a habit, a passion, for reading—not flying from book to book with the squeamish caprice of a literary epicure, —but read systematically, closely, and thoughtfully, analyzing every subject as you go along, and laying it up safely and carefully in your memory.

"Determine with yourself that no application shall be wanting to lift you to the heights of public notice; and if you find your spirits beginning to flag, think of being buried all your life in obscurity, confounded with the gross and ignorant herd around you. But there are yet more animating and more noble motives for this emulation: the power of doing more extensive good—the pure delight of hearing one's self blessed for benevolent and virtuous actions, and as a still more unequivocal and rapturous proof of gratitude, 'reading that blessing in a nation's eyes'; add to this, the communicating the beneficial effects of this fame to our friends and relations; the having it in our power to requite past favors, and to take humble and indigent genius by the hand, and lead it forward to the notice of the world. These are a few, and but a few, of the good effects of improving one's talents to the highest point, by careful and constant study, and aspiring to distinction."

On reviewing his past life, at this period, Mr. Wirt seems to have been forcibly struck with the warning and encouragement which it presented to young men.

"I have, indeed," says he, "great cause of gratitude to Heaven. * * * In reviewing the short course of my life, I can see where I made plunges from which nothing less than a Divine hand could ever have raised me; but I have been raised, and I trust that my feet are now upon a rock. Yet, can I never cease to deplore the years of my youth, that I have murdered in idleness and folly. What a spur should this reflection be to young men!"

The eloquent author of the Life of William Wirt says: "We have remarked of Wirt, that his life is peculiarly fraught with materials for the edification of youth. Its difficulties and impediments, its temptations and trials, its triumphs over many obstacles, its rewards, both in the self-approving judgment of his own heart, and in the success won by patient labor and well-directed study; and the final consummation of his hopes, in an old age not less adorned by the applause of good men, than by the serene and cheerful temper inspired by a devout Christian faith; all these present a type of human progress worthy of the imitation of the young and the gifted."

But this "progress" is not to be made without constant effort. Wirt in his figurative style thus describes it:

"You will find it pretty much of an Alp-climbing business. The points of the rocks to which you cling will often break in your hands, and give you many a fall and many a bruise; but instead of despairing at the first fall, or the twentieth, remember the prospect from the summit and the rich prizes that await you. Up with a laugh, catch a better hold next time, and try it again.

"The law is to many, at first, and at last, too, a dry and revolting study. It is hard and laborious; it is a dark and intricate labyrinth, through which they grope in constant uncertainty and perplexity—the most painful of all states of mind. But you cannot imagine that this was the case with Lord Mansfield or with Blackstone, who saw through the whole

fabric in full daylight in all its proportions and lustre."

The pleasure with which Wirt entered into a trial of legal strength, after he had "toiled and moiled" in his profession for many years, is thus expressed:

"I have some expectation of going to Washington in February to plead a cause. I shall be opposed to the Attorney-General, and perhaps to Pinckney. 'The blood more stirs to wake the lion than to hunt the hare.' I should like to meet them."

To the friend to whom he has so frequently addressed stimulating arguments, Mr. Wirt again writes:

"You must read, sir; you must read and meditate like a Conestoga horse—no disparagement to the horse by the simile. You must read like Jefferson, and speak like Henry. If you ask me how you are to do this, I cannot tell you, but you are nevertheless to do it.

"By the way, there is one thing I had like to have forgotten. One of the most dignified traits in the character of [Patrick] Henry, is the noble decorum with which he debated, and the uniform and marked respect with which he treated his adversaries. I am a little afraid of you in this particular, for you are a wit and a satirist. Take care of this propensity. It will make you enemies, pull a bee-hive on your head, and cover your forensic path with stings and venom. Let it be universally agreed that you are the most polite, gentlemanly debater at the bar. That, alone, will give you a distinction, and a noble one too; besides, it is a striking index and proper concomitant of first-rate talents.

"For two or three years you must read, delve, meditate, study, and make the whole mine of the law your own.

"Let me use the privilege of my age

and experience to give you a few hints, which, now that you are beginning the practice, you may find not useless.

"1] Adopt a system of life, as to business and exercise; and never deviate from it, except so far as you may be occasionally forced from it by imperious and uncontrollable circumstances.

"2] Live in your office; that is, be always in it except at the hours of eating and exercise.

"3] Answer all letters as soon as they are received; you know not how many heart-aches it may save you. Then fold neatly, and file away neatly, alphabetically, and by the year, all the letters so received. Let your letters of business be short, and keep copies of them.

"4] Put every law paper in its place as soon as received, and let no scrap of paper be seen lying for a moment on your writing-chair or tables.

"5] Keep regular accounts of every cent of income and expenditure, and file your receipts neatly, alphabetically, and by the month, or, at least, by the year.

"6] Be patient with your foolish clients, and hear all their tedious circumlocution and repetition with calm and kind attention; cross-examine and sift them until you know all the strength and weakness of their cause, and take notes of it at once, whenever you can do so.

"7] File your bills in Chancery at the moment of ordering the suit, and while your client is still with you to correct your statement of his case; also, prepare every declaration the moment the suit is ordered, and have it ready to file.

"8] Cultivate a simple style of speaking, so as to be able to inject the strongest thought into the weakest capacity. You will never be a good jury lawyer without this faculty.

"9] Never attempt to be grand and magnificent before common tribunals,— and the most you will address are common.

"10] Keep your Latin and Greek, and science, to yourself, and to the very small circle which they may suit. The mean, envious world will never forgive you your knowledge, if you make it too public. It will require the most unceasing urbanity and habitual gentleness of manners, almost to humility, to make your superior attainments tolerable to your associates.

"11] Enter with warmth and kindness into the interesting concerns of others— not with the consciousness of a superior, but with the tenderness and simplicity of an equal.

"12] Be never flurried in speaking, but learn to assume the exterior of composure and collectedness, whatever riot and confusion may be within; speak slowly, firmly, distinctly, and make your periods by proper pauses, and a steady, significant look.

"You talk of complimenting your adversaries. Take care of your manner of doing this. Let it be humble and sincere, and not as if you thought it was in your power to give them importance by your fiat. These maxims are all sound; practice them, and I will warrant your SUCCESS."

Chapter 7

The Economic Currents

ECONOMIC America altered more swiftly during the 1850s than in any decade before. It changed in two ways. First of all, there was more of nearly everything, from cotton lint to Tuscan houses. There was almost twice as much cotton lint, for example, produced in 1860 as there had been in 1850. Secondly, there were more kinds of things, for instance, more kinds of new machines. The same held in human terms: there were many more people than before and they were of many different nations, classes, and conditions. Most were born in America but hundreds of thousands were immigrants who entered during the decade.

During much of this decade the dreams of success that Horatio Alger would later put into print turned into reality. The economy expanded to a degree that carried millions of Americans at least a step or two up the ladder. The nation's attitude was one of optimism, and understandably so. After all there had not been a real business depression—or a panic, to use the term of those days—since 1837. There finally was one in 1857 but the Panic of 1857 was actually a spasm, relatively short and not very sharp. We see it reflected in the consumer price index. With the year 1860 as 100, the index figure was 92 in 1851, 105 in 1857 (the effect of the panic was just beginning to be felt), and 100 in 1859.

Throughout the 1850s the mills and factories continued to pour out their products. Their share in the nation's commodity output grew all the time. In 1839 it had been less than one fifth. In 1859 it was one third. The pictures of factories with chimneys puffing and long lines of workers tending machines are no exaggeration. Nevertheless, it is probably worth repeating that agriculture still dominated America's economic life. And one section, the South, had almost nothing but agriculture.

If talk about economic trends has a forbidding sound, it is good to remember that the trends translated into people: people who worked on the farm or in the factory, people white and black, young and old, poor and rich. Some of them are shown in the pictorial documents that follow.

Source: Lawrence, Mass. Drawn by J. B. Bachelder and lithographed by Endicott & Company, 1856.
The Harry T. Peters "America on Stone" Lithography Collection,
The Smithsonian Institution

The foreground is farmlike. A gardener bends at his work while a little boy watches. A man reaches up into the branches of a low tree, perhaps for a piece of fruit. The place is actually a park, a pleasant one. Across the road from it stand houses and outbuildings but still with plenty of trees and grass.

However, the panorama above it is the point of the picture. For it shows a bustling, industrial city which reaches from one end of the lithograph to the other. We see the Merrimack River which furnishes the waterpower and provides the mills and factories with their reason for being there. The lithograph itself lists some of the biggest plants as well as showing them: the Lawrence Machine Shop, the Duck Mill, the Pemberton Corporation, and the Atlantic Corporation among them. The most imposing thing to the observer is the sheer size of the major buildings. These immense factories housed thousands of workers, male and female, and were in the process of altering the economy of the nation.

It was an economy that was shifting from the country to the town, and the artist has symbolized the fact in his lithograph. On the conscious level Bachelder dedicates the lithograph, with a bow, to the citizens of Lawrence. But unconsciously perhaps he makes the city a mere ribbon across his picture. Fully half of the picture shows the delights of rusticity if not of farm life—or, in present-day terms, the delights of suburbia: green lawns, trees, space, openness, leisure, affluence. Most of the other half of the picture is sky, nothing but sky. By its vastness it dwarfs the industrial town and flattens it.

We can guess that Bachelder betrays the ambivalence which marked America of the 1850s. He admires industrialism, is impressed by it, and pays tribute to it. But he cannot escape a love for other than industrial values; he still feels that God made the country and man made the town.

Source: Cover for "Farewell Old Cottage" Lithographed by Sarony & Major and issued by Firth, Pond & Co., 1851.
Reproduced from the Collections of the Library of Congress

There is no doubt where Stephen Foster's heart was. It was in the country rather than in the town. He swelled with sentiment at the thought of a farm or meadow. Here in one of his enormously popular ballads he laments the leaving

LAWRENCE, MASS.

of the young for the city. The young man's heart may be breaking but he ambles away from home anyhow. In fact the lyrics suggest that he has already left it and is merely returning for a visit.

Though it would be easy to push Foster's picture too far, it can still stand as a symbol. As we have noted the population of the 1850s was growing urbanized. Inevitably it was the young who were leaving. And not only young men but young women. Especially in New England the mill towns were attracting the farm girls. In addition, the immigrants of all ages were settling in greater numbers in the cities than in the country.

The cover for "Farewell Old Cottage" is in the usual mode of kitchen-calendar art. Everything is gentle, mellow. The background has been hazed; the contrast of light and shade is soft. The components of the picture are standard Romantic: placid water, leafy trees, a blasted trunk, a cottage, a dog, a horse. A mood of melancholy permeates the scene. The only possible exception may be fanciful: the dog seems to look with a touch of indignation at his departing master. The composition is triangular in its form, basically rather simple but given some interest by the zigzag laterals in the lower lefthand corner. The general movement in the picture is to the right, with the dog's head repeating the direction of the horse's. The artist has added to the pace of the picture by having the country road lead slightly downhill toward the right margin.

Source: W. S. & C. H. Thomson's Skirt Manufactory.
Harper's Weekly, February 19, 1859

As America waxed affluent, more of its clothing was manufactured instead of being made at home. A mass market gradually emerged, first for men's attire and then—in spite of the continuing busyness of the housewife's needle—for women's as well. And though the dressmaker came regularly to the middle-class home, she was beginning to feel the competition of the factory too. Specialization was setting in: here we have a business devoted solely to skirts. The illustration from *Harper's Weekly* has a number of things to show us.

It shows us the spread of urban industrialism, for one. The Thomson factory, located in New York, has drawn hundreds of hands, and not simply from the city itself. We see row after row of workers and they are all young women. Even the supervisors are women, though we cannot be quite sure about the figure on the platform at the far end of the big room. The girls in some of the rows bind the hoops with tape. Others sew the cloth at the sewing machines. The room is large, lighted by windows and skylight. It does not seem a bad place to work—it is no ghetto loft—though we may wonder when the standing girls can sit down.

The Puritan ethic appears plainly. Work is good in itself and so is commercial prosperity. The Thomsons are benefactors of mankind. They provide jobs for those who need them. They make a product that is useful, certainly, and that at the same time forwards the delightful doctrine of conspicuous consumption. It is not a doctrine that has originated in the United States but the United States will perfect it. Here it is

COVER FOR "FAREWELL OLD COTTAGE"

exemplified by the skirts that use up twice as much cloth as they need to. Modesty and comfort would still be served even if the skirts did not billow out in all directions.

The watchword on the wall is taken from the Puritan ethic. "Strive to Excel" the sign says to the girls whenever they raise their heads to look at it. And strive to excel in industry in particular. Work longer, harder, and more carefully than the rest. The result will not only be higher profits but better girls. Though the Thomsons may not have said so, it was a staple of belief among the New England millowners that if you worked a girl till she was bone-tired she would have no energy left for sin.

Source: Cotton-Gin—Ginning Cotton.
Harper's Monthly, March 1854

Whatever the trend in the rest of the country, the South remained firmly agricultural. It was indeed the Cotton Kingdom. Spendthrift in its land, it forced its cotton plantations and tobacco farms steadily westward. By 1850 a large part of Virginia, for instance, east of the Blue Ridge mountains was made up of abandoned farm land covered with little but underbush. The demand for cotton was increasing and international. British mills and British buyers wanted it as much as the ones in New England. The invention of the cotton gin and the existence of fresh farmland to exploit allowed the South to balloon its yield. The value of the cotton lint produced in 1850 was $118,000,000. The value of the cotton lint of 1860 was $217,000,000. Profits soared for the plantation owners and the cotton factoring firms.

It paid the plantation owners to gin the cotton at home. The machinery, devised by Eli Whitney in 1793 and then gradually improved, was uncomplicated. The way it worked is shown in the present illustration. One slave is pushing the newly gathered cotton bolls down a chute while another rakes them into the hopper. Within the hopper, and concealed from our eye, a number of circular saws are set on an axle and rotate swiftly. Part of each saw protrudes through an iron grid. The raw cotton in the hopper is drawn in by the teeth of the saws. The teeth pull the cotton lint through the grid and into a chute under the floor. The cotton seed is too big to go through the grid and drops beneath the floor at the other side. By means of this process the cotton is readied for spinning.

The composition of the picture is a balanced one, with the spate of cotton as the center of interest. The artist repeats the diagonals of the chute in the diagonals of the window framed against the sky and the top of the tilted basket. The human figures are symmetrically disposed, with one slave at each corner. The dark masses are as usual at the bottom of the picture except for the dark loft which frames the slave pushing down the cotton. The modeling of the figures is routine; the whole picture is a piece of hackwork. But its appearance evidenced the national interest in cotton. And in a sense it represents both agriculture and industry, the two main ways through which America made its living.

W. S. & C. H. THOMSON'S SKIRT MANUFACTORY

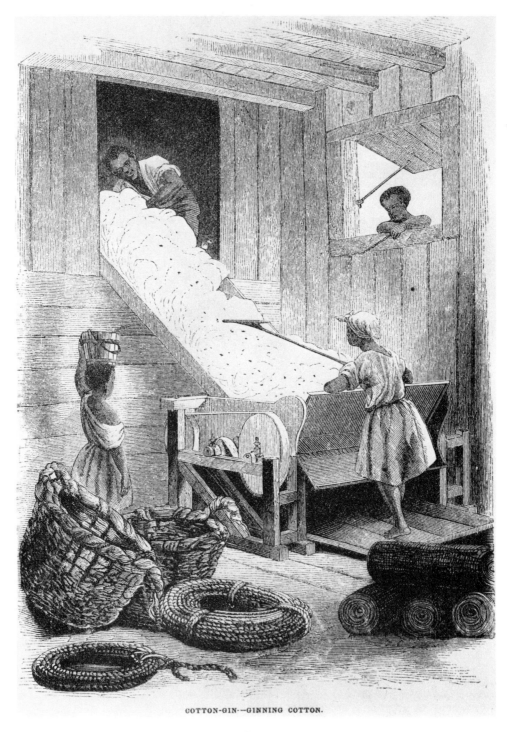

COTTON-GIN.—GINNING COTTON.

COTTON GIN—GINNING COTTON

58

III. *The American Home*

Chapter 8

The House Itself

THE physical setting for the family carries its own message. The typical American home during the 1850s was still a farmhouse, so a plan for such a house—made by someone mindful of the implications involved—has a good deal to tell us. In *Rural Architecture,* a book published in New York in 1852, Lewis F. Allen pictured, planned, and described farm homes for people of various incomes. The book as a whole is distinguished by two things: his interest in the social relationships of the family as they affect the house, and his general good taste.

The selection reprinted here gives us the specifications for a sensible machine for middle-class rural living. The house is the major part of the plan but Allen also describes the outbuildings. Taken together, they constitute a self-sufficient unit. The effect of the house and its attachments is pleasant. Thanks to shifts in style, it looks more attractive to us now than the boxy New England farmhouse of an earlier day; for Allen's house resembles a modern rambler, long, low, and informal. It even has a kind of breezeway. Allen estimates that the house will run to between $1,000 and $1,500, the outbuildings between $400 and $600—somewhat less relatively than they would now.

Allen's plan is based on a farmhouse he himself occupied, so it has been tested by experience. He realizes, for example, that the kitchen is the heart of the house, or as he puts it "the grand room." It has a big fireplace complete with hooks and trammels to support pots or kettles over the fire. The fireplace has an oven next to it. The biggest bedroom in the house opens into the kitchen. So do closets, pantries, and passageways. It does not take much imagination to see the kitchen filled with bustle and savory activity while Sunday dinner is being prepared.

The rest of the house and outbuildings complete the machine for living. Their modules include the parlor, for state occasions; a number of garret chambers, to be used either as bedrooms or storage space; a wash-room, a wood house, a stable, a piggery—and a water closet.

Source: Lewis F. Allen, *Rural Architecture*
(New York, 1852), pp. 84, 87–88, 90–94.

DESIGN II

This is the plan of a house and out-buildings based chiefly on one which we built of wood some years since on a farm of our own, and which, in its oc-cupation, has proved to be one of ex-ceeding convenience to the purposes intended. As a farm *business* house, we have not known it excelled; nor in the ease and facility of doing up the house-work within it, do we know a better. It has a subdued, quiet, unpretending look; yet will accommodate a family of a dozen workmen, besides the females engaged in the household work, with perfect convenience; or if occupied by a farmer with but his own family around him, ample room is afforded them for a most comfortable mode of life, and suf-ficient for the requirements of a farm of two, to three or four hundred acres.

This house is, in the main body, 36 × 22 feet, one and a half stories high, with a projection on the rear 34 × 16 feet, for the kitchen and its offices; and a still further addition to that, of 26 × 18 feet, for wash-room. The main body of the house is 14 feet high to the plates; the lower rooms are 9 feet high; the roof has a pitch of 35° from a horizontal line, giving partially-upright chambers in the main building, and *roof* lodging rooms in the rear. The rear, or kitchen part, is one story high, with 10 feet posts, and such pitch of roof (which last runs at right angles to the main body, and laps on to the main roof), as will carry the

peak up to the same air line. This addi-tion should retreat 6 inches from the line of the main building, on the side given in the design, and 18 inches on the rear. The rooms on this kitchen floor are 8 feet high, leaving one foot above the upper floor, under the roof, as a chamber garret, or lumber-room, as may be re-quired. Beyond this, in the rear, is the other extension spoken of, with posts 9 feet high, for a buttery, closet, or dairy, or all three combined, and a wash-room; the floor of which is on a level with the last, and the roof running in the same direction, and of the same pitch. In front of this wash-room, where not cov-ered by the wood-house, is an open porch, 8 feet wide and 10 feet long, the roof of which runs out at a less angle than the others—say 30° from a hori-zontal line. Attached to this is the wood-house, running off by way of L, at right angles, 36 × 16 feet, of same height as the wash-room.

Adjoining the wood-house, on the same front line, is a building 50 × 20 feet, with 12 feet posts, occupied as a workshop, wagon-house, stable, and store-room, with a lean-to on the last of 15 × 10 feet, for a piggery. The several rooms in this building are 8 feet high, affording a good lumber room over the workshop, and hay storage over the wagon-house and stable. Over the wagon-house is a gable, with a blind window swinging on hinges, for receiving hay, thus relieving the long, uniform line of roof, and affording ample accommodation on each side to a pigeon-house or dovecote, if required.

The style of this establishment is of plain Italian, or bracketed, and may be equally applied to stone, brick, or wood. The roofs are broad, and protect the walls by their full projection over them, 2½ feet. The small gable in the front roof of the main dwelling relieves it of its otherwise straight uniformity, and affords a high door-window opening on to the deck of the veranda, which latter should be 8 or 10 feet in width. The shallow windows, also, over the wings of the veranda give it a more cheerful expression. The lower *end* windows of this part of the house are hooded, or sheltered by a cheap roof, which gives them a snug and most comfortable appearance. The veranda may appear more ornamental than the plain character of the house requires; but any superfluous work upon it may be omitted, and the style of finish conformed to the other. The veranda roof is flatter than that of the house, but it may be made perfectly tight by closer shingling, and paint; while the deck or platform in the centre may be roofed with zinc, or tin, and a coat of sanded paint laid upon it. The front chimney is plain, yet in keeping with the general style of the house, and may be made of ordinary bricks. The two parts of the chimney, as they appear in the front rooms, are drawn together as they pass through the chamber above, and become one at the roof. The kitchen chimneys pass up through the peaks of their respective roofs, and should be in like character with the other. . . .

Interior Arrangement

The front door of this house opens into a small entry or hall, 9 × 6 feet, which is lighted by a low sash of glass over the front door. A door leads into a room on each side; and at the inner end of the hall is a recess between the two chimneys of the opposite rooms, in which may be placed a table or broad shelf to receive hats and coats. On the left is a parlor 22 × 15 feet, lighted on one side by a double window, and in front by a single plain one. The fireplace is centrally placed on one side of the room, in the middle of the house. On one side of the fireplace is a closet, three feet deep, with shelves, and another closet at the inner end of the room, near the kitchen door; or this closet may be dispensed with for the use of this parlor, and given up to enlarge the closet which is attached to the bedroom. Another door opens directly into the kitchen. This parlor is 9 feet high between joints. The sitting-room is opposite to the parlor, 19 × 15 feet, and lighted and closeted in nearly the same manner, as will be seen by referring to the floor plan.

The kitchen is the grand room of this house. It is 24 × 16 feet in area, having an ample fireplace, with its hooks and trammels, and a spacious oven by its side. It is lighted by a double window at one end, and a single window near the fireplace. At one end of this kitchen is a most comfortable and commodious family bedroom, 13 × 10 feet, with a large closet in one corner, and lighted by a window in the side. Two windows may be inserted if wanted. A passage leads by the side of the oven to a sink-room, or recess, behind the chimney, with shelves to dry dishes on, and lighted by the half of a double window, which accommodates with its other half the dairy, or closet adjoining. A door also opens from this recess into the closet and dairy, furnished with broad shelves, that part of which, next the kitchen, is used for dishes, cold meat and bread cupboards, &c.; while the part of it adjoining the window beyond, is used for milk. This room is 14 × 6 feet, besides the L running up next to the kitchen, of 6 × 4 feet. From the kitchen also opens a closet into the front part of the house for any purpose needed. This adjoins the parlor, and sitting-room, closets. In the passage to the sitting-room also opens the stair-way leading to the chambers, and beneath, at the other end of it, next the outside wall, is a flight leading down cellar. The cellar is excavated under the whole house, being 36 × 22, and 34 × 16 feet, with glass windows, one light deep by four wide, of 8 × 10 glass; and an outer door, and flight of steps outside, under either the sitting-room or kitchen windows, as may be most convenient. A door opens, also, from the kitchen, into a passage 4 feet wide and 12 feet long leading to the wash-room, 18 × 16 feet, and by an outside door, through this passage to the porch. In this passage may be a small window to give it light.

In the wash-room are two windows. A chimney at the far end accommodates a boiler or two, and a fireplace, if required. A sink stands adjoining the chimney. A flight of stairs, leading to a garret over head on one side, and to the kitchen chamber on the other, stands next the dairy, into which last a door also leads. In this wash-room may be located the cooking stove in warm weather, leaving the main kitchen for a family and eating room. A door also leads from the wash-room into the wood-house.

The wood-house stands lower than the floor of the wash-room, from which it falls, by steps. This is large, because a plentiful store of wood is needed for a dwelling of this character. If the room be not all wanted for such purpose, a part of it may devote to other necessary uses, there seldom being too much shelter of this kind on a farm; through the rear wall of this wood-house leads a door into the garden, or clothes-yard, as the case may be; and at its extreme angle is a water-closet, 6 × 4 feet, by way of lean-to, with a hipped roof, 8 feet high, running off from both the wood-house and workshop. This water-closet is lighted by a sliding sash window.

On to the wood-house, in a continuous front line, joins the workshop, an indispensable appendage to farm convenience. This has a flight of stairs leading to the lumber-room above. . . . Next to the work-house is the wagon and tool-house, above which is the hay loft, also spread over the stable adjoining; in which last are stalls for a pair of horses, which may be required for uses other than the main labors of the farm—to run to market, carry the family to church, or elsewhere. A pair of horses for such purposes should always be kept near the house. The horse-stalls occupy a space of 10 × 12 feet, with racks and feeding boxes. The plans of these will be described hereafter. The door leading out from these stalls is 5 feet wide, and faces the partition, so that each horse may be led out or in at an easy angle from them. Beyond the stalls is a passage 4 feet wide, leading to a store-room or area, from which a flight of rough stairs leads to the hay loft above. Beyond this room, in which is the oat bin for the horses, is a small piggery, for the convenience of a pig or two, which are always required to consume the daily wash and offal of the house; and not for the general *pork* stock of the farm; which, on one of this size, may be expected to require more commodious quarters.

The chamber plan of this house is commodious, furnishing one large room and three smaller ones. The small chamber leading to the deck over the porch, may, or may not be occupied as a sleeping room. The small one near the stairs may contain a single bed, or be occupied as a large clothes-closet. Through this, a door leads into the kitchen chamber, which may serve as one, or more laborers' bed-chambers. They may be lighted by one or more windows in the rear gable.

If more convenient to the family, the parlor and sitting-room, already described, may change their occupation, and one substituted for the other.

The main business approach to this house should be by a lane, or farm road opening on the side next the stable and wagon-house. The yard, in front of these last named buildings, should be separated from the lawn, or front door-yard of the dwelling. The establishment should stand some distance back from the traveled highway, and be decorated with such trees, shrubbery, and cultiva-tion, as the taste of the owner may direct. No *general* rules or directions can be applicable to this design beyond what have already been given; and the subject must be treated as circumstances may suggest. The unfrequented side of the house should, however, be flanked with a garden, either ornamental, or fruit and vegetable; as buildings of this character ought to command a corresponding share of attention with the grounds by which they are surrounded.

This house will appear equally well built of wood, brick, or stone. Its cost, according to materials, or finish, may be $1,000 or $1,500. The out-buildings attached, will add $400 to $600, with the same conditions as to finish; but the whole may be substantially and well built of either stone, brick, or wood, where each may be had at equal convenience, for $2,000 in the interior of New York. Of course, it is intended to do all the work plain, and in character for the occupation to which it is intended.

Chapter 9

The Art of Homemaking

THE book *Home Comforts* is a pleasant little tour de force. Published in 1855 by a writer using the pseudonym Lillie Savery, it makes household hints sound as sprightly as a story. The opening chapter, "Economy Illustrated," reprinted here, gives us a sketch of the ideal housewife. It is the industrious, ingenious Mrs. Savery herself. Her income is small—her husband is only a mechanic—but what she does with it is awe-inspiring. She makes shoes for herself out of some old soles and some parts of her husband's pantaloons; she bakes a cake that costs only three cents; and she feeds and dresses her two healthy children on next to nothing. She has brought up her children in her own image. They are both busy as bees, the daughter doing chores in the kitchen or garden, the son mowing grass to trade for milk. The father naturally is no less industrious. He is up early spading the ground for the garden before he goes to work; on his return he labors with undiminished zest. And the hired girl, Susan, is a paragon who apparently never sleeps.

The foil for Mrs. Savery is Mrs. Doolittle. Pompous, wasteful, wealthy (she is married to the richest merchant in town), she saves the chapter from cloying by her snobbishness. She tells her interlocutor, Mrs. Lovewell, about her visiting the Savery household. As Mrs. Doolittle goes on with her description, Mrs. Lovewell, amiably using the Socratic method, gets her to admit that Mrs. Savery is right in everything she does and Mrs. Doolittle is completely wrong. At the end of the chapter Mrs. Doolittle has been converted. She announces that she is going to put her daughter Salinda to school with Mrs. Savery, so that Salinda can learn some of Mrs. Savery's secrets. Mrs. Doolittle adds, blushing slightly, that Salinda herself is going to marry a mechanic.

The story carries not only a freight of general principles of domestic economy but also specific recipes. For example: "First she mixed it with *a little super carbonate of soda";* and so on. And it is all made palatable by the play of the author's wit.

Source: Lillie Savery, *Home Comforts*
(New York, 1855), pp. 9–23.

ECONOMY ILLUSTRATED

"Oh, dear me, Mrs. Lovewell, I am heartily tired of visiting that Mrs. Savery. What do you suppose I found her doing yesterday afternoon, when you know it was so pleasant that everybody was in the street? Oh, you need not guess; I am sure you never would think of the right thing."

"Indeed, I don't know that I could, but I have no doubt it was something useful. Practicing some of her arts of economy, I suppose."

"Economy indeed! Why, it is downright meanness. I should be mortified to death, if I was caught at such a piece of business."

"Why, Mrs. Doolittle, you alarm me. Pray, what was she about?"

"About, indeed! Why, she was making a pair of shoes."

"Slippers, you mean, I suppose; I often do that for my husband."

"Oh, yes, worsted work; that is a very different thing. No, it was a pair of *shoes* for herself. She had taken a pair of old shoe-soles, from which the tops had been worn out, and had cut new uppers from an old pair of her husband's black lasting pantaloons. Did you ever hear the like! I was really disgusted to hear her talk about it."

"Why, what did she say."

"Why, she said, 'There now, Mrs. Doolittle, I sat down after dinner, and commenced the job, with Susan to help me rip off the old soles and bind one of the new shoes, and now you see I have got just as good a pair of shoes, and for aught I see, just as good looking as the old pair that I paid a dollar and a half for. And that is what I call economy. Now I will go and show Susan how to make a new corn cake for tea. Don't you want to learn?'

"I told her no indeed; when I got so poor, and I put a real meaning emphasis upon the word—when I got so poor that I could not keep a cook that knew how to do her own work, I would come and learn the trade."

"Was she offended? Indeed Mrs. Doolittle, you were rather rude. You might have learned how to make a very nice cake."

"Well I must acknowledge that I did; no, she was not the least offended, but insisted that I should go down with her to the kitchen and see how it was done. I had a good mind to refuse, for I expected that I should get a grease spot on my new silk, just as like as not. I am sure I should in my kitchen; but would you believe it, hers is as clean as a new pin. Why the very floor looks as white and clean as a table. I do think she must keep that Susan of hers scrubbing all the time. For my part I don't see how she ever gets through all the work and do the washing too. I wish I could get such help."

"Mrs. Savery says it is by economy. Economy of time, as well as everything else. But about the nice corn cake?"

"Oh yes. Well I never; why it was just nothing to make. I could have made it just as well as she did."

"If you had known how."

"Why yes, to be sure; but it is nothing to learn; and then to hear her count the cost. Why she would feed a whole family for sixpence. In the first place she took a cup of Indian corn meal, not over three-cents worth, she said, and white at that—I always use yellow meal—it has more taste than the white—and put it in a clean wooden bowl, and what do you think she mixed with it, to make her cake? Water; nothing but water. Yes a little pinch of salt; but that she said she could not count the cost of, it was so small; and then she mixed, and stirred, and beat the meal and water together as though she was beating eggs, until she got it into a smooth batter, that would just pour into a shallow tin pan, about an inch deep. The cake when done was about as thick as my thumb. She first put the pan into a very hot oven and let it cook until the batter got stiff, and then she opened the stove doors and set the cake up edgeways right before the glowing coals until it got a nice delicate brown crust, and then drew it back and let it bake slow a long time—half an hour or more I should think."

"And was it good?"

"Good! why I declare I never tasted anything so delicious in all my life. I wouldn't have believed it, that just meal and water could be made so good. But that is not all. Just as she had got her cake turned up before the fire, in came her two children—such pictures of health—did you ever see the like!"

"She says that is 'the economy of health.' It is cheaper to keep them

healthy than sick, as well as more comfortable. You found them very neat, too."

"Neat! I never saw the like. But it's no wonder; look at the pains she takes with them. Why, it must keep Susan busy all the time."

"Then who does the work?"

"Well, I don't know. I can't understand it. I wish I could get along so. But then my children are always sick. Hers are always well and that makes the difference."

"No, the difference is in always keeping them well. But you were going to tell us something more about the cake."

"Oh, yes. When the children came in, Lillie said,

'Oh mother, will you let me bake a sweet cake for brother Frank and me?'

'Yes, if you will run up to your room and put away your things, and get on your aprons.'

"Directly down they came, and as I live, both of them with check aprons on. I should not like to see my children dressed in check aprons. It looks so common, and sort of countryfied. Then Lillie took the bowl of batter, and got a part of a teacupful of molasses, and a spoonful of ginger, and stirred it in, and then she got a cup of sour milk; and what do you think that was for?"

"I suppose to put in the cake."

"Yes, but first she mixed with it a little *super carbonate of soda,* until she set it all foaming, and then stirred it into the batter, with a little more meal to thicken it again, and poured it into an iron pan about twice as deep as the other, and clapped it right into the hot oven, where it baked until we had almost done tea, and then Susan brought it in smoking hot, and Mrs. Savery cut it up into squares, opening each piece and laying on a little lump of sweet butter, and so serving it round to each one; and would you believe it, in a respectable family, that that was the only cake on the table. I declare I had no great opinion of corn meal sweet cake, it seemed to look so mean; and then I had already eaten hearty of the plain cake, and did not think I would touch this one, but Lillie, with her insinuating little coaxing way— I don't know who could resist her—said I must taste her cake, and with that she asked me to take my knife and lay it open, and then she took a spoonful of juice out of the quince preserves, and spread over it, and I began tasting and tasting, and would you believe it, the first I thought about what I was doing, I had cleared my plate, and Lillie was helping me to another piece; she was so delighted to see me eat it with such a relish, when I only intended to 'give it a taste, just out of compliment.' "

"Then it was good?"

"Good! I never tasted anything more delicious. I have often had a cake upon my table that I paid a dollar for that did not give half as much satisfaction; the bakers are getting to cheat so dreadfully. I could have forgiven her about her meanness—don't you think it is meanness?—in making shoes, or putting check aprons on her children, if she had not preached me one of her sermons upon economy, and actually proved to me that the supper, delicious as it was, had literally cost nothing—that is next to nothing. There was the meal three cents —the molasses and salt and soda, three cents—the tea, two cents—the sugar and milk, two cents—the butter—butter is high now, but that was not over four cents—and let me see, was that all?"

"You mentioned some quince preserves."

"Oh, yes, but she said they actually cost less than nothing. About eleven years ago—it was to commemorate the first birthday of Frank—she planted a quince bush, and then she told how she made it grow, and bear fruit. She said she always kept the ground loose and covered in the summer with straw, which she wets with soap suds and dishwater, and last year her quince tree bore more than she wanted; and so a friend of hers came and brought her own sugar, and did all the work, and put up the quinces at the halves, while Mrs. Savery was away on a visit in the country. So she proved, you see, that they really did cost nothing. I wish I could live so."

"I don't see why you could not, you have got a nice place for a garden."

"Yes, full of bushes and flowers, but I have got no quince tree."

"But you must do as Mrs. Savery did; plant one."

"Yes, and I might not live till it bore fruit. And besides, I never could do as she does. We hire all our work, and I often tell Mr. Doolittle it costs more to raise a few roses and flowers than it would to buy them. But then our girls must have a garden."

"Don't you know how Mrs. Savery works hers?"

"Oh, yes: her husband is a mechanic, and knows how to work, and don't mind it, and he spades up the ground before breakfast, and then Mrs. Savery and the children, and Susan all work at it, and that is the way they make their things cost nothing. We live different, you know."

"Perhaps they make it a pleasure, instead of toil. I recollect going in there one day last summer—the door was open, and it was just at sundown, so I walked in and through the house—the tea-table was standing, just as they left it, and all hands were out in the garden as busy as bees. I recollect Lillie was saving safron, which Mrs. Savery said would sell for enough to pay for all the medicine they used in a year.

"Frank was cutting his third crop of grass from the borders, which he sold to old Capt. Peabody, for I don't know how many quarts of milk. The old lady, you know, makes a living from her two cows. I declare there was not a spot in that garden that hadn't something useful growing in it. But that was not all; I do believe that garden is the great secret of health of those children.

"As soon as Lillie saw me, she ran up and shook hands, and said 'she was so glad I had come, for father was just wishing that some of our friends would come in, and then he would cut the big melon.'"

"Melons! why, do they raise melons upon that little patch of ground?"

"Why no, I cannot say they do exactly, for the seed was planted in a barrel of earth set on the flagging, and the vines were trained up on top of a little flat roof building in the yard, and there they grew six or eight feet from the ground, some sweet delicious water-melons. That was what Mr. Savery said was the economy of space. It was 'economy of space' indeed; for underneath the barrel of earth, was one full of ashes, saved from their chamber stove, where they burn wood, and that barrel used to run off a little lye to soften the hard water of their well."

"Oh, I always buy potash."

"And she always saves it. A gallon of lye will soften a large kettle full of hard-water, and as you see, said Mr. Savery, takes up no room, and the leached ashes make excellent manure. That is what makes Frank's grass grow so rank, and our fruit trees look so thrifty."

"Well, did you eat the melon?"

"Oh yes, as soon as Lillie mentioned it,

her father got up and brought it down, and Susan drew a pail of cold water and put it in; and Frank said then he would run over and ask Aunt Mary and the girls, to come and join the water-melon party; and upon my word, I do think it was the sweetest melon, and sweetest family circle I ever got into in all my life."

"And was it big enough for all of you?"

"Oh yes. I have often paid three or four shillings for one nothing like as good. And while we were eating—or rather while we were talking, after satisfying all of our appetites, Susan and all, Mr. Savery told Lillie to get her little account book, and show me, not only how she was learning to keep accounts, but how much they were indebted to the garden. Really I never could have believed it. But the best of all, said he, it teaches my children habits of industry and economy."

"Oh yes, that word *economy* always comes in."

"Well, I am sure it is a very good word, and at this time particularly necessary for all to learn, and to practice too. It would save much suffering among the poor."

"Yes, it may be necessary for mechanics, and such sort of folks, to be always saving, but thank fortune, my family are able to live without working like common laborers in the garden every day. Besides, my children ain't able to do it; they are very delicate."

"Perhaps, Mrs. Doolittle, it is the garden, and check aprons, and thick shoes, and corn bread, and all that, that makes Mr. Savery's children so healthy. And certainly, when they are dressed for church, there are none that look prettier, or attract more attention by their pretty behavior; if they do work in the garden and get ruddy faces, and dirty fingers."

"Well, well, if you ain't getting to be a convert to the Saverys' economy. I shall expect to see you soon, making your own shoes."

"I don't know as to that, but I will tell you what you may see me doing—and I intend to begin to-morrow—and that is taking lessons in the art of house-keeping. You know my daughter, Salinda, is soon to be married, and I think we had better give Mrs. Savery five hundred dollars of her portion, for some lessons in the economy of house-keeping, the practice of which in time will pay it back, twice over."

"And so you are going to get her to give your daughter the finish of her education, after all you have done for her. Well, well, I am beat now."

"I shall certainly make her the offer.

I have been thinking about it for some time; and now what you have told me has fully convinced me that a quarter's tuition from Mrs. Savery, will be worth more than any quarter she ever had at boarding-school, or from her music master or French teacher; for to be candid with you, Salinda is going to marry a mechanic."

"A mechanic! Oh my! the richest merchant's daughter in town, going to marry a mechanic. Well now I must go, and tell the news. What will my girls think! Good bye."

"Good bye. Yes, yes, Mrs. Doolittle, tell your girls, and all the rest of your acquaintance, that Salinda Lovewell, is going to take lessons of economy of Mrs. Savery, and then marry a poor mechanic. Well, we shall see, whether that won't be good economy.

Chapter 10

The Businessman at Home

IN antebellum days it was acknowledged that the husband was the head of the household, the source of its strength, and the font of its wisdom. Perhaps because of this self-evident truth few books appeared which told the husband what to do. The volumes of instruction on, or observation about, family life ordinarily included a chapter concerning him; but the tone was that of equals addressing equals. Not so when it came to addressing the wife or children. Most books were probably printed with them in mind, for it was felt that they needed considerable instruction in their duties.

Among those authors who did remind the male of his domestic responsibilities was the Reverend H. A. Boardman. We met him before when he was explaining how to be a good clerk. In his *The Bible in the Counting-House* he also included a homily on the role of the merchant at home.

Boardman's theme is that the merchant should be a true Christian in every phase of his life. Despite a nineteenth-century prolixity, he makes his points. Most of them prove to be surprisingly modern, though the dependence on God that Boardman preaches sometimes seems less fashionable today than dependence on astrology or psychiatry. In dealing with marital relations, Boardman advises the merchant not to treat his wife as a servant or plaything but to share his problems with her. Even when his problems are financial or commercial—and even today it is part of the sexist's creed that a woman cannot understand business—Boardman's advice is "tell your wife."

He is equally enlightened in dealing with the father's relation to his children, as we can see from the selections printed below from Lecture 8, "Domestic Life." Today the commuting father sees little of his children; in the 1850s the long hours he spent in business had the same result. So Boardman warns the father to make the best use of the time he has: to talk at home not about making money but about things that will better his children's character, and to be kind to his children rather than harsh or imperious. And he must do these things now, or the children will grow up and be lost to him. "In the education of your children, it is 'now, or never.'" He will have missed "the purest felicity" left to him if he neglects them. Boardman ends with a quotation from Coleridge urging that the happiness of life comes from little, domestic joys.

All this sounds like copybook maxims, but Boardman's vigorous mind and steady, thumping style still keep some of their original attraction. He is not pontificating; he is talking to his merchant man to man.

Source: H. A. Boardman, *The Bible in the Counting-House* (Philadelphia, 1853), pp. 259–65.

DOMESTIC LIFE

It will not do to forget that the responsibilities which attach to the head of the family, are intransferable; and that while you occupy that position, you must be held accountable for the proper discharge of its duties. This consideration must at times press with great solemnity upon the minds of thoughtful men who are much separated from their children. The training of those children is going forward alike in your presence and in your absence. Day by day, their faculties are maturing, their principles becoming established, their habit-forming, and their whole characters assuming the essential type they are to bear through life —possibly, through eternity. This is your trust—the most sacred, the most momentous, trust, God has confided to you. To fulfil it wisely and well, is of more importance to you than the acquisition of a fortune or the attainment of any other secular end. Nor is it within the compass of any human abilities to do this, unless aided by the Spirit of God. That source of help is, happily, open to you. "If any of you lack wisdom, let him ask of God, and it shall be given him." Every parent who appreciates the relation, will gratefully avail himself of the assistance so freely tendered him in this delicate and difficult duty. But he will not rest here. The temper of mind which sends you to the throne of grace for succour, will put you upon using all the appliances within your reach, to multiply the attractions of home to your families, and to keep their affections in a fresh and healthful state. To do this, you will need, not only to give them as much of your society as you can, but to make your intercourse with them pleasant and improving. For example, it cannot fail to injure them if the whole burden of your conversation at home, is about business, and stocks, and money, and the like; or if they see that you have no relish for any pursuits except those which derive their value from dollars and cents. If *this* is to be the sum and substance of your companionship with them, it is of little moment that you hurry home from your counting-rooms to see them: your absence will do them no harm. Or if, again, you habitually carry into domestic life a fretful or an imperious temper, if you are lavish of harsh words or cross looks, it would be as well to remit the training of your families to other hands. Neither these, nor any other, practical errors on your part, will be harmless. Such is the authority impressed upon the headship of the house, that your every act and word and look and gesture—and what you leave unsaid and undone, no less than what you say and do—will go to fashion the moral lineaments of those deathless beings around you. This would be a serious matter, if it was for this life only they were to be trained. But we cannot limit our parental responsibilities thus. Our obligations extend alike to the bodies and the *souls* of our children. And they who consider the difficulty of extricating one soul from the bondage of sin and the snares of the world, will understand something of the charge involved in preparing a household for heaven. Surely, your children have a claim upon you for all the help you can afford them in combating the temptations of life: and it is neither generous nor just to withhold from the *mothers* that co-operation they are entitled to in the education of your offspring.

It is another weighty consideration bearing upon this point, that unless you avail yourselves of present opportunities, you may miss altogether that endearing and salutary intercourse with your families which I am inculcating. The period you are anticipating, when a discharge from business is to leave you full scope for the culture of domestic pleasures, may never arrive. How many of your contemporaries and neighbours have been arrested by death in the midst of their cares and their traffickings! While you are preparing to enjoy the society of your families, the relentless reaper, who spares no age nor condition, may cut you down. At the very moment, possibly, when your plans have been brought to a successful consummation, and you are ready to *begin to live,* a vacant seat at your table may mark the transitoriness of all human expectations.

Nor is this the only contingency. Should your life be spared, your release from business may come too late both as to your families and yourselves. Too late for them: because their training may be completed. In the education of your children, it is "now, or never." You may bend the sapling, but you cannot bend the oak. You may mould the clay, but you cannot mould the pottery. Your seed will germinate if cast into the genial lap of Spring, but it will get no sustenance from the rugged bosom of Winter. If you mean to have any useful agency in fashioning the characters of those children, this is the time to exert it.—Your prospective season of leisure may come too late for yourselves. When the time arrives for domestic enjoyment, your domestic sympathies and attachments may have become so blunted, that you will be insusceptible of this kind of happiness. There are other things besides iron, which will *rust* from want of use: other attributes of humanity besides bone and muscle, which depend upon exercise for healthful vigour. A neglected home is apt to become an undervalued home. The bird that is long away from its nest, may not care to return to it. And it is somewhat hazardous for a man to discover that, after all, he can "get on" and really enjoy life, without being dependent upon the pure and simple pleasures of his own fireside. The way to shun such untoward discoveries, is to keep the flame burning brightly upon your domestic altars, from the time it is first kindled, until death; to let nothing but the damp of the grave extinguish or enfeeble it. To neglect this, is to forego the purest felicity which the fall has left us. Those who have practised it, have found that life was too short to exhaust the stores of elevated enjoyment bound up in the domestic constitution; too fleeting for that sacred fellowship of home, "So friendly to the best pursuits of man,/Friendly to thought, to virtue, and to peace!"

This is not, unhappily, as well understood as it ought to be. There are no adequate pains taken to perpetuate the freshness of early affection, and to cherish, as time wears on, the sentiments and habits which consecrate the earlier experiences of married life. "A person may be highly estimable on the whole, nay, amiable as neighbour, friend, housemate, in short, in all the concentric circles of attachment, save only the last and inmost; and yet from how many causes be estranged from the highest perfection in this! Pride, coldness, or fastidiousness of nature, worldly cares, an anxious or ambitious disposition, a passion for display, a sullen temper, one or the other, too often proves 'the dead fly in the compost of spices,' and any one is enough to unfit it for the precious balm of unction. For some mighty good sort of people too, there is not seldom a sort of saturnine, or, if you will, *ursine* vanity, that keeps itself alive by sucking the paws of its own self-importance. And as this high sense, or rather sensation, of their own value, is for the most part grounded on negative qualities, so they have no better means of preserving the same but by negatives, that is, by *not* doing or saying any thing that might be put down for fond, silly, or nonsensical, or (to use their own phrase), by *never forgetting themselves,* which some of their acquaintances are uncharitable enough to think the most worthless object they could be employed in remembering. The same effect is produced in thousands, by the too general insensibility to a very important truth; this, namely, that the Misery of human life is made up of large masses, each separated from the other by certain intervals. One year, the death of a child; years after, a failure in trade; after another longer or shorter interval, a daughter may have married unhappily; —in all but the singularly unfortunate, the integral parts that compose the sum total of the unhappiness of man's life, are easily counted, and distinctly remembered. The Happiness of life, on the contrary, is made up of minute fractions, the little soon-forgotten charities of a kiss, a smile, a kind look, a heartfelt compliment in the disguise of playful raillery, and the countless other infinitesimals of pleasurable thought and genial feeling."

Chapter 11

Making Good Boys and Girls

IN the multiplying manuals on family life there are two main concerns: the relation of the parents to each other and the proper upbringing of the children. When the writers deal with the relation of husband to wife the silence about clinical sex, incidentally, is awesome. When they deal with how to raise children, they sound to us less old-fashioned. In spite of today's permissiveness the directions they give often have, even to us, a certain internal logic and persuasiveness. There is a chapter called "Management of Children" in Mrs. L. G. Abell's book *Woman in her Various Relations* (1851) that is a model of its kind. The tone is brisk, the suggestions sensible for that time and specific. The mother is advised to be loving but firm.

According to Mrs. Abell the main job of the mother is to rear her children. A corollary is that the best place for a woman is in the home. Yet Mrs. Abell is aware that there is more to being a woman than acting as wife or mother. We see in her book a touch of the feminism that will be found in the selection after this one, from *Woman and her Needs*. Nevertheless, Mrs. Abell's emphasis is on the homemaker. Here, in the selection printed below, the homemaker is told how to raise good boys and girls.

Source: Mrs. L. G. Abell, *Woman in her Various Relations*
(New York, 1851), pp. 228–37.

MANAGEMENT OF CHILDREN

It is always well to adapt punishment to the nature of the offense, if possible. For instance, if a child insists upon climbing on a table, it will cure him entirely to set him out on the table in the middle of the room, and spread the leaves, as it will be impossible for him to get down. His situation in no time will become so very irksome, that he will have no desire to repeat the offense.

If he betrays selfishness at table, let him be served last for this reason. If he hurt any one with a whip or plaything, it must be taken from him entirely for a season; and so on, in all the little and frequent *faults*.

Watching opportunities to curb the first determined risings of willful rebellion is an important consideration. With most children there is an era, and this often happens when the child is about emerging from babyhood, in which a struggle is made for the mastery, and the question has to be promptly decided, who is to *rule* — the child or the parent? Vigorous measures will be necessary at this juncture, and punishment, decisive and repeated, until submission on the part of the child is complete, will only answer the end desired. But one struggle will not suffice, without care, to insure obedience afterward.

Speaking of their faults has a disheartening effect, and has an unhappy influence on the feelings. Reproving a child severely in company, or holding any of its habits up to ridicule, is not well, and will tend to discourage and depress the mind.

Mere accidents should be overlooked, with a caution or warning, and the parent should discriminate between a fault and an inadvertence.

Lying and disobedience are serious faults, that may never be passed over; but the disposition and moral sense will be injured if the small offenses are treated with the same severity.

Never keep a child in suspense, and say, "I will think of it," unless you intend to grant the request, for when the expectation has been thus raised, it is harder to bear *denial*.

Great patience is necessary in all our intercourse with children. From some hidden cause, irritability and fretfulness must often be borne with, after all that we can do for their comfort. Unmoved serenity is all-important in such cases, as it can never be overcome by opposition or impatience, for it is often the result of some bodily infirmity.

Selfishness is a sin of early growth. We see it in the smallest child that stands upon its feet. He claims his own chair, his own wagon, his own toys, his own mother, if his rights are in any way invaded; and it grows with the growth, and strengthens with the strength. It is only to be overcome by an unceasing watchfulness to improve all opportunities to call out the tender feelings of kindness which all children occasionally display. It cannot be destroyed by authority, nor uprooted by commands; but can be regulated and subdued, in a measure, by calling into exercise the better feelings.

Affection should be cultivated. Parents are apt to be satisfied with the love they feel for the child, without thinking it necessary to call the same reciprocating emotion from them. The foundation of *family affection* is laid during the first ten years of childhood, and should be cherished as a plant of most tender growth. I have seen it wither and droop, for the want of care and nurture, till it became a blight upon all enjoyment, and a sting to every pleasure.

A tyrannical, and domineering, and revengeful spirit should be early crushed, or it will become a source of intolerable evil. The gentleness of Christ, the tenderness and compassion He felt, and exhibited, and taught, will touch the hearts of children, and produce the strongest impressions on their minds. It should be the maxim at all times, "Do unto others as you would have them do to you." *What can we do for children without the Bible?*

Benevolence should be taught and inculcated early. If the seed is not sown, there will be no harvest. It may be made a source of pleasure to a child to relieve the wants of the destitute. Send a child with some comfort to a poor neighbor, or a sick friend; it will bring a two-fold blessing. Accustom them to lay up their money to give to some poor object of pity, or to send Bibles to the heathen. They must be encouraged to give something that would cost them some sacrifice.

As you value a child's happiness and well-being in this life, preserve it from all unnecessary fears. Never startle them with sudden noise, or strange appearances, or ghost stories. They will do them injury that will continue for years. One alarming tale of murder, robbery, sudden death, mad dogs, etc., will leave an impression lasting as the life. We must not only do what we can to secure from alarming impressions, but cultivate resolution and fortitude to meet pain, sicknes, danger, and sorrow, and to be useful in the various engagements of life. When our children are sick, while we do our utmost to relieve, to solace, and comfort them, we should mingle resolution with our tenderness, and, if necessary, combine discipline with the kindest attentions.

A sense of importance is imbibed by children, unless there is care and pains taken to learn them "to take the lowest place," and to yield in all things to superiors. We naturally incline to consider the child's comfort and happiness so *important* that we are apt to forget that the child is receiving the same impression, and will never lose the feel-

ing that his own wants are *pre-eminent,* unless we sacrifice a little of our own feelings of tenderness to establish a better feeling in them than supreme and entire *selfishness.*

Too many playthings have a bad effect. The child who may be allowed a few simple things, and taught to use them in various ways, leaving room for the mind to act, will find more real pleasure than that afforded by the most costly toy. Disgust and dissatisfaction with every thing is often produced by too great an effort to please a child.

The sooner a child can be taught to help himself, and to help others in any little way, the better. Such exercise strengthens the faculties both of body and of mind, and will be the beginning of a habit.

"I can't" is often used as an excuse for indolence or disobedience, and should rarely be admitted, as upon resolute exertion depends success. The child can be taught to put up his own playthings, to dress himself in part, to pick up things for any one, and to wait on those who are busy, to some trifle. It will amuse and please a child more than much done merely to amuse and pacify him. It has an influence on the affections, and learns a child to help as well as to be helped, and makes him happy in pleasing others.

Teasing children has a very bad influence on their tempers and feelings. Catching them up from their play, interrupting them in their harmless and innocent pursuits and amusements, annoys and vexes them, and should never be practiced. The lives of some children are embittered, and the sunshine of their glad existence clouded, by a continuation of such unkind and injudicious treatment by mothers, or older members of a family. I have seen those that seemed to take great pleasure in this kind of amusement, but it partakes of a nature that finds its pleasure in giving pain, and is in any one a fearful trait of character.

Delicacy is a plant of choicest value, though of tenderest growth. Correct moral tastes and feelings are the greatest safeguards to all character, and nothing on this point can be correct that is not delicate. Even little children will indulge, in a small measure, in conversation bordering on indelicacy, to amuse each other and excite a laugh; but the least tendency to such a practice should be carefully watched and corrected, and, if persisted in, should be treated with severity.

An improper trick, even in infancy, should be frowned upon, and a look of serious reproof will manifest a disapprobation that will be remembered. It is only by strict and nice attention to little things that modest and refined habits are ever formed. Tell a child that God destroyed the inhabitants of Sodom for such bad behavior, and it will save them from all impure thoughts and conduct when old enough to understand.

Manners are next to religion and virtue, and should be constantly watched over, as one of the essentials in any character. Teach a child to "honor all men," to oblige, to be kind, to be respectful, and he will be pleasing of course. But allow him to follow an opposite behavior, to talk while others are conversing, to be noisy and rude, disobliging, and disobedient, and he will, of course, become an object of *disgust*. Loud talking and laughing, violent exclamations, as terrible! awful! dreadful! etc., induce a roughness of manner, as well as coarseness of mind, and will lead to vulgar habits and demeanor.

Mimicry is amusing, but will lead to an improper turn of mind, and ridicule should never be allowed.

It is essential to good breeding that children be taught by "line upon line" to express themselves well, and to speak clear, distinctly, and grammatically.

Children should be taught to sit down and rise up from the table at the same time, to wait while others are served, to be quiet, and to see delicacies without asking for them, and only to speak when they need something or are spoken to, as forwardness in talking makes children bold and unpleasing.

Chapter 12

Woman and Her Needs: Minority Report

ALTHOUGH it is hard to realize, the family of the fifties was changing, particularly where the wife and mother was concerned. There were stirrings beneath the surface. The intelligent woman did not always feel satisfied with a life which revolved around a man, and the more education she received the more articulate she was apt to become about her lot. There had always been feminists in America who urged that women be granted more rights, if fewer privileges, but in the middle of the nineteenth century they spoke with new determination. In 1848 four feminists led by Mrs. Elizabeth Cady Stanton organized the first women's rights convention. Meeting in Seneca Falls, New York, it discussed votes for women and adopted a resolution that women be given equality as citizens with men.

Many feminists found their hands full campaigning for political equality. But the boldest ones advocated social and moral equality as well. Of this small group, most were too shrill to get a public hearing. An exception was Mrs. Elizabeth Oakes Smith. She was witty and compassionate as well as fervent. Her abilities let her become a well-known lecturer on the lyceum platform. Though a feminist she was also feminine. When she lectured in Concord, for instance, an irritated Henry Thoreau had to escort her, and she teased him by making him carry her lecture script in her perfumed handkerchief.

In 1851, the same year that she lectured in Concord, she published a feminist manifesto. Called *Woman and her Needs*, it was in its urbane way a highly subversive document. The very title is significant, for the emphasis is on what should be done for women rather than on what they should do for others. In Chapter VIII, abridged below, of her slender volume she denies that marriage should be the goal of every girl, that woman is at her best as the sweet-tempered servant of her spouse, and that she should be kept in any way from developing her talents. But she adds that women are not all alike: many are fit for marriage and nothing else. The point is that she believes that the human character can be molded and that the female character has been molded by the dominating male. The historical ideal of womanliness has been concocted by man. After all, as she says ironically, "The lions have written the books." And to her that sort of womanliness is not nearly enough.

Source: Mrs. E. Oakes Smith, *Woman and her Needs*
(New York, 1851), pp. 80–86, abridged; 88–92, abridged.

CHAPTER VIII

IT IS often said, "A womans' world is in her affections, her empire is home." This is only in part true, and true only to a part of the sex. There are thousands of men, and women, too, entirely unfitted for the family relation. Men, so dull and imbecile, where the social affections are concerned, that they can neither minister nor be ministered to in this way, but who are clear, good abstract reasoners, apt at invention, and capable of advancing science—though cold, selfish, and unsympathizing; women, too, dogmatic, ambitious, antagonistic, who would value some intellectual triumph worth a thousand hearts, and dearer than any recognition of the affections. These have nothing in themselves to bring them into harmony with the family relation. Their attempts at tenderness look foolish, and any lapses into coquetry strike you as a downright attempt at a fraud. You recoil from it as untruthful, if not sinister; while this womanly weapon, in the hands of another, may appear not only becoming, but attractive.

Far be it from me to undervalue the slightest grace of my sex; it is because I recognize individuality, and reverence it, that I will not apply the same laws to all. . . .

[Many] types there are—women of ample gifts to hold the most affluently endowed of the other sex in thrall—such as a Cleopatra, a Heloise, and so on from the most celebrated to the most obscure. Now, will any one pretend that the same laws apply to all of these? Where is their world? Can it be narrowed down to the four walls of the saloon or the nursery?

Let us put these aside. Even in a lower scale of being there is a large class to whom the affections hold a very subordinate part—women who find it irksome to sustain the relations of wife and mother, and who would never have assumed them, but because public opinion has made it desirable, and the unequal action of labor, necessary. I even heard of a poor woman who witnessed the inordinate grief of a neighbor over the death of a child, with utter astonishment, and remarked that "she was sure she did not feel so bad when her child died, for she hadn't had to work near so hard since." Now, this is pitiful enough, and the naturalness of the expression shows she was entirely deficient in the emotion so predominant in the other.

The lions have written the books, and having persisted in making that part of our character which brings us in relation to themselves the prominent subject of comment, they have ignored our other attributes, till there is a vague feeling engendered that a woman is the worse for large endowments of any kind whatever. Iago's narrow and coarse exposition of her vocation, "To suckle fools, and chronicle small beer," is not far from the popular estimate. Genius and beauty, God's crowning gifts, are looked upon with distrust, if not with dread. The fear that a woman may deviate the slightest from conventionalism in any way, has become a nervous disease with the public. Indeed, so little is she trusted as a creation, that one would think she were made marvellously beautiful, and endowed with gifts of thought and emotion only for the purpose of endangering her safety—a sort of spiritual locomotive with no check-wheel, a rare piece of porcelain, to be handled gingerly—in fact, a creature with no conservative elements within herself, but left expressly thus, that men might supply them, and lead and guide, and coerce and cajole her, as it pleased him best. She is a blind angel, neither adapted to heaven nor earth in herself, but, if submitting graciously to man's guidance, capable of filling a narrow, somewhat smoky, and very uncertain nook on this small planet, and possibly to win heaven through the perfection of suffering here.

Let her assert the laws of her being, let her say she is capable of more than this narrow sphere, that she grieves and frets in the cage, and the fault is grievous. She is ill-tempered, ambitious, unwomanly— as though womanhood had but one signification. It is even a reproach for her to have a will of her own. The voice of her own soul within her crying for space and recognition must be suppressed, lest she should be less subservient as a wife, and less humdrum as a mother; and yet the heroes of their age were not born of your tame women. The fathers of Wes-

ley and Washington and Napoleon were far from being superior men; indeed we should rather call them very orderly, sensible, dull people; while their mothers were each brilliant, individualized, strongly marked characters, with fine health and great personal beauty.

It seems strange that we should need to enter a plea for the faculties that God has given us; but so it is. The persistent use of the obnoxious word *female* in our vocabulary is proof of the light in which we are regarded.

Read but a tithe of the twaddle written by the other sex in regard to our nature, and it will be seen how little we are understood. Take up a common newspaper, which may be regarded as an exponent of the popular voice, and see how we are talked of—as creatures, one would suppose, belonging to a different race. Here is a paragraph from the first paper at hand, in illustration:

Woman's Character.—No trait of character is more valuable in a *female* than the possession of a sweet temper. Home can never be made happy without it. It is like the flowers that spring up in the pathway, reviving and cheering us. Let a man go home at night wearied and worn by the toils of the day, and how soothing is a word dictated by a good disposition. It is sunshine falling upon his heart. He is happy, and the cares of life are forgotten.

Far be it from me to gainsay the expiring, lackadaisical truth of the sentiment herein expressed. But would one be quite sure the being spoken of was a woman?—would it not rather seem it might be some dangerous creature shut up in a very dull and somewhat unfurnished chamber—said creature being apt sometimes to exhibit quite the contrary manifestations? . . .

If men do not understand us, and do

not describe us as we are, women have not done much better, they having looked abroad to see what others have said, rather than having descended into their own bosoms for light and truth. If Mrs. Ellis is really serious in much of the advice she gives married women, their husbands ought by no means to feel flattered, for they are surely little better than *great babies*, to be humored and got along with, or unruly animals, who, having the power, must be so managed as to be left as little dangerous and troublesome as possible. Away with this flimsy, sickly kind of recognition! It is no wonder the world is so evil, and stupid, and imbecile, while we thus nurse up old follies, and make pets of what ought to be exploded errors. Men and women both need a thousand-fold more courage than they now have, in order to search earnestly for Truth, and recognize her when found. . . .

Let it be understood, I do not disparage the home affections, the circle of home duties. God forbid! I only wish to assert that we must not be limited to these; that we must and ought to be true to the talents committed to our keeping. If our circle has been ordained in a limited sphere, fill it joyously—if in a larger, take up its glorious burdens nobly, and bear them to the throne of the Eternal. Every creature is happy in its own atmosphere. Let us find wherein our great strength lies, and break the withes of custom, if need be, to assert our power; let us arise from the cords of bondage unscathed, lest we find ourselves, from too long slumber, feeble and blind, and covered with scorn, our beautiful fabric of life reeling to its fall.

The woman with but the one talent is praiseworthy for putting it to account— and she with the ten is culpable for their

neglect. That word happiness has a most weak and undefined meaning, as ordinarily used—exemption from grief and solicitude is one meaning; and to very many, enough to eat and drink, and "civilly merry" friends, is another; success in trade, "to swing upon a gate all day," irresponsibility, as in the slave, &c., &c. Now, one must be infinitely weak and inconsequential in his reason, to say that any or all of these bring happiness. No, that can have no law, except as it springs from the construction of the being itself. There is something beyond these externals, that imparts it, and *this something lies in the bosom of the Infinite Father, who calls upon us to be like Him, perfect in our being,* and to grow in the grace of all its harmonies. We must and will feel the stirrings of a great nature if it be great, and we are happy only as we obey its monitions. We are not happy in a half life, a half utterance; for the wealth struggles for its power; the smothered fire burns and consumes till it find room for its healthful glow. A thousand women are ill-natured and miserable, not from positive ills about them, but from compression; they have that within, demanding space and indulgence, and they pine for its freedom—the laws of their life are not comprehended, and they sink to imbecile complaints, only because there is no voice to call them forth to freedom and light. When I say freedom, I do not mean the violation of any one ordering of society. I say, reverence these—but awake to the God-light within you, and follow its guidance. It is his law, even in the external world, to bring all creations into an appropriate sphere—the dews of the mountain even tire of its isolation, and mount upward to the sky, where they rejoice in the rainbow—the seed struggles mightily in the dark earth, for the green leaf and the beautiful blossom lie folded within, calling for the light—the worm sickens at the dust of its dim way, for the wings of the butterfly call for a higher life; and everywhere the great voice of God from within cries "where art thou?" and yet we bide ourselves, and find excuses for our fear and our inaction.

Hereafter, in the progress of events, I see no reason why the influence of woman should not be acknowledged at the ballot-box: indeed, when we consider the disorder and venality prevailing there, it would seem that her voice may be the great element needful to reform. The fact of her dropping a ticket into a receptacle of the kind, does not look hazardous to her femininity; she might seem to do this with little or no commotion, and return in conscious dignity to her household, and there infuse a braver cheer, and instill into the immature judgments of those committed to her care nobler lessons of life. Shakespeare's Portia is not the less engaging at Bellmont for having plead the cause of her friend with lawyer-like sagacity. In Europe the fashion of Queens has made it not an infrequent thing for a woman to speak in legislative halls, and Victoria's domestic abilities seem not the least impaired by her occasional appearance there. But in our country, where it might be supposed a certain degree of courage would keep hand-in-hand with reform, men appear to think the worst disasters would befall them by even discussing the question. If a woman does so, she is met, not as a thinker—one capable and willing to consider abstractly a question of human good, which can be of no possible advantage to herself, for she will be long in her grave before her views would be acknowledged, if at all—but she is met by unmanly strictures upon her sex, and foolish flings at *"female* politicians." Pardon the phrase, it is a quotation—I recognize only the appropriate term of woman. But this is aside from my subject.

Our right to a full life—to the exercise of full life—is the foundation of a plea—not that of the nursery and kitchen merely—not that of the luxurious saloon, the haunts of fashion merely—for disguise it as men and women may, this perpetual adulation, this fostering of our pettiness, our vanity, our love of luxury, is but the mode of holding us in the pupilage of sex—recognizing only our relation in one aspect of life, and ignoring all other claims. I do not undervalue the harmonies of love—every woman owes much of the graces of her life to these—the affections are all holy and beautiful, but the laws of these are as diverse as the mental character of their owners; and while to some they may be all, to others, however strong, they are but the framework, the foundation of a great and harmonious superstructure.

Chapter 13

Family Affairs

IN pictures and poetry, in song and story, in county histories and little weekly newspapers, we find evidence that the family was the central institution of the society of the 1850s. The church and the school were both of great importance but the family stood ahead even of them.

The little cluster of visual documents which follows tells us something about several sides of family life. The companies which sold lithographs to the people during the 1850s have left meager records, yet there is no doubt that family matters were a favorite subject for their art. It is worth remembering that these lithographs were bought because they stood for the idea of family. They were not like the daguerreotypes which would soon be made and bought in numbers—after all they were the likeness of a particular family. That was a matter merely of having one's picture taken, while the purchase of a lithograph was a tribute to the institution.

In their highly different ways each of the accompanying lithographs idealizes familial life. Though there was more to it than they reveal, much of that is shown in the five prose selections which precede the pictures. Some of it is not. For example: infant mortality. It remained high; and here and there you could still purchase a lithograph of a gravestone, with a place on it to write the name of the dead baby. Another of the hard realities of family life, omitted in the pictures but suggested in the prose selections, was the dominance of the husband and father. He had all the law on his side. His wife was, legally at least, a vassal; she passed from the control of her father to that of her husband. His children were equally devoid of legal rights. He could mistreat them with impunity.

Of course he was not always a strict ruler. The point was that he could be, for the culture was on his side. So far as we can tell, most fathers were humane. For that matter, some were docile. Many a joke was told about "henpecked" husbands. Many an American child, as Count de Gurowski suggested, exerted more power than a European one. America already appeared a country of youth to censorious European eyes, and a country as well where women seemed to rule, despite the complaints of feminists like Mrs. Oakes Smith.

Nevertheless, we should know that what we read in the selections or see in the pictures fails to show much of the underside of American family life. The 1850s now qualify as the good old days; they were, no doubt, but not to the extent that appears.

Source: Married. Lithographed and issued by Kellogg & Comstock, 1850.
The Harry T. Peters "America on Stone" Lithography Collection,
The Smithsonian Institution

Marriage was a favorite subject in the lithographer's trade. It was seldom satirized; there was more sentiment attached to it than to any other subject except death. Its various stages all sold well, from the wedding itself to the silver-haired couple surrounded on the farm by throngs of grandchildren. Here of course we see the young parents and their brood.

For anyone who savors bad American art, this lithograph constitutes a classic. It manages to avoid all extremes of excellence and remains unblushingly maladroit. If it were a primitive it might have a Grandma Moses charm. But the artist evidently has had just enough instruction to take the bloom off his artistic innocence. He has been taught that a picture should have some structure to it, as well as a focus and a conscious attention to light and shade. In this lithograph his lines lead inward, and his light and shade are consistently contrasted. Even the plushy window-hangings set off one another.

But his figures have all the animation of wooden models. They sit or stand like dolls. The lines of each figure are either vertical or horizontal, except for those of the father, which slant daringly toward the center. The expression in each face is completely vacuous. Husband and wife look emptily at each other on one spatial level of the picture; below them, on the next level in space, the two girls stare blankly at their little brother (he must be a boy—the mores demand it). The doll which one little girl holds is no more doll-like than the little girl herself. Or, to put it in another way, the doll looks as human as the family.

The family before us is middle-class. The clothes are an idealization of Sunday-best; the furnishings, in their way, are too. It is probably the parlor which is the setting, with its oppressive drapes, its horsehair chair, its fringed sofa, and its Romantic picture in the upper right-hand corner.

Here is the ancestor of the suburban family of today, a century and more before the patio, the outdoor grill, and the splashy clothes. Doubtless a century from now we will look equally odd in the few Polaroids that have been preserved.

MARRIED

Source: Cover for "Willie we Have Missed you." Lithographed by Sarony & Co. and issued by Firth, Pond & Co., 1854.
Reproduced from the Collections of the Library of Congress

Stephen Foster stayed in the mainstream of American sentiment. He celebrated both its joyful and its tearful occasions, though it must be confessed that he preferred the tearful ones. Here, however, he sings of the joy of reunion. The family is together again.

Husband and wife actually embrace, unlike the pair in the previous picture, who sit sedately apart. As a matter of fact, Willie has simply dropped his handbag and stovepipe hat on the floor while he hugs his wife. In spite of the modest size of his luggage, the warmth of greeting suggests that he has just returned from a considerable journey. It is late at night; the toys resting in front of the fire (drum, horse, top) suggest a little boy, who is doubtless already asleep.

What permeates the song and is reflected in the picture is the sentiment. The artist has captured it successfully. The faces are unremarkable except that the wife has stronger features—a sharper nose and chin than an artist would give her today. Little about the room they stand in sets it off but the landscape we see through the open door has some interest. In its smooth forms and molded structure it reminds us of the Iowa scenes by the artist Grant Wood. Once again it is a Romantic landscape and yet its curious stylizing makes it more memorable than the major scene within the house.

Source: The Wedding Night. Lithographed by J. Schutz and issued by N. Currier, probably in 1850.
The Harry T. Peters "America on Stone" Lithography Collection, The Smithsonian Institution

Our first pictorial document, "Married," displays no emotion whatsoever. The second, "Willie we have Missed you," shows the joy and relief of reunion. The third, "The Wedding Night," shows a kind of joyous carnality that no American lithographer would have depicted without much hesitation. That marriage meant sex was undeniable in actuality but unacceptable in theory. American mores either ignored the fact of it or else uneasily denied its importance. In an age of the double bed and large families, sex was as taboo as a social subject then as death is now. Illegitimate sex was simply considered not to exist but even legitimate sex, in marriage, was considered an unfit subject for any sort of public expression.

The extent of the suppression of sex from the surface of American society is amazing. Overtly pornographic sex is absent. The usual idea is that if a society suppresses sex on the surface, it

COVER FOR "WILLIE WE HAVE MISSED YOU"

THE WEDDING NIGHT

will show itself in subsurface ways, one of which is pornography. However, even the Kinsey Institute, with one of the largest collections of pornography in the world, has almost no American pornography for the 1850s.

"The Wedding Night" was the closest thing to pornography that an antebellum American was apt to see. It embodies a view that few Americans admitted holding: that sex could be enjoyable—to both partners. But the lithograph is so patently European in flavor that even censorious Americans would be apt to excuse it. After all, it was well known that Europe was a sink of depravity. The artist, Schutz, was a European and he attired his bridal pair in elaborate foreign dress. He even hung an earring on the groom. Schutz worked for Nathaniel Currier in 1849–50 and was probably a sport in Currier's otherwise circumspect shop. At any rate Currier allowed him some artistic license, with the interesting result we see.

The most vivid thing about the picture is the expression on the two faces. The groom unlaces his new wife's stays with a lip-licking smile. The bride bends her head to look back at him. Her expression is one of amiable expectation. She stands, hands on hips, almost coquettishly and is far from the timid virgin that the American male was supposed to initiate into the duties if not the pleasures of sex. Legitimate though the delights of bed promise to be in this case, it is significant that they are delights and that they will be shared, to repeat, by both partners.

The artist of "The Wedding Night" knew what he was about. His lithograph, with the bed bulking large behind the lovers and the twin pillows close together, with the tassels intertwined and the folds of the bed's drapes all too labial, played on American prurience. But the picture is not scruffy; Schutz treats his topic with a bland good-humor that would invite even a Puritan to smile.

Source: Res. of John Agnew.
The Harry T. Peters "America on Stone" Lithography Collection,
The Smithsonian Institution

In any struggle to present the average in American life, the odds are against us. It is not the average that survives. The average is taken for granted more often than not; no newspaper reports it, no artist pictures it. For that matter, no historian chronicles it; he is seldom interested in our daily doings.

The result is that when we look for everyday life we have to use a sort of triangulation or, to change the metaphor, an extrapolation. This is as true for the houses people lived in as for the people themselves. We have already read a description of the plans for one farmhouse which, according to its designer, will be cheap enough so that the average farmer can afford to build it. But the average house actually occupied in the 1850s, in town or country, has by now been torn down. And few pictures of it survive. Most lithographs preserve the atypical: the mossy cottage under the moon, the big farmhouse at Thanksgiving, or the stately mansion of the town banker.

Here, however, in a single lithograph,

we are fortunate to find an average house as well as an above-average one. Even the above-average one is no mansion. It is the home of a respectable manufacturer of glass; behind it stands a shed with its glass-furnace smoking. Some day his firm would grow formidable, as part of a major American corporation, but meanwhile it simply let him make a decent living. Though American Gothic was the fashionable architectural style, there is nothing Gothic about John Agnew's residence. The house is almost if not quite plain New England.

The design is simple and symmetrical, without bargeboards or gewgaws of any description. The only decorative touch is furnished by the shutters, and they were probably useful as well as ornamental. We see the house, in all probability, in summer; at a guess it is an idealized Sunday afternoon. The men and women wear their best clothes. The buggy in the lower left carries two couples who, like the middle-class, middle-aged couples of today's suburbia, segregate by sex. The men sit in the front seat, the women in the back. On the Agnew lawn three people will start a game of croquet as soon as the fourth

joins them. The fourth in question is a lady, doubtless late, who is now hurrying to join the others.

The grounds betray the fact that Agnew has more money than the house might suggest. The fountain, in particular, is a rather expensive touch. The flagpole, tall though it is, cost less but it clearly evidences Agnew's patriotism.

To its left we have the average house. Much smaller than the Agnew home, it probably contains five rooms. What it lacks in size it tries to make up in style. Its architecture is Tuscan, the fashion which was competing with American Gothic and would shortly replace it. The hooded tower is omitted because the house is a cheap one. But the brackets are there, joining the roof and the outer walls; the window treatment is simplified Tuscan; and the bay window has Tuscan touches. The lawn is smaller than the Agnews's and the lawn ornament is modest. But it is there: a pedestal, topped by a vase, with some undistinguishable flowers in it. The residence seems suitable for a relative of Agnew's, perhaps a brother-in-law, who never quite made the success expected of him.

RES. OF JOHN AGNEW

93

IV. The World of Knowledge

Chapter 14

The American Mind

FEW writers of the 1850s addressed themselves fully to the challenging subject of the American mind. They shrank from the breadth of the topic if not from its depth. Count Adam de Gurowski, however, had no hesitation. He charged in readily. He devoted a chapter entitled "The American Mind" in his *America and Europe* to his views about the complexion of our thought. He surveyed the origins of the American mind, its peculiarities, its powers, its overflow into art, language, and literature, its odd attitude toward the past, and its delight in inventions.

In the parts of the chapter reprinted here, he begins with a series of bold generalizations. Some of them sound hollow. Abstraction follows abstraction, with often an old-fashioned air to us because of Gurowski's belief in faculty psychology. On the other hand, most of his generalizations are at the least plausible. They fit in with other evidence of the time that we can discover.

When he compares the mind of the Old World, which he has left, to that of the New World, where he is living, the advantage is all on the side of the New World. Except in literature. Most American literature remains an imitation of English literature—"a few productions excepted, as for example Longfellow's Evangelina." Yet even the literature has something to say for itself. In assessing it, Gurowski has the wit to realize the importance of regional differences; he understands that the literature of New England, for instance, varies from that of the West. In the final part of his chapter he dwells on our fascination with machines, the same characteristic which Horace Greeley showed in his *Art and Industry* of 1853.

He does all this while wrestling amiably with American syntax—"as is it the popular song," he writes for instance.

Source: Adam G. de Gurowski, *America and Europe*
(New York, 1857), pp. 333–36, abridged, 339–41, abridged; 346–49, abridged; 351–52, abridged.

THE AMERICAN MIND

The American mind tends pre-eminently towards the objective, at times however being given to the subjective, even to abstract speculation. It is singularly impulsive and receptive, seizes eagerly upon the most antagonistic objects, and embraces them with considerable elasticity. Expansive, and at times daring, it is less disciplined and subdued by routine, than is the case with the English mind. Hitherto the American mind has not reached the elevated standpoint of an absolute, intuitive individuality. Stimulated by the fulness and vigor of intuitiveness, but open to the breathing influences of outward nature, to the ever freshly pouring combinations of events, the mind ascends slowly, step by step, into the expanding region of normal self-consciousness. It is inquisitive, analytic, dismembering, and still eager often to discover, to comprehend a general law, to accept general formulas and axioms, and to submit to them. It grapples willingly with difficulties, but is not however always enduring or patient enough to overcome and subdue them, above all when the difficulties are founded in merely abstract, speculative combinations. Evoked to self-conscious activity, the American mind was thrown at the start into a stern and rough medium, and cut off from the motherland; it was obliged to direct all its intensity to struggles with nature, with destructive matter, was forced to choose and decide swiftly, to act, and not to remain in musing contemplation.

Immediate practical results are more attractive for the American mind, although not exclusively, than the charms of imagination. In its intellectual, positive turn, it yields easily to the pressure of outward events and combinations. Intellect finds more food, more stimulus, in externalities and therefore it overpowers the spirit, the imagination, as well as the tendency to abstract, interior contemplation. Of great mobility, expansive but not deep, the American mind as yet seems unable to seize thoroughly and penetrate deeply into the infinity of intuitive ideas, engrossed as it has hitherto been by sensations. The social condition, the primitive state of nature, opening uninterruptedly her wider and wider circles before the Americans, challenge and attract the intellectual powers, carry away the activity into one general, explorative, mechanical, commercial current. But then even, a certain inborn elasticity redeems and saves it from utter degradation. And so, notwithstanding this seemingly all-absorbing commercial propensity, the mind of the people at large does not become eaten up or narrowed, as is the case, for example, with the immense majority of the various commercial classes in Europe. The so-called petty shopkeeper spirit does not prevail in America to the same extent as in most of the European parent countries.

Excitability, omnipotent in the American character, scarcely affects the activity of mind. The keen internal perception of the object strongly resists excitability or nervousness, and dispels the mist that has been aroused. If the Americans do not resist but yield to the current of excitement, it is more from want of independence, than from want of a sound, internal, mental judgment. Comparatively rapid and comprehensive in assimilation and combination—far more so than the English—the American mind seems to be indifferent to method; at the same time, by a striking contrast, the intellect is disciplined by it in most of its mechanical dealings with the realm of matter. Though not absolutely rigorous in its operations, the American mind is earnest, giving fixity and ballast, and forming a counterpoise to the often febrile unrest of character.

The various peculiarities of the American mind, the outbursts of its originality and independence, are manifested more generally and freely in the people at large, in its promptings and impulses, than in those which are commonly considered as the representative minds, the literary stars, or any other exponents of the spiritual or imaginative faculties. Among the people likewise, as for example among that of New England, that of the West, gushes out and is domestic the rich vein of humor, which constitutes a trait of originality, distinct from the English humor, and from that of other European nations. . . .

There must have been poetry of action and of endurance in the American primitive life, as there was in the sacrifices of the Puritans, although it found no vent in songs and other productions. The poetical spark slumbered during the colonial time. Colonial existence seems never to have been favorable to any kind of poetical effusions. So the ancient colonies of Greece, in Italy, Sicily, Marseilles, repeated the songs of the mother country, but no fresh genuine strain flowed from them. It might even have been also, that the climate here, assimilating and identifying to its influences the new comer, repressed at the start the poetical effluence. No spring, but rapid transition from winter to summer; so the individual here passes from childhood at once to manhood; so the people unknown, unconsidered yesterday, took at once, in full activity, its place among the oldest and grown up nations of the world. Among the people of the Old World, even material poverty, transformed into a chronic normal state, sometimes formed a source of poetical inspiration. There the youth of the poorer class, in forced self-contentment, abandons himself often to reveries or to the inward life of the heart, to soft, lovely emotions; here the child in the cradle, the tender youth, have striven and strive to free themselves from the withering embrace of poverty, plunge at once into the current of the prosaic but active world. Not spring but autumn charms and attracts the Americans; not the bud—as is it the popular song—but the ripened fruit, the carefully worked out art, characterize American poetry.

As soon as independence was asserted by the nation, the activity of mind became evoked in all directions; poetry and literature began to be a domestic American product. Lyrical poetry preëminently pours out abundantly, in powerful streams and often full of grace, freshness and charm. The lyric productions of acknowledged American poets, men and women, as well as many accidental effusions, can fairly stand beside, and some above the lyricism of other nations. Many of the little fiery or graceful poems, that have been evoked by events of national, domestic character, bear the mark of originality.

Generally, however, their literature, with its poetical and ephemeral creations, is not original in conception, not stamped with individuality, to the same degree, as are the life of the people and its political institutions. Emancipated as a nation, the Americans remain mentally, by their literary productions, in the colonial dependence upon England. They have outstripped the Old World in most of the productions of intellect, in mechanical arts and inventions, impressing on them, to a certain degree, the stamp of originality; *per contra* in literature, they with difficulty take an independent start. Many are the natural as well as the conventional reasons and causes which account for the phenomenon, that in reality there does not exist— a few productions excepted, as for example Longfellow's Evangelina—an original American literature, but only an imitation, or a continuation of the English literature. Hitherto literature seems rather to be engrafted on, than to sprout out of the vitality of the nation. . . .

The mental dependence upon England is so wide-embracing, that even in the judgment of the most cultivated Americans, familiar with the literatures of other European nations, as well as with their development, march, and history, England still represents the whole of Europe. So when, in any matter whatever, they look for a term of comparison, or seek to elucidate a problem, either scientific, literary, or social, by correlative facts existing in Europe, they generally limit their assertion or comparison to England, firmly believing that it is the

same as if they were drawing the necessary evidences from any other European nation. Few hitherto can clearly realize and comprehend the immense difference existing between the social and mental culture, the customs, habits, modes of life, on the Continent of Europe and those of England; few are acquainted to that extent with the historical and chronological development and concatenation of various sciences and learning, as to be aware that, in this transmission and development, many of the sciences have originated or have been carried forward elsewhere than on the English soil. The people at large are less under the influence of this mental mirage, and in the thus extensive intercourse with Europe, are less ruled and influenced by the reverence for England. But as the faithful wander to Mecca and Rome, paying their worship to the pope and cardinals, so American literators of every degree and hue visit and pay homage almost exclusively to their English models and masters.

Literature being a reflection of the modes, the habits of life, as well as of a certain current of notions and ideas, its character, even in serious productions, corresponds to the character, nay, even to the locality, of the people. American literature was started, almost born in New-England, and has been developed principally in Boston. The authority of Boston, which prides itself on its close resemblance to some secondary features of the English life, as well as on its literary deference to England, has checked, in the otherwise independent mind of the people of New England, the impulse of originality and of individuality. But emancipation dawns. The people at large more and more diverges from Old England, and carries away literature.

Further, the West elaborates a new social and mental life. There the man must fall back upon his inborn resources and faculties; the inner and the outer world equally inspire and urge him to individuality, to independence. The mind and imagination have no bounds there. Elements of the most varied and strongly dissimilar character, mingle and fuse with each other in the West. Their shock and fusion will produce new luminous sparks, new phenomena. The West seems therefore destined to mark a new epoch, to give a new and original start to American literature.

The American mind, the American people, has the greatest capacity of consummation, a capacity unequalled and unparallelled by any other people in the history of the human race. The very considerable literary home production in America is increased by the English literature, and by translations from other languages. The people at large, and not only certain portions of them, read; and thus there exists an inexhaustible demand for new products. Almost all the branches of mental and intellectual activity, good, bad, or indifferent, find issues, and are absorbed by the reading public. There are large masses, however, of either poor or illiterate, and scarcely rudimentally instructed whites in the Slavery States, who are not attracted to mental occupation, or who cannot buy books. Not less considerable is the mass of illiterate Irish, who therefore do not contribute to stimulate the demand for domestic or imported literary productions. The Germans, amounting likewise to several millions, confine themselves mostly to German literature. About sixteen millions of inhabitants in the United States—principally of the Free States—constitute the kernel of the population, which absorbs domestic and English literature, and foreign imports. Not any European country, not even several of the most civilized ones combined, and accordingly greatly outnumbering America, proffers in proportion so large and remunerative an outlet for literary productiveness.

The mental pursuit of book-writing preserves the prominent characteristic of all other pursuits in America. It is principally, if not exclusively, an object of material gain, and the aim is the sale. Such is the case even with productions of serious scientific purport or contents. European *savants*, in giving to the world the fruits of their—often life-long—protracted speculations, investigations and studies, yield more to an inward, moral desire to reveal and throw into the world a new generating idea, by which others may become enlightened, or stimulated to a new and fresh activity. They have in view scientific and literary fame, more than the pecuniary advantages to be obtained from their arduous labors, all serious, scientific books of whatever range meeting generally with a rather limited demand. In America, even productions in that department are in proportion by far more remunerative.

Theology and history stand foremost among the more elaborate indigenous literary products. The numerous various confessions, the unlimited religious freedom, and the innumerable independent spiritual communities and associations which it creates, the religious element still powerful in the composition of American society, the mental and social standing and influence of the clergy, sufficiently explain this prolificness.

Mythical traditions, legends, lays and tales, preserved religiously by oral transmissions, have been the living fountains of history for all nations. America, born in positive times, and in the epoch of print, could not surround her cradle with such dim but venerated recollections. But for that, the May-Flower, or even the vessels which brought to these shores Smith, Raleigh and the other first settlers, might have rivalled the Argo in their mythical halo. But for that, the daring discoverers of the buffalo tracks in the undulating lands of Kentucky, in the prairies of the West; Fremont, the pathfinder, upon the Rocky Mountains, such men might stand before posterity as a Hercules, Theseus, or Odin. The recollection of the deeds of the past, charms and attracts the human mind. Man likes to tear them from oblivion. This tendency of the mind is evidenced strongly in America. With eager diligence the Americans make up the deficiency of not being covered by the myths and the dust of many centuries, by chronicling the most minute details of the action of the first settlers, the records of the first settlements, and of the establishment of towns, cities, colonies, and their expansion into States. Thus every village, nay, almost every spot has its positive history, its chronicler. Those simple accounts, how society, how communities, communes were born and organized here, how natural, simple causes, and the combination of events with human activity, human social and material wants, almost insignificant at the start, in their subsequent normal concatenation, have expanded and founded States and a nation—these facts by inference aid to explain the origin of elder and ancient nations, which is wrapped in mist. . . .

The industrial and mechanical arts which bear directly on the necessities of existence, and urged by these necessities have generated the most multifarious results. They have reached in America an expansion almost unrivalled by any other European nation. All such inventions, answering to immediate demand, become a specialty with the Americans. They directly increase the material wealth, the forces and the power of the nation, producing the expansion of prosperity among the masses of the people. Democratic in their nature, origin and results, benefiting thereby the greatest number, they stand foremost in popular appreciation, and excite general and intense interest. In harmony with the state of society, and with its urgent necessities, they constitute the salient feature of the American mind. And so it happens that millions will pass unnoticed a work of the Fine Arts, when an industrial and mechanical invention would throw them into a feverish excitement. . . .

Chapter 15

Growing Pains in the Schoolhouse

As the 1850s went along, the American public school system steadily expanded and improved. The census of 1850 showed that out of every hundred children of school age, forty-seven were in school. The census of 1860 showed that the number had risen to fifty. But these, it should be added, were white children; only two out of every hundred Negroes were in school. However, even the education of white children could stand improvement, and this was true in even the most advanced of Northern states, Massachusetts.

The school system still had to go far to satisfy its best friends. One of those friends was a vigorous Massachusetts politician named George Boutwell. After gaining the governorship of the state and serving creditably there, he became secretary of the State Board of Education. During his time as secretary he collected some of his reports and occasional papers and published them in 1859 as *Thoughts on Educational Topics and Institutions*. The thoughts on "Elementary Training in the Public Schools," reprinted in part below, originated as one of his annual reports to the board.

His writing is marked by an honest appraisal of schooling in Massachusetts and a high ideal of what public education should be. In this selection both the criticisms and the recommendations are, contrary to much educational practice, quite specific.

He wants an education that is not only intellectual but moral and physical. He believes that the school should inculcate discipline in the child; indeed he says that it should "chasten" him. Furthermore, the school should help the child to gain the sound body needed for a sound mind. Boutwell wants a heavy emphasis on reading and spelling, though he also thinks that writing is important—as well as two curiously old-fashioned subjects, music and drawing. He believes in inductive grammar rather than in grammar as a set of rules. He believes in the "New Mathematics" of his day both because it is relevant and because it trains the mind. And he is at his most progressive in announcing that he believes in higher pay for teachers.

Source: George S. Boutwell, *Thoughts on Educational Topics and Institutions*
(Boston, 1859), pp. 131–32, abridged; 134–35, abridged; 143–47, abridged; 149–51.

ELEMENTARY TRAINING IN THE PUBLIC SCHOOLS

We are still sadly defective in methods of education. Until recently teaching was almost an unknown art; and we are at present struggling against ignorance without any well-defined plan, and attempting to develop and build up the immortal character of children, without a philosophical and generally accepted theory of the nature of the human mind. There are complaints that the duties and exactions of the schools injure the health and impair the constitutions of pupils; that the progress in intellectual attainments is not always what it should be; that the training given is sometimes determined by the wishes of committees against the better judgment of competent teachers; that the text-books are defective; that the studies in the common schools are too numerous; that the elements are consequently neglected; and that, in fine, too much thought is bestowed upon exhibitions and contests for public prizes, to the injury of good learning, and of individual and general character. For these complaints there is some foundation; but care should be exercised lest incidental and necessary evils become, in the public estimation, great wrongs, and exceptional cases the evidence of general facts. . . .

When the child is a member of the school, what shall be done with him? He must first be taught to take an interest in the exercises by making the exercises interesting to him. That the transition from home to the school may be easy, he should first occupy himself with those topics and studies that are presented to the eye and to the ear, and may be mastered, so as to produce the sensation that follows achievement with only a moderate use of the reasoning and reflective faculties. Among these are reading, writing, music, and drawing. This is also the time when object lessons may be given with great advantage. The forms and names of geometrical solids may be taught. Exercises may be introduced tending to develop those powers by which we comprehend the qualities of color, size, density, form, and weight. Important moral truths may be presented with the aid of suitable illustrations. In every school the teacher and text-books may be considered a positive quality which should balance the negative power of the school itself. In primary schools text-books have but little value, and the chief reliance is, therefore, upon the teacher. Instruction must be mainly oral; hence the mind of the teacher should be well furnished, and her capacities chastened by considerable experience. As the pupils are unable to study, the teacher must lead in all their exercises, and find profitable employment for the children, or they will give themselves up to play or to stupid listlessness. Of these alternatives, the latter is more objectionable than the former. . . .

Assuming that the principal work of the primary schools, after moral and physical culture, should be to give instruction in reading, spelling, writing, music and drawing, it is just to say that special attention should be bestowed upon the two branches first named. So imperfectly is reading sometimes taught, that pupils are found in advanced classes, and in advanced schools, whose progress in other branches is retarded by their inability to read the language fluently and intelligently. When children are well educated in reading, they find profitable employment; and they are, of course, by the knowledge of language acquired, able to comprehend, with greater facility, every study to which they are called.

Pupils often appear dull in grammar, geography and arithmetic, merely because they are poor readers. A child is not qualified to use a text-book of any science until he is able to read with facility, as we are accustomed to speak, in groups of words. This ability he cannot acquire without a great deal of practice. If phonetic spelling is commenced with the alphabet, he will be accurately trained in that art also. It is certain that reading, writing and spelling have been neglected in our schools generally.

If there is to be a reform, it must be commenced, and in a considerable degree accomplished, in the primary schools. These studies will be taught afterwards; but the grammar and high

schools can never compensate for any defect permitted, or any wrong done, in the primary schools. Reading is first mechanical, and then intellectual and emotional. In the primary schools attention is first given to mechanical training, while the intellectual and emotional culture is necessarily in a degree postponed. When the first part of the work is thoroughly done, there is no ground for complaint, and we may look to the teachers of advanced classes and schools for the proper performance of the remaining duty. The ability to spell arbitrarily, either in writing or orally, and the ability to read mechanically,—that is, the ability to seize the words readily, and utter them fluently and accurately,— must be acquired by much spelling and much reading.

This work belongs to the early years of school-life; and, if it can be faithfully performed, the introduction of textbooks in grammar, geography and arithmetic, may be wisely postponed. But it is a sad condition of things, which we are often compelled to contemplate, when a pupil, who might have become a respectable reader had the elementary training been careful, accurate and long-continued, is introduced to an advanced class, and there struggles against obstacles which he cannot comprehend, and which the teacher cannot remove, and finally leaves the school without the ability to read in a manner intelligible to himself, or satisfactory to others. It is the appropriate work of primary schools, and of the teachers of primary classes in district schools, to develop and chasten the moral powers of children, to train them in those habits and practices that are favorable to health and life, whether anything is known of physiology as a science or not, and to give the best culture possible to the eye, the ear, the hand and the voice. This plan is comprehensive enough for any teacher, and it will be found sufficient for any pupil less than ten years of age. Nor am I speaking of that culture which is merely preparatory for the life of the artist, but of that practical training which will enable the subject of it so to use his powers as to render his life valuable to himself, and valuable to the world. There will be, in the exercises comprehended by this outline, sufficient mental discipline. It will, of course, be chiefly incidental, and it may well be doubted whether studies that are merely disciplinary should ever be introduced into our schools. There are useful occupations for pupils that, at the same time, tax and test the mind sufficiently. The plan indicated does not exclude grammar, geography and mental arithmetic, but text-books will not at first be needed. Grammar should be taught by conversation, and in connection with the exercises in reading. Grammar is the appreciation of the power of the words of the language in any given relations to each other, and a knowledge of grammar is essential to the ability to speak, read and write properly. Therefore, grammatical rules and definitions are, or should be, deduced from the language. Hence children should be first trained to speak with accuracy, so that habit shall be on the side of taste and science; next the offices which words perform in simple sentences should be illustrated and made clear. And thus far without textbooks; when, finally, with their help, the pupils in the higher schools may acquire a knowledge of the science, and, at once, as the result of previous training, discern the reason for each rule and definition. . . .

The introduction of Colburn's Intellectual Arithmetic was an epoch in the science. It wrought a radical change in the ability of the people to apply the power of numbers to the practical business of life. Its excellence does not consist in rules and illustrations by which examples and problems are easily solved, but in leading the mind of the pupil into natural and apparent processes of reasoning, by which he is enabled to comprehend a proposition as an independent fact. Herein is a mental discipline of great value, not only in the sciences, but in the daily affairs of men of all classes and conditions. It is to be feared that equally satisfactory results have not been attained in what is called written arithmetic. This partial failure deserves consideration. The first cause may be found in an erroneous opinion concerning the difference between mental and written arithmetic. Written arithmetic is mental arithmetic merely, with a record at given stages of the process of what at that point is accomplished. But, as written arithmetic tends to lessen the power of the pupil for the performance of those operations that are purely mental, he should be subjected, each day, to a searching and rapid drill in mental arithmetic also. This neglect on the part of teachers explains the singular fact that pupils, well trained in mental arithmetic, after attending to written arithmetic for three or six months, appear to have lost rather than gained in their knowledge of the science as a whole.

The second cause of failure may be found in the fact that rules, processes and simple methods of solution, contained in the books, are substituted for the power of comprehension by the pupil. He should be trained to seize an example mentally, whether the slate is to be used or not, and hold it until he can determine by what process the solution is to be wrought. Nor is it a serious objection that he may not at first avail himself of the easiest method. The difference between methods or ways is altogether a subordinate consideration. There may be many ways of reaching a truth, but no one of them is as important as the truth itself. The text-books should contain all the facts needed for the comprehension and the solution of the examples given; the teacher should furnish explanations and other aids, as they are needed; but the practice of adopting a process and following it to an apparently satisfactory conclusion, without comprehending the problem itself, is a serious educational evil, and it exerts a permanent pernicious influence.

The remarks I have now made upon methods of teaching, which may seem to have been offered in a spirit of severe criticism, should be qualified and relieved by the statement that our teachers are as well educated as any in the country, and that they are yearly making progress in their profession. Indeed, I am encouraged to suggest that better things are possible, by the consideration that many instances of distinguished success in teaching the alphabet, reading and grammar, are known to me; and that teachers are themselves aware that the work is, upon the whole, inadequately performed. If, as is generally conceded, the highest order of teaching talent is required in the primary schools, then that talent should be sought out by committees; the persons possessing it should enjoy the best means of preparation; they should receive the highest rewards, both in money and public consideration, and they should be induced to labor, without change or interruption, in the same schools and among the same people.

Chapter 16

Adult Education

THE salient characteristic of American education was its democracy. We aimed increasingly at education for all. The main agency was the always expanding and usually improving public school system. Besides the school there were often some library resources and—perhaps even more important in antebellum days—the lyceum. The library was beginning to establish itself as a supplementary school and the lyceum with its series of inexpensive lectures during each winter was a genuine educational institution. Henry Thoreau said of the one in his neighborhood that no money was better spent than the $125 used each year to maintain it. Through such means Americans could benefit from a continuing education, from education by night if not by day.

The alert professional educator clearly saw the opportunities for service. Here is Samuel Hall, author of one of the standard books on school-teaching, *The Instructor's Manual*, describing with vision and vigor the possibilities of relating out-of-school to in-school education. The selection given below is from "Lecture XII," which like the others is addressed to young teachers. Though Hall's book had been originally issued a good twenty years before, its points were still valid and help to account for its continued popularity. In the part reprinted here Hall concentrates on describing a step-by-step plan for starting a school lyceum, patterning it after the many thriving adult lyceums which had sprung up in the towns and villages of the United States. These pages both testify to the success of the lyceum movement and afford a model of how it operated.

Along the way Hall takes the opportunity to decry reading for pleasure only, in particular the reading of fiction. Sounding like a critic of today's television he says somberly, "Nothing is accounted interesting, to a class of readers, but that which abounds with incident, adventure, and catastrophe."

Source: S. R. Hall, *The Instructor's Manual*
(Boston, 1852) pp. 223–33.

LECTURE XII

Popular education is exciting new interest in the country; and many, who once looked upon themselves as having outlived the time of improvement, are now learning that they may, by efforts easily made, retrieve some of the losses heretofore sustained.

The spirit of improvement ought certainly to be carried into your schools. In accomplishing this, you are to take the lead in the districts to which your labors are devoted. Any school may become a lyceum. It may not, indeed, assume all the features of a town or county society, but still be a society for mutual improvement. An easy and certain method may be devised for awakening an interest in every neighborhood.

When we recall to mind the names of a long list of self-taught and self-made men, and examine the results of their efforts and labors, we have the strongest encouragement to direct the attention of those under our influence, to what *they* may achieve. It is unquestionably true that many, who otherwise would be discouraged by the difficulties which they meet, or observe in the prospect before them, may, however, be stimulated and assisted to pursue such a course as will lead them to respectability and usefulness: *this* is to be done by the intellectual discipline and the practical knowledge which they may acquire at the period, and especially by the means within their reach.

But, you will ask, how can this be accomplished? I will suggest some of those means which occur to me as easy and practicable.

In the first place, having succeeded in establishing order in your school, extend an invitation to those scholars who are willing to make uncommon efforts for acquiring knowledge, to meet you on some evening. Say to them, expressly, you wish none to attend but those who are willing to exert themselves to make attainments in useful knowledge, beyond the usual subjects introduced into school. In this way attention will be excited, and you will find but few who will stay away. When you meet them, it may be useful to read or repeat to them the history of some individual, like Franklin or Rittenhouse; or, perhaps, give account of some of the improvements which have been made in facilitating labor or promoting the convenience of man. The wonderful powers of steam, and the uses to which it can be and is applied, in propelling vessels, conducting railroad cars, turning machinery, forging anchors, spinning cotton, printing books, or any of its thousand well-known uses, will be to the point. The object is, to arouse attention and promote thought. If you can excite young persons to *think*, a most important object is gained, and the door is effectually opened for improvement. Till this is done, but little can be accomplished towards benefiting them in any important degree.

After you have gained this point, you

may next present some particular subject for an exercise. It may be connected with the studies of the school or business of life. It ought not, however, to interfere with the school exercises, or tend to take off attention from those subjects which are of primary importance. The following outlines of a system upon this subject are offered for the consideration of teachers.

On the first evening, let those who are disposed to attend, be requested to state everything they can concerning the history of the town in which they live; and if any are sufficiently acquainted with drawing, they can give a map of it. As a preparation for this historical exercise, they may be requested to visit and converse with some of those who have been inhabitants of the place for a long period of time. The oldest residents will be able to relate many particulars very interesting to the young. This exercise, attended with suitable remarks from the instructor, will be both pleasant and useful to the school, and others who attend. It would certainly add to the interest of the exercise on the part of the pupils, if an intelligent citizen, well acquainted with the history of the town or neighborhood, should attend and relate the most important facts with which he is familiar.

Then let one be requested to write an account of some interesting historical event, such as the discovery of this country, the battles of Lexington, Bunker Hill, Bennington, Saratoga, etc. To a second may be assigned some other historical subject. It will be necessary to assign exercises sufficient to occupy the evening. Another evening, let each one be requested to give, as far as proper, an account of the business in which he, or the family to which he belongs, may be engaged; stating its profits, and its difficulties or facilities. A third evening may be devoted to rhetorical exercises; and another, to free remarks on some important question. Another may be spent in reading interesting accounts of some parts of our own country, or of some other part of the world, time being allowed for making remarks on the subjects. Let an evening be assigned also for the purpose of answering questions proposed to you by the pupils.

It will not be necessary to have these exercises confined to males. The females have often more knowledge, and are better scholars, than any of the young men found in a district. In all cases, where practicable, females should be urged to take a part in the School-Lyceum, and to be present at the meetings.

It will be useful to them and interesting to others, to give some account of housewifery. A description of the process of making cheese, an account of the best mode of making butter, or even of the manner of making a loaf of bread, or brewing beer, would be heard with pleasure, and not without advantage, in almost any place. Domestic economy generally, is a proper subject of attention, and one on which they may, with the utmost propriety, be requested to read compositions. Many other exercises will claim the attention of females, as much as that of young men. All the subjects which I shall hereafter mention are of this class.

I have been the more particular in these remarks, from the fact that sufficient attention is not usually paid to female improvement.

After proper attention has been given to the exercises already mentioned, and others of the same kind, you can proceed to introduce some of the more important principles of natural philosophy, and chemistry, with simple experiments. Moral philosophy claims particular attention. The younger members may, at the same time, have lessons in geometry, and its applications to the business and purposes of life. "Holbrook's First Lessons," accompanied with a card of diagrams, will afford great amusement, and be highly profitable to scholars of eight or ten years of age. By the same class, the "Little Philosopher; or, Infant School at Home," might be used with great advantage. It is an admirable work.

When sufficient attention has been given to such studies, the way will be prepared for the regular formation of a lyceum, on the general principles of these institutions. The importance of apparatus will now be perceived. You will, of course, make it a subject of early attention. To obtain this will be an object of high importance, as it will be a means of facilitating the operations of the lyceum, and will make it a common property.

Another means of increasing the interest felt by your scholars in these subjects, will be to give or engage others to give familiar lectures, furnishing food for reflection, and throwing light on the subjects of study connected with the business and the wants of life. Is there a physician in your vicinity? engage him to give some familiar lectures on the human system, the means of preserving health, or some other theme within the range of his profession. Is there a lawyer? he may point out the several principles of the common law; the distinction between this and statute law; the necessity to every citizen of a certain amount of legal knowledge, etc. Is there an ingenious mechanic? he may tell some-

thing about the nature, importance, and uses of his trade. The minister may be requested to give a lecture on the importance of moral philosophy, or he may explain the nature of the Christian religion, the value and influence of the Bible, etc. etc. By thus engaging foreign assistance, you will be conferring a double benefit. First, the instruction given will be important and highly useful of itself; and secondly, by engaging the attention of those who take a lead in society, you will render the lyceum popular.

You may also confer an important benefit on the neighborhood in which you are employed, by promoting the formation of a library of scientific and useful books. The attention of the young is not sufficiently given to reading of the most useful kind. Young persons are generally better pleased with works of fiction, than with those best calculated to discipline their minds, and to cultivate a good taste. The prevalent taste for reading is, in a degree, vitiated; and whoever is instrumental of correcting it, in a single neighborhood, will unquestionably be a public benefactor. The proportion of light reading, which has been patronized for a few years past, is altogether too large. The "Annuals," "Albums," novels, etc., etc. which have recently been eagerly sought after and read, are exerting a ruinous influence, especially by becoming the occasion of corrupting the taste, and leading the young to neglect those books which would be highly beneficial. I cannot but urge it, therefore, as highly important, that you exert an influence in favor of a more useful kind of reading. Whenever you can direct the attention of your scholars to those books which will lead to a habit of close thinking, you will deserve the thanks of every friend to the young. I am fully persuaded, that neither parents nor instructors are sufficiently awake to the effects of the prevalent light reading of the present day. Nothing is accounted interesting, to a class of readers, but that which abounds with incident, adventure, and catastrophe. A love-tale, or something of similar character, is woven into almost everything written for the young, and has charms for many, (must I say for some professedly pious youth?) greater than a book of travels, voyages, history, or geography. To such, a scientific book has ordinarily few charms. Is there no danger on the whole, that what has been gained on the score of a better mode of teaching, is in danger of being counterbalanced and lost by an injudicious course of reading? Is there not room to fear, that a desire to *please* the young, has overbalanced a desire to *instruct* them? If my fears are well founded, you will confer a great benefit on those whom you can persuade to provide, and read attentively, books calculated to promote a knowledge and excite a love of the sciences.

It is my purpose, at this time, to make suggestions only; your own reflections will furnish you with many things connected with the subjects on which I have spoken. Let it be an object with you to adapt your mode of operations to the exigences of your situation. I am aware, that the directions which I have given cannot be followed in all cases. If a lyceum already exists, or if a course of exercises has been marked out, you will need to pursue that mode which will have the best effect, considered with reference to existing circumstances. In some cases, it may be impracticable to attempt anything more than to call your scholars together, and instruct them in geometry,

by the help of the First Lessons and cards before mentioned. But, by all means, do *something* towards effecting the objects contemplated by lyceums. All of you *may* do something, and must be governed by circumstances as to the best mode. Let not the season pass, however, without making the attempt. Absolute failure, on your part, is preferable to inactivity. Should you not succeed, you will have the pleasure, at least, of reflecting that you have tried to benefit the members who compose your important charge. It will certainly be in your power to disseminate some important intelligence on the subject of popular education. The seed thus sown, may spring up hereafter, under the influence of a warmer sun. Discouragement is not to be indulged, till your efforts have absolutely failed; and if you go forward with your work steadily, manfully, and perseveringly, you may be assured that they will not fail.

Permit me to say, in the conclusion of this lecture, that much will depend on the impression you make on the parents of your scholars. If you can interest them, there will be but little doubt of your success in interesting their children. Be careful, then, to have your objects thoroughly understood by them in the first place. A demand on their purses would be improper, till you have convinced them both that they ought to do something more to benefit their scholars, and also how this may be effected.

Having once convinced them of the utility of apparatus, the means for procuring it will generally be obtained without great difficulty. Let the scholars themselves become the advocates for appropriations. Some encouragement from yourself, will afterwards be necessary; and, in a majority of cases, I have no doubt it will be attended with success. If parents are parsimonious here, their unreasonableness ought to be fully shown. It is certainly true that parsimony is frequently bad economy; and it may be made to appear so. A few dollars expended for apparatus or judicious books, may prevent the young from forming a habit of seeking amusement in a more expensive manner. In a word, satisfy parents what is their true interest, in regard to their children, and your work is accomplished.

Yield to no discouragements which you may encounter. The object you have in view, is too important to be abandoned in consequence of small obstacles. Remember the maxim, "Labor conquers all things." If success does not attend your first efforts, let it be a stimulus to greater exertion, rather than a reason for discouragement. Resolve to succeed, and maintain your determination; if your efforts are discreetly directed, some success will inevitably follow. The interest thus awakened in a single winter has been followed by very cheering results.

Chapter 17

The Scientific Revolution

THE old science was vanishing; the specific was crowding out the general. What the schools still grandly called "natural philosophy" was being cut up into particular fields such as chemistry, botany, biology, and geology. And the fields themselves were swiftly becoming more complex; what they were losing in breadth they were gaining in depth. The geology, for instance, of the running argument on "Geology vs. Genesis" was being altered into a highly technical, informational discipline.

A vivid example of the fight between the new and the old, of the transition from natural philosophy to individual sciences, can be encountered in a review in the *American Journal of Science and the Arts* for May 1855. The magazine, edited chiefly by the noted chemist Benjamin Silliman and his son, set a stiff standard for judging scientific publications. The book being reviewed is Professor Ebenezer Emmons's *American Geology,* Part 1. The main problem is that Emmons's work shows a highly inept mingling of the old and new, and the result is a savage attack by the anonymous reviewer. Above all, Emmons has interspersed geological fact with ethical exhortation. He sees science as affording moral instruction. Also, though he himself is only a geologist, he has ventured into zoology and mineralogy as well as morals.

To the outraged reviewer he is not only merely a geologist but a bad one. Many of his facts are wrong. And his method is marked by slipshod analysis, faulty interpretation, and bad logic. His very grammar is outrageous.

Although both the book and the review are more than a century old, they prove to us that by the 1850s science was no longer something the layman could understand. It takes a trained geologist to comprehend what Emmons is saying and his reviewer is criticizing. The result is that the few pages of the review given here are mainly symbolic. The point is not to try to comprehend what those pages say but to see that they show how formidable, how esoteric, science was becoming even in the 1850s.

Source: "Art. XL.–Emmons on American Geology,"
American Journal of Science and the Arts, 2nd ser., vol. 19 (May 1855), pp. 397, abridged; 404–6, abridged.

ART. XL.–EMMONS ON AMERICAN GEOLOGY

The laborious investigators of our American geology can scarcely find time for the preparation of popular treatises, which shall embody the results of their researches, and the consequence too often is that this labor is left for those who are most unfit for the task. It is but a few months since another pen than ours called attention to Mr. Marcou's poor caricature of a geological map of North America, and showed that both the map and the accompanying text are full of errors and mis-statements, calculated to give foreign readers most erroneous ideas, not only of the state of American science, but of the true geological structure of the country. We recall this with more regret, because we observe that Sir R. I. Murchison was deceived by Mr. Marcou's pretensions, and lent to the map a certain sanction in the pages of Siluria, before he was apprized of its worthlessness. The fact that Mr. Marcou is a comparative stranger in our country may explain his ignorance though not his presumption; but we regret to say that no such excuse can be urged in behalf of the author whose name appears at the head of the article. Dr. Ebenezer Emmons is known to the American public as having been the geologist charged with the examination of the northern district of the State of New York, and as the author of the so-called Taconic System; besides which, as geologist to the State of North Carolina, he has given us two or three reports, which we may notice further on. With these antecedents, he presents to the world the first part of a work on American Geology.

The author seems to have sat down to his task without any well defined plan, and hence the promiscuous arrangement, repetitions, obscurities, and contradictions of the volume. As to scientific accuracy, style, or even English grammar, the work is filled with errors.

Mr. Emmons conceives that the Taconic and Champlain rocks west of the Green Mountains are wedge-shaped masses, which in a breadth of a few miles are reduced from a thickness of several thousand feet to nothing, and it is along the overlapping edges of these extraordinary formations, that he fixes his "line of weakness," which corresponds to the imaginary line of fracture and disturbance. Comment upon this is unnecessary.

The detailed description of the hydroplastic rocks is not given, but we have, to compensate for this deprivation, some eighty pages devoted to mines and mining, which we can only say are worthy of the author. We pass over his crude notions about the theory of metallic veins, and the economics of mining, expressed in his usual style, and shall confine ourselves to pointing out some two or three errors. The iron ores of the Laurentian rocks are described as forming veins, while they in all cases form beds interstratified, with limestone and gneiss, and affected by all the undulations of the accompanying strata. The drawings given by the author, (pp. 140–150), are sufficient to illustrate this, and to prove the incorrectness of his view. At p. 141 he attempts to explain the position of the iron by supposing that the strata have been folded since the formation of the veins.

The lead mines of Wisconsin and Iowa are said by Mr. Emmons to belong "to the Cliff limestone, the lower part of which is equivalent to the Niagara limestone of New York." This is an old error which was corrected some years ago by Mr. Hall, and it is now well known that the lead-bearing limestone of these regions rests upon the Trenton limestone and is overlaid by the Hudson River group. The lead mines of Missouri however occur in the Calciferous sandrock.

In his description of the copper mine of Bristol, Conn., we are told by Mr. Emmons that the ore is gray copper, with yellow sulphuret, and that the locality is remarkable for its fine crystals of gray copper. The crystals of *copperglance* or vitreous copper ore from this mine are well known to mineralogists, but *gray copper, (fahlerz)* which Emmons confounds with this species, is a very rare ore in this country, and has never yet been found at Bristol. He also informs us that Chatham Co., N. C., affords veins of gray copper (copperglance), "which is probably an altered yellow sulphuret." But this is not the only instance where his mineralogy is at fault; on page 53, leucite is classed with

the zeolites, although it is a feldspar and has no affinities with that class. Steatite is said by our author scarcely to differ from talc; but the only analysis given in the illustration of this similarity, is the following,—Silicia 48·30, magnesia 26·65, oxyd of iron 2·00, alumina 6·18, and water 9·05, which is the composition of saponite; the true steatites contain upwards of 60 p. c. of silica, with but little water and no alumina.

Mr. Emmons's zoölogy is however still worse than his mineralogy. We quote a few samples from a glossary of scientific terms appended to his report on the Geological Survey of North Carolina, 1852.

"*Belemnite*—a fossil of a cylindrical form, tapering rapidly to a point, *and at one end or the other it has a conical cavity; it is the backbone of an extinct animal allied to the cuttle fish.*

"*Mammalia—animals which furnish glands for the secretion of milk.*

"*Mastodon—see mammoth.*

"*Mammoth*—an extinct thick-skinned animal allied to the elephant."

He thus confounds the two distinct genera *Mastodon* and *Elephas*. And these we are ashamed to say, are from the pen of a man, who is now, and has been for thirty years, Professor of Natural History in an American college.

Whatever else may be objected to our author, it must be conceded, that in endeavoring to enliven the technicalities of geology by excursions into other fields, he does not disdain to enrich his pages with gleanings from kindred sciences, and even to summon poetry and philosophy to compensate for his shortcomings in English grammar. We shall take the liberty of transcribing a few specimens for the gratification of our readers. In his preliminary sketch of the physical geography of North America, he thus discourses of the ocean. "The profound depths of the ocean are tenantless wastes, except for the dead who have here found resting places, where no wind or wave can move them, or bring up their sacred relics to light, and cast them once more upon a troubled shore."—p. 26. The belts of sand which skirt our Atlantic coast, "in time support a scanty vegetation and *admit of pasturage* for mules, horses, and sheep. The horses which run wild upon these semi-deserts belong to the pony breed; *but* they are tough and hardy," and our author naively adds, "They invariably refuse corn when first taken."—p. 12.

The moon "that luminary which shines with such silvery light and appears so plane and even" to Mr. Emmons, and which he calls "a smaller pattern of our earth" appears to have exercised a strong influence upon his imagination; he gives "a diagram from the Penny Cyclopedia," in order that the student "may *locate* the volcanic peaks," some of which he tells us "exceed one and a-half miles in height." We may remark that according to the accurate measurements of Beer and Maedler there are six of these mountains which are over 19,000 feet and more than twenty, over 15,000 feet in height. A little farther on, the moon's mass and density being given, we are told, "Hence a body weighing six pounds at the earth, would weigh one pound at the moon, *if each weight retained its terrestrial gravity*"!—p. 119.

In his report on North Carolina just quoted, he compares the cycles of the heavenly bodies with geological periods, and adds, "for us space is a unit, and it gives us a measure of time, so that time is space, and space is time, but geology cannot convert time into space, nor space into time." He then in the style of Mr. Chadband inquires "why geology gives us no unit" of time, and consoles himself with the reflection that "the inquiry is futile, and we can only say, that *it can have no final cause;* it can have no practical use."—p. 86.

As he draws to the close of the first part of his American Geology, and alludes to the progress of the science, our author speaks approvingly of the "inquiry after causes," and he tells us:

What is to be discouraged are the attempts to leap the wall at a single bound. We are to climb, and the steps are to be cut by labor. Proceeding in this way, even the essential nature of things may be opened before us. And who shall forbid inquiries into the essential nature of spirit? Step by step we climb the ascending pathway. Light gleams up in the distance. The essence of cause, the essence of God, may faintly illume the horizon of our prospects. It is the goal of man's hopes and aspirations.—p. 193.

This is sheer nonsense, or it would be blasphemy, of which we are willing to acquit the author. But we have copied enough of this, and our only object in calling attention to such a production has been to utter a protest, in which we are sure that every one who has the honor of his country or the advancement of science at heart, will unite, against Mr. Emmons and his book as exponents of American Geology.

Chapter 18

Pseudolearning

IN any picture of the learned world of antebellum days it would be wrong to ignore the faddists and scientific frauds. A weird variety of quacks and medicine men, supplemented by some obviously sincere zealots, flourished before the Civil War. The illuminati of the cold-water cure jostled the advocates of animal magnetism. The dowsers with their wands could be as impressive as the apostles of Sylvester Graham with their coarse bread and icy douches. Of all the pseudosciences, phrenology made the widest appeal. Like physiognomy it was an import from Great Britain. Convinced that the skull in its convexities (it was vulgar to call them bumps) reflected the organs of the brain, the phrenologists preached a gospel of human character which proved very attractive. It promised a quick, easy way to the understanding of human nature; and everyone hoped for that. The businessman wanted to assure himself of honest employees; the suitor wanted to be certain of getting a loving wife; the politician wanted to be able to sway the voter at will.

Appealing to the American itch for applied science, the Fowler brothers, Orson and Lorenzo, advertised themselves as "practical phrenologists"—useful not theoretical. But they promised more than that. Though phrenology reigned as the queen of the pseudosciences, the Fowlers were shrewd enough not to devote themselves to it exclusively. They advertised themselves as adept not only in reading the bumps on the skull but also in the even more dubious exercise of detecting the character through face and figure. Their *New Illustrated Self-Instructor in Phrenology and Physiology* (1859) includes some statements about physiology which made phrenology look sane. In the sections reprinted below, the Fowlers begin by explaining the resemblance between man and animals and end by praising physiognomy as a true science. We can start with Section 16, "Resemblance between Men and Animals."

Source: O. S. and L. N. Fowler, *New Illustrated Self-Instructor in Phrenology and Physiology*
(New York, 1859), pp. 49–53, abridged; 55–56, abridged; 58, abridged.

RESEMBLANCE BETWEEN MEN AND ANIMALS

That certain men "look like" one or another species of animals is an ancient observation. And when in looks, also in character. That is, some have both the lion, or bull-dog, or eagle, or squirrel expression of face, and likewise traits of character. Thus, Daniel Webster was called the "Lion of the North," from his general resemblance in form, having shoulders, hair, and general expression to that king of beasts; and a lion he indeed was, in his sluggishness when at his ease, but power when roused; in his magnanimity to opponents, and the power of his passions.

He had a distinguished contemporary, whose color, expression of countenance, manners, everything, resembled those of the fox, and foxy indeed he was, in character as well as looks, and introduced into the political machinery of our country that wire-working, double-game policy and chicanery, which has done more to corrupt our ever-glorious institutions than everything else combined, even endangering their very existence. Freemen, hunt it down.

Those who resemble the bull-dog are broad-built, round favored, square-faced, round-headed, having a forehead square, and perhaps prominent, but low; mouth rendered square by the projection of the eye or canine teeth, and smallness of those in front; corners of the mouth drawn down; and voice deep, gutteral, growling, and snarling. Such, if fed, will bark and bite *for* you, but, if provoked, will lay right hold of you, and hold on till you or they perish in the struggle. And when this form is found on female shoulders, "the Lord deliver you."

Tristam Burges, called in Congress the "Bald Eagle," from his having the aquiline or eagle-bill nose, a projection in the upper lip, falling into an indentation in the lower, his eagle-shaped eyes and eyebrows, . . . was eagle-like in character, and the most sarcastic, tearing, and soaring man of his day, John Randolph excepted. And whoever has a long, hooked, hawk-bill, or Roman nose, wide mouth, spare form, prominence at the lower and middle part of the forehead, is very fierce when assailed, high tempered, vindictive, efficient, and aspiring, and will fly higher and farther than others.

Tigers are always spare, muscular, long, full over the eyes, large-mouthed, and havé eyes slanting downward from their outer to inner angles; and human beings thus physiognomically characterized, are fierce, domineering, revengeful, most enterprising, not over humane, a terror to enemies, and conspicuous somewhere.

Swine—fat, loggy, lazy, good-dispositioned, flat and hollow-nosed—have their cousins in large-abdomened, pug-nosed, double-chinned, talkative, story-enjoying, beer-loving, good-feeling and feeding, yes-yes humans, who love some easy business, but hate HARD WORK.

Horses, oxen, sheep, owls, doves, and even frogs, etc., also have their men and women cousins, with their accompanying characters.

These resemblances are plain, but more difficult to describe; but the voice, forms of mouth, nose, and chin are the best bases of observation. . . .

LAUGH AS CORRESPONDING WITH CHARACTER

Laughter is very expressive of character. Those who laugh very heartily have much cordiality and whole-souledness of character, except that those who laugh heartily at trifles have much feeling, yet little sense. Those whose giggles are rapid, but light, have much intensity of feeling, yet lack power; whereas those who combine rapidity with force in laughing, combine them in character. One of the greatest workers I ever employed, I hired just because he laughed heartily, his giggles being rapid *and* loud. But a colored domestic who laughed very rapidly, but LIGHTLY, took a great many steps to do almost nothing, and though she worked fast, accomplished little. Vulgar persons always laugh vulgarly, and refined persons show refine-

ment in their laugh. Those who ha, ha right out, unreservedly, have no cunning, and are open-hearted in everything; while those who suppress laughter, and try to control their countenances in it, are more or less secretive. Those who laugh with their mouths closed are non-committal; while those who throw it wide open are unguarded and unequivocal in character. Those who, suppressing laughter for a while, burst forth volcano-like, have strong characteristics, but are well governed, yet violent when they give way to their feelings. Then there is the intellectual laugh, the love laugh, the horse laugh, the philoprogenitive laugh, the friendly laugh, and many other kinds of laugh, each indicative of corresponding mental developments.

THE MODE OF SHAKING HANDS

Also expresses character. Thus, those who give a tame and loose hand, and shake lightly, have a cold, if not heartless and selfish disposition, rarely sacrificing much for others, are probably conservatives, and lack warmth and soul. But those who grasp firmly, and shake heartily, have a corresponding whole-souledness of character, are hospitable, and will sacrifice business to friends; while those who bow low when they shake hands, add deference to friendship, and are easily led, for good or bad, by friends. . . .

COLOR AND TEXTURE OF HAIR, SKIN, BEARD, ETC.

Everything in nature is colored, inside and out; and the color always corresponds with the character. Nature paints her coarse productions in coarse drab, but adorns all her finer, more exquisite productions with her most beautiful colors. Thus, highly-colored fruits are always highly-flavored; the birds of the highest quality are arrayed in the most gorgeous tints and hues.

So, also, *particular* colors signify particular qualities. Thus, throughout all nature black signifies power, or a great amount of character; red, the ardent, loving, intense, concentrated, positive; green, immaturity; yellow, ripeness, richness, etc. Hence all black animals are powerful, of which bear, Morgan horse, black snake, etc., furnish examples. So black fruits, as blackberry, black raspberry, whortle berry, black Tartarian, cherry, etc., are highly-flavored and full of rich juices. So, also, the dark races, as Indian and African, are strong, muscular, and very tough. All red fruits are acid, as the strawberry; but the darker they are the sweeter, as the Baldwin, gillifleur, etc.; while striped apples blend the sweet with the sour. But whatever is growing, that is, still immature, is green; but all grasses, grains, fruits, etc., pass, while ripening, from the green to the yellow, and sometimes through the red. The red and yellow fruits are always delicious. Other primary colors signify other characteristics.

Now, since coarseness and fineness of texture indicate coarse and fine-grained feelings and characters, and since black signifies power, and red ardor, therefore coarse black hair and skin signify great power of character of some kind, along with considerable tendency to the sensual; yet fine black hair and skin indicate strength of character, along with purity and goodness. Dark-skinned nations are always behind the light-skinned in all the improvements of the age, as well as in the higher and finer manifestations of humanity. So, too, dark-haired persons,

like Webster, sometimes called "Black Dan," possess great power of intellect and propensity, yet lack the finer and more delicate shadings of sensibility and purity. Coarse black hair and skin, and coarse red hair and whiskers, indicate powerful animal passions, together with corresponding strength of character; while fine, or light, or auburn hair indicates quick susceptibilities, together with refinement and good taste. Fine dark or brown hair indicates the combination of exquisite susceptibilities with great strength of character, while auburn hair, with a florid countenance, indicates the highest order of sentiment and intensity of feeling, along with corresponding purity of character, combined with the highest capacities for enjoyment and suffering. And the intermediate colors and textures indicate intermediate mentalities. Curly hair or beard indicate a crisp, excitable, and variable disposition, and much diversity of character—now blowing hot, now cold—along with intense love and hate, gushing, glowing emotions, brilliancy, and variety of talent. So look out for ringlets; they betoken April weather—treat them gently, lovingly, and you will have the brightest, clearest sunshine, and the sweetest, balmiest breezes; but ruffle them, and you raise—oh, what a storm! a very hurricane, changeable, now so very hot, now so cold—that you had better not ruffle them. And this is doubly true of auburn curls; though auburn ringlets need but a little right, kind, fond treatment to render them all as fair and delightful as the brightest spring morning. . . .

PHYSIOGNOMY A TRUE SCIENCE

That nature has instituted a SCIENCE of Physiognomy as a *facial* expression of mind and character is proclaimed by the very instincts of man and animals. Can not the very dog tell whether his master is pleased or displeased, and the very slave, who will make a good, and who a cruel master—and all by the expressions of the countenance? The fact is, that nature compels all her productions to proclaim their interior virtues—their own shame, even—and hoists a true flag of character at their masthead, so that he who runs may read.

Thus, all apples both tell that they possess apple character by their apple shape, but what *kind* of apple—whether good, bad, or indifferent—by their special forms, colors, etc.; all fish, not only that they are fish, but whether trout or sturgeon, and all humans that they are human by their outline aspect. And thus of all things.

Moreover, though all human beings have the general human form and features—though all have eyes, nose, mouth, skin, etc., yet every one has a *different* face and look from every other. And more yet, the *same* person has a very different facial look at different times, according as he is angry or friendly, etc.

And always the *same* look when in the same mood. Of course, then, something *causes* this expression—especially, since *all* who are angry, friendly, etc., have one general or *similar* expression; that is, one look expresses anger, another affection, another devotion, another kindness, etc. And since nature always works by means, she must needs have her *physiognomical* tools. Nor are they under the control of will, for they act *spontaneously*. We can not *help,* whether we will or no, laughing when merry, even though in church, pouting when provoked, and expressing all our mental operations, down even to the very innermost recesses of our souls, in and by our countenances. And with more minuteness and completeness than by words, especially when the expressions are intense or peculiar. Spirits are said to converse mainly by their expressions of countenance—to *look* their thoughts and emotions, instead of talking them.

Chapter 19

Further Education

AS WE survey the 1850s we can see why many Americans believed that no nation in the world was more interested in learning than ours. Democratic education still had far to go but it was clearly on the way. Only in the South, enmeshed in slavery, did education remain feeble and limited. Elsewhere, a variety of evidence can be unearthed to testify to the interest both in formal and informal education. It is true that little of the evidence is exact. The school statistics for the United States do not begin to be gathered till 1870. The antebellum statistics on the number of books published are shaky: individual publishers liked to boast that they were printing and selling more books than they really were. The statistics on newspapers and magazines can be deduced but only approximately. The census for 1850 counts 254 daily papers; the census for 1860 counts 387. In each case, however, the enumerators add a note to the effect that these figures include a "small number" of periodicals.

Yet we do not need exactness to see that education for young and old, for rich and poor, for white if not for black, was plainly part of the American dream. We see it in spelling books, in primers, in lyceum lectures, in library associations, in new elementary schools, academies, institutes, and colleges. We see it in periodicals of all varieties and in a wide range of books. We see it in the proliferating editions of the most popular book of all, the Bible. We see it in inventions and new machines, in the expertise that planned the Niagara bridge and the *Flying Cloud*. It almost seems that we can see education everywhere. And we can surely see it in the pictorial documents that follow.

Source: View of Antioch College. Sketched by J. R. Hamilton
and issued by Sarony & Major, after 1852.
Reproduced from the Collections of the Library of Congress

No picture shows the extension of education during the 1850s better than this one. Of course the number of schoolhouses was multiplying; the network of both primary and secondary schools was spreading over the country. But this kind of extension was horizontal. It was the vertical kind which was most striking. The dramatic appearance of higher education on the American scene came in the 1850s. It is certainly true that a small variety of colleges, led by Harvard, had existed before that; and it is equally true that though they educated only a tiny number, that number was an elite. However, it was not till shortly before the Civil War that America in general apparently became aware of higher education.

The evidence for this impression runs from the most direct to the most tangential. We have such direct evidence as the founding of new colleges and the burgeoning of old. Among the new ones, in the 1850s to take just a few: Adrian College in Michigan, Beaver in Pennsylvania, Berea in Kentucky, Butler in Indiana. Meanwhile, the old ones steadily added more students. And we have such indirect evidence as the increase, according to one content analysis, of references to college in the domestic novels of the 1850s.

The most striking symbol of the extension is Antioch College. Established in Yellow Springs, Ohio, in 1852, it represented the logical development of the foremost trends in our education. Its

president was the distinguished Massachusetts educator, Horace Mann, who went to Yellow Springs with the courage of any western pioneer. He was breaking as much new ground as they did. The extent of it can be observed in the lithograph reproduced here.

This lithograph is a promotional piece for the new college and by its very existence testifies to the new day. Though Harvard would have been horrified by such advertising Antioch embraced it. In fact Antioch even appointed a New York agent, whose name is listed in the lower righthand corner. The promotion is artful, enticing. Because Antioch attracted national interest there are a number of engravings and lithographs of it before the Civil War. But in none of those does the college look as handsome. In the others the trees as a rule seem smaller, the campus barer, the buildings less elegant. In our "View of Antioch College" the artist has done all that art can.

The legend beneath the title adroitly marries tradition and innovation. It reads: "This institution was founded by the Christians in 1850. Incorporated in 1852. It is located at Yellow Springs, Ohio. In its privileges, there is no distinction in regard to Sex. The laws of human health & Life will be practically taught, and enforced upon all! It will exert no sectarian influence over its pupils."

Tradition is shown in the fact that its founders are termed religious and that everyone will be expected to conform to

VIEW OF ANTIOCH COLLEGE

the regulations. Innovation is shown in the fact that it will admit women and give them equal rights (Antioch will be the first in the country to do this), that it will teach the "laws of human health & Life" practically (practical education will lead to a pioneering plan in which students split their time between jobs and books), and that it will be non-sectarian (though here it will not be unique).

J. R. Hamilton has wrung all he can from the scene before him. He has framed the college buildings with a piece of Romantic landscape on the left and at least some Romantic rock on the right. However, he also shows a train puffing into the picture at the right margin. He has made the buildings massive partly through making the few human beings antlike. He has dressed the architecture —a weird conglomerate with Tuscan predominating—to considerable advantage. Here, then, is education of the 1850s, at its most inviting.

Source: Front page of the *New York Ledger*, October 11, 1856.
Reproduced from the Collections of the Library of Congress

In the world of knowledge newspapers and magazines played an increasingly prominent part. During the decade the number of weekly newspapers rose by more than a third, from 2,048 in 1850 to 2,971 in 1860. The number of magazines rose with equal sharpness but then fell off when the Panic of 1857 set in. The magazine proprietors learned the hard lesson, which every American depression would teach anew, that magazines were expendable. In 1850 the census counted over 600 magazines while in 1860 it found only 575; but there is no doubt that throughout most of the decade the magazines flourished. Two of the most durable of all American magazines started within this decade, *Harper's Monthly* and the *Atlantic Monthly*.

The decade also saw the founding of what is today the main daily newspaper, the New York *Times*. Dailies appeared most often in the Northeast and even in the 1850s New York was already the principal newspaper town. It had Horace Greeley's crusading *Tribune* at one extreme and James Gordon Bennett's gamy *Herald* at the other. The *Herald*'s advertising was sensational. One sample will do; it comes from the medical testimonials: "You cured me in one day of an old gonorrhea—D. M. Corbyn." The ordinary American was shocked.

Midway between the magazine and newspaper, the "mammoth weekly" reared its bulk. Specializing in sentimental fiction, it acquired an immense popularity during the 1840s but then lost it in the 1850s to the "story weekly." The genius of the story weekly was an Irish immigrant named Robert Bonner. He bought a little sheet called the *Merchants' Ledger*, renamed it the *New York Ledger*, and converted it within the space of a few years into the nation's most popular weekly. His main drawing card was still sentimental fiction, and he had the wit to buy the best—or rather, the most effective. He hired the leading literary weeper of her time, Mrs. E. D. E. N. Southworth, and serialized her soggy novels week by week. But he sea-

THE NEW YORK LEDGER

DEVOTED TO CHOICE LITERATURE — ROMANCE — THE NEWS — COMMERCE

VOL. XII. R. BONNER, EDITOR AND PROPRIETOR, NO. 44 ANN-STREET.　　NEW YORK, OCTOBER 11, 1856.　　TERMS, {$2 PER ANNUM. FOUR CENTS A COPY.}　　NO. 31.

ORION, THE GOLD BEATER;

OR,
TRUE HEARTS AND FALSE.

A TALE OF CITY LIFE.

BY SYLVANUS COBB, JR.,

AUTHOR OF "THE GUNMAKER OF MOSCOW," "THE STORM SECRET," &c. &c.

CHAPTER I.

ORION—A CURIOUS ADVENTURE.

ORION BESET BY THE RUFFIANS, GLICKER AND SLUMPKEY.

soned her fiction with brisker literature, including the witty sketches by Fanny Fern. In addition he often added homilies intended to make better men and women of his readers, as well as a variety of other printed matter. The slogan of the *Ledger* proved accurate enough in its way: "Devoted to Choice Literature, Romance, the News, and Commerce."

The *Ledger* widened the world for its readers and they rewarded it amply, making Bonner a millionaire. The front page for the issue of October 11, 1856, is reproduced here. It is given over to the first chapter of a novel, *Orion, the Gold Beater,* by a well-known hack writer, Sylvanus Cobb. Though the printing in the reproduction is too small to decipher, it is worth mentioning that the novel is a little gem of bad literature. Its hero, Orion Lindell, is described by Cobb as being "true, pure, and noble." In Manhattan he will be beset by all sorts of misadventures; but no reader needs to be a prophet to predict that, in spite of lurking villains or threatening ruffians, truth, purity, and nobility will win out.

Source: Jas. B. Smith & Co's. Philadelphia Blank Book Manufactory. Drawn and lithographed at A. Kollner's Lithography, 1850.

Here we see another evidence of the spread of knowledge in antebellum America. At its simplest the lithograph testifies to the fact that enough Americans could write and read so that there was a substantial market for blank books. A big enough market, in fact, so that every now and then a whole factory could be found making them. The flowing figures of some bookkeeper could go into a new Smith ledger; so, for that matter, could great literature. Henry Thoreau, writing in his blank books of the 1840s and fifties, complained that the only ones he could buy were already ruled for figures. But he wrote literature in them nevertheless.

The different steps in blank-book making are shown around the margin of the central illustration; some of them survive today. Beyond the left-hand margin is a list of the many kinds of books the Smith Company made, ranging from day books to dockets. Beyond the right-hand margin is a list of the stationers' supplies the firm made, as well as still more kinds of blank books. The supplies include sealing wax, black sand (for blotting), lead pencils, wrapping paper, curtain paper, inks, and writing slates.

The lithograph tells us that the Smith Company was also a bookseller. By 1859 the bibliographer Orville Roorbach could publish a list of 2000 booksellers throughout the United States. Though there were few in the South, in the rest of the country they developed into a network of knowledge, of instruction as well as amusement. Books could be bought likewise by subscription or direct from publishers, but the bookstore was an ever-growing social agency. The business records of the Boston publisher Ticknor & Fields have survived and we find the extent of the network through them. Northern New England bought its Tick-

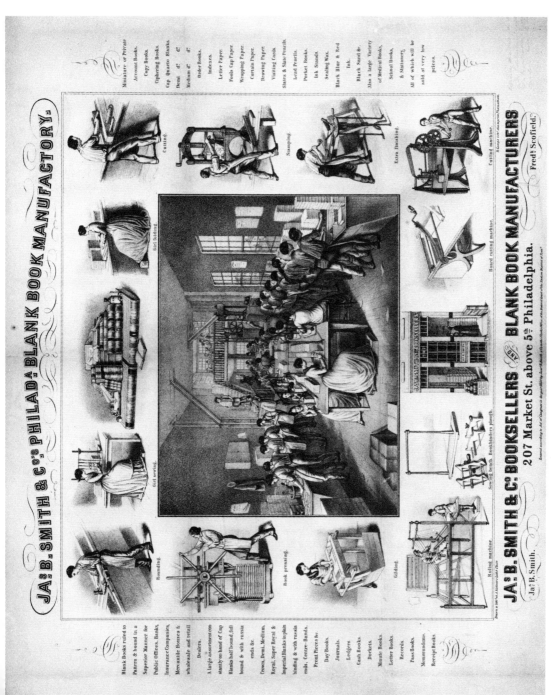

JAS. B. SMITH & CO'S. PHILADELPHIA BLANK BOOK MANUFACTORY

129

nor & Fields books through booksellers in Bangor, Portland, Portsmouth, and Keene. In Massachusetts the Boston stores were supplemented by those of Worcester and Springfield. Southern New England bought in New Bedford, New Haven, and Hartford. And the system worked in the same way, though not to the same degree, in other parts of America. Even in the South, which bought the fewest books, we know that there were booksellers functioning in Richmond, Raleigh, Charleston, and New Orleans.

Many books, it should be stressed, were intended to teach. The most popular were manuals, how-to-do-it books. They ranged from manuals on how to progress in life, for example W. A. Alcott's phenomenally popular *Young Man's Guide,* which reached its twenty-first edition in 1858, to a manual on (believe it or not) how to fly. This was Wise's *System of Aeronautics,* issued in 1850. America had to know how to do things. When it could not learn by observation or word of mouth, it turned to books; and it turned more and more readily.

Some census figures sum the matter up. In 1850 the value of books manufactured was $5,900,000. In 1860 the value was $9,500,000. The tide of printers' ink was rising all the time.

Source: Photograph of Ralph Waldo Emerson. By Curtis & Cameron, ca. 1855.
Reproduced from the Collections of the Library of Congress

America's foremost intellectual of the 1850s looks thoughtfully away in this superb portrait. As a writer and thinker he preached a doctrine which curiously mingled American individualism with an esoteric spiritual culture. Throughout the decade he remained one of the most sought-after of platform speakers. He read his Transcendental lectures from Maine to Missouri, and his audiences listened and thought they learned. Newspaper reports tell us that Emerson's hearers were unsure of exactly what they had heard but they were convinced that it was good. Going home, they felt that greatness had at least brushed close to them. And this is not mere rhetoric: we have enough newspaper stories and journal entries to know that it was no rare response.

The decade saw Emerson passing his prime. The two noble series of essays were already out, but two more of his memorable books appeared during the decade. One was *Representative Men,* in which he wrote about such great figures as Plato and Montaigne, not for themselves but because they gave him a vehicle for communicating his ideas. Though the book was dated 1850, the chapters had done yeoman service as lectures first. The other book was *English Traits,* published in 1856. The result of his visiting England and ruminating on it, it proved to be the best book about the English up to that time. And as the decade ended he turned another impressive series of lectures into the book *The Conduct of Life,* which would appear in 1860.

PHOTOGRAPH OF RALPH WALDO EMERSON

131

V. The House of Worship

Chapter 20

Religion, American-Style

THE more deeply we look into the decade before the Civil War, the more we see that the Christian religion had an importance then that it does not have now. Whether it was religion manifested in the individual or the group, institutional or not, its influence was pervasive. There was a massive interaction between it and other elements in American civilization. We find an illuminating example in the interaction between Christian idealism and one of the master ideas in America, the idea of progress.

The American adjustment is perhaps clearest in the Reverend William R. Williams's *Religious Progress*. As he observed the American scene he found material progress—and the belief in it—everywhere. He found it, in fact, to an inordinate degree. But he also detected religious progress. What interested him as a practical American was the application of religious progress to the improvement of character. He composed a series of lectures on the subject for his congregation and from the lectures prepared his book. Its theme appealed to many readers; the first edition of the book appeared in 1850 and further editions followed during the decade. "Religion a Principle of Growth" is the opening lecture; selections from it are printed below.

Williams begins by announcing firmly that religion is "a principle of perpetual progress." God is our perfect model and we can grow, both as individuals and as a nation, toward His perfection. Williams observes acidly, in passing, that everyone does not agree about this. But the enemies of Christian progress are infatuated. This is not to deny that both the church and its adherents can be improved—in fact, that is exactly the reason for laboring at Christian progress.

Some of the most notable progress is being made outside the country. This is an era of foreign missions and the cross is being carried into heathendom everywhere. Pagan religions are reeling: for instance, "China has shuddered to see the long dominion of her Confucius and her Boodh invaded by the gospel of Jesus the Nazarene." It is to keep them reeling that we need to strengthen our church in America, for our missionary effort will falter if it is not sustained at home.

Lastly, Williams discusses in the selections given here two forces which are also growing but which are potential enemies of religious growth. The first is physical science, led by geology in its repeated attempt to discredit Genesis. The second is social reform. The right road to social reform is through moral reform; and moral reform, as Williams might say, begins in our own bosoms. "It is the reform of our own individual lives, as growing out of a change sought at Christ's feet, and from God's almighty grace." Both physical science and social reform must be dealt with wisely, Williams concludes.

Source: William R. Williams, *Religious Progress*
(Boston, 1850) , pp. 13–17; 21–23; 25–26, abridged.

RELIGION A PRINCIPLE OF GROWTH

Our age is writing "progress" on its banners, and sends along the benches of its schools, and the ranks of its combatants, as the watchword of the times: "Onwards." It bids us to forget the things that are behind, as incomplete and unsatisfactory, and to press toward those which are yet before us. We believe that the gospel, and it alone, adequately, and to the full content of the heart, meets this deeply-seated craving of our times. Religion is a principle of perpetual progress. Not that it distends and pieces its old creed by constant innovations; or retracts the severity of its early warnings and restrictions; or makes Fashion its Sinai. Not that it is the docile handmaid of Philosophy, or the contented retainer and serf of worldly rulers, wearing their livery, taking their wages and orders, and acting merely as a higher branch of their police,—a spiritual constabulary force. If it grew thus with the growth of secular systems and governments, it must on the other hand share in their decay, and perish in their fall, like a parasitic plant blasted by the death of its sturdier supporter.

But setting before us, as the great end of our existence, and as the only perfect model of moral excellence, the Infinite Jehovah, it requires, and it also ministers an ever-growing conformity to Him. And yet the Exemplar, thus to be approached, is ever above the highest soarings of our adoration, gratitude, and love. The elevation of our moral ascent towards him widens continually the horizon of our knowledge, and deepens the sense of our dependence and deficiency,—and earth and self are thus made continually to dwindle. Mere terrene virtue becomes soon giddy and haughty, in proportion to the height of its real or imaginary flights. But the grace of Christ Jesus makes lowliness and self-renunciation to increase in proportion with the increase of true wisdom and goodness. As it spreads more canvas to the breeze, it steadies with new and heavier ballast the keel. And the more humbly and deeply this grace is imbibed, the richer are its effects on the individual heart, and on the character and well-being of the nation, and on the movements and destinies of the age. Each new trial of its infinite resources displays still new depths of truth adequate to every emergency of every people, and of every time. The infatuation of its enemies disputes this fact. They would compliment the religion of the cross into the grave, as an old-world excellence, that is now obsolete; or, others of them, hoot it out of sight as a detected and spent imposture. The remissness of its friends suppresses or obscures this same character of permanent development in true piety. But we suppose the times in which we live, eminently to need that Christians remember and act upon the principle, that their religion is a law of moral and interminable growth. "Grow in grace," is the apostle's injunction to all recipients of that grace. It is the secret and rule of personal reform, constantly advancing, and of social amelioration, enfranchisement and elevation. For the gospel alone it is that can meet the world's wants in their highest and fullest sense; coming to right the wronged, and to guide the darkling, and to relieve the wretched, and to uplift the down-trodden. Compared with its high aims, the loftiest quarry of earthly ambition is but low and poor. The saint wins victories that an Alexander might have coveted in vain, for better is he that ruleth his spirit than he that taketh a city. And the negro, who in the low, dark slave-hut, breathes out confidingly his departing soul, trusting the Saviour and entering heaven, has a glory which all his armies and all his

conquests would of themselves fail to give to the expiring Napoleon.

This trait in the gospel,—its character as a principle of steady and indefinite growth, and of limitless advancement,—needs to be pondered. Our business is now indeed, not so much with the influence of this religion on the community, as on the individual heart and character. But the individual elevated, uplifts necessarily the family and state and age of which he forms a part, and in which he is a necessary and vital element. There is much in the present condition of the churches, and much in the present aspect of the world, that makes this progressive energy of Christianity, a lesson needing now to be especially urged by the teachers and heeded by the disciples of this faith.

The church, we said, needs in this age, to be kept in mind of the great truth, that there remains yet much land to be possessed, not only as the common heritage of the faithful, but as the personal allotment, and homestead, so to speak, of each one of the faithful. The churches, re-discovering a long neglected duty, are now attempting to evangelize the heathen. It is an *age of Missions*. The islands of the Pacific have heard the cry after the lapse of eighteen centuries, that our earth has been honored and blessed by the coming of a Divine Redeemer. China has shuddered to see the long dominion of her Confucius and her Boodh invaded by the gospel of Jesus the Nazarene. The Shasters of Braminism find their sacred Sanscrit tongue employed, by the diligence and fidelity of missionary translators, to utter the oracles of that One True God, who will banish from under the heavens which they have not made, and which He has made, all the hundred thousand gods of the Hindoo Pantheon, with all the other idols of the nations, however ancient and however popular. The tinglings of a new life from on high seem, along the coasts of Asia and of Africa, shooting into nations that Paganism held for centuries senseless and palsied. Is not Ethiopia soon to be, as the prophetic eye of the Psalmist long ages ago saw her, stretching out her hands unto God? But whilst each Christian church, each band of spiritual disciples, in lands long evangelized is thus lengthening the cords of her tent to take in the Gentiles under its broad canopy, she must in consequence, and as it were in counterpoise, of the extension, strengthen her stakes at home, to bear the increased tension and the extended shelter. Her supports must be proportionately augmented at home, by a deepening piety and a sturdier vigor of principle in her discipleship, or the work will soon come to a stand abroad. A sickly and bedwarfed Christianity here will not furnish the requisite laborers, or the needful funds. Expansion without solidity will bring upon our Zion the ruin of the arch unduly elongated and heavily overloaded. Christendom itself must be more thoroughly Christianized, before Heathendom will relinquish its old character and worship, and learn our creed and love our Saviour. Already the zeal and heroic sacrifices of some of our recent converts shame and should stimulate the comparative worldliness and lukewarmness of the churches that had first sent to them the missionary and the Bible. . . .

The world, falsely or with justice, is shouting its own progress, and promising in the advancement of the masses, the moral development of the individual. It is an age of eager and rapid discovery in the *Physical Sciences*. The laws and uses of matter receive profound investigation, and each day are practically applied with some new success. But some of the philosophers thus busied about the material world, seem to think that the world of mind is virtually a nonentity. As Geology scratches the rind of our globe, some are hoping to dig up and fling out before the nations a contradiction to the oracles of the earth's Creator; and to find a birth-mark on the creature that shall impeach the truth of its Maker's registers as to its age and history. Others, in the strides of Astronomy along her star-paved way, hope to see her travel beyond the eye of the Hebrew Jehovah, and bringing back from her far journey a denial of the word that His lips have uttered. Yet Physical Science can certainly neither create nor replace Moral Truth. The crucible of the chemist cannot disintegrate the human soul, or evaporate the Moral Law. The Decalogue, and the Sermon on the Mount; Conscience and Sin; the superhuman majesty and purity of Christ; the Holy Ghost, and the Mercy Seat, would remain, even if a new Cuvier and another Newton should arise, to carry far higher and to sink far deeper, than it has ever yet done, the line of human research; and even if these new masters of physical lore should blaspheme where the older teachers may have adored. Some claim that Revelation must be recast, to meet the advances in Natural Science. They overlook the true limitations, as to the power and prerogatives of mere Material Knowledge. And what are the new and loftier views of man's origin and destiny which these reformers propose to substitute for those views which they would abolish? On the basis of a few hardy generalizations upon imaginary or distorted facts, and by the aid of some ingenious assumptions, a system is excogitated that is to strip the race of immortality, conscience and accountability; and that represents us as but a development of the ape, to be one day superseded by some being of yet nobler developments than our own, and who will have the right to rule and kill us, as we now rule and kill the beasts of the forest. And is it thus, that Philosophy reforms upon the Bible? No—in the endeavor to out-grow Revelation, it has but succeeded in out-growing reason and brutifying humanity. No—let science perfect yet more her telescopes, and make taller her observatories, and deeper her mines, and more searching her crucibles; all will not undermine Jehovah's throne, or sweep out of the moral heavens the great star-like truths of Revelation, and least of all the Sun of Righteousness. God's omniscience is never to be ultimately brought down to, and schooled by man's nescience, as its last standard and test. The last and greatest of the world's scholars will, we doubt not, be among the lowliest worshippers, and the loudest heralds of the crucified Nazarene. The gospel is true—true intensely, entirely and eternally: and all other and inferior truth, as it shall be more patiently and thoroughly evolved, will assume its due place and proportion, as buttressing and exalting the great, pervading, controlling and incarnate Truth —Christ the Maker, the Sovereign, the Upholder, and the Judge, no less than the Redeemer of the world. . . .

It is again, even in lands and governments where political revolution is not needed or is not desired, an age of *social reform*. And in such a time, when the operatives, the proletary class, to use a word of French thinkers, the men living on the day's wages, the laborious and the begrimed, the doers of hard and honest work, are crying out because of the long neglect and cruel oppression which they deem themselves to have endured on the part of their richer brethren,—is it not especially the season, when alike all those who seek and all those who dread such changes, should study, in the scriptures emanating from the Former and Ruler of Society, man's duties to man, and his obligations to his God? The law of human brotherhood is there illustrated as no where else, spread as it is not only over Christ's teachings, but enforced and exemplified by Christ's sacrifice. There we see how the most radical of all reforms is also the most quiet and the most accessible to us all. It is the most radical, for it alters, to the inmost centre and to the outermost circumference, our relations to ourselves and to our race, to the universe, to eternity and to God. It is the most quiet, because it comes not with garments rolled in blood and the confused noise of the battle-field, but in the depths of the heart and with the still, small voice of God's Spirit, "not by might nor by power, but by my Spirit, saith the Lord of Hosts." It is the most accessible, for it waits not for the will of majorities, the success of some favorite candidate, or the action of some busy cabal; it stays not for protocol or senate, or cabinet, but in the solitude of our own closets, and in the secrecy of our own bosoms, it does its lonely, personal and uncontrollable work. It is the reform of our own individual lives, as growing out of a change sought at Christ's feet, and from God's almighty grace, and by the energy of His renewing Spirit, in our own individual hearts. A freedom thus won, what tyrannous invader shall ever reconquer?

Chapter 21

The Protestant Way

THE typical American was still a Protestant. And the typical Protestant was more apt to be a Methodist than anything else. The census of 1850 counted nearly 1,190,000 Methodists to an (estimated) 415,000 Southern Baptists and 207,000 Presbyterians. The next census, for 1860, showed that the growth of Methodism had slowed up when compared with the growth of the other denominations but it still added nearly half a million members.

The Reverend John Scarlett was a leading Methodist minister in New Jersey. He was a convert and the enthusiasm of the convert has often been commented on. He nearly always admires his adopted creed with more zeal than those born to its usages, and he sometimes sees it more clearly. In 1854 Scarlett published *The Life and Experiences of a Converted Infidel*. There he described his youthful wallowing in skepticism and deism, followed by his ascent into Christianity. He left no doubt that the Methodism he had been converted to was the best of all possible sects. At the end of his book he outlined the main points of the Methodist creed and pattern, and in doing so revealed how well it suited American civilization.

His basic premise is clear: whatever Methodism does is right. When other denominations agree, they are right too. When they disagree, as the Presbyterians do in keeping some vestiges of Calvin's narrow creed, they are wrong. Any Methodist knows that everybody has free will, despite Calvin; everybody can be saved, again despite Calvin, at any time.

Methodism is an open, democratic religion, and a powerhouse for good. To other denominations it has "been a battery, from which they have received light and fire." With the passing of the centuries, Methodism has grown, not only in religious but also in secular life. Its role has been especially significant in America: "we have good reason to believe that these United States are much indebted, under God, to Methodism, for their superior greatness over other nations."

Scarlett closes his book with a resounding statement of his belief in the progress of Methodism. Like William Williams he believes in religious progress. He predicts that the "Kingdom of God"—in his view, the Methodist church—must and will advance until the "Church shall have met and conquered every foe."

Source: John Scarlett, *The Life and Experience of a Converted Infidel*
(New York, 1854), pp. 264–70, 272–74.

CONCLUDING REMARKS

I cannot avoid the conclusion that METHODISM is a Church form of godliness, with a power the nearest in resemblance to primitive Christianity of any other in modern times. Methodism is a system consistent with itself, and consistent with the Bible: is suitable to the universal wants of mankind: and harmonizes in every part with Christian experience. Its true definition is its best recommendation; and the less it is departed from, by those within its fold, the better for them, and the world around them, and other Churches; and the more will God be glorified by their adherence to its original forms. Methodism could not be improved by exchanging any of its peculiarities for those of other Churches.

In the distinctive doctrines of the Methodist Episcopal Church we see something that "commends itself to every man's conscience in the sight of God." These doctrines are:—

The necessity and universality of the atonement made by the sacrificial death and sufferings of Jesus Christ.

The free moral agency of man, by free and universal grace given.

The justification of the ungodly by faith, exclusively and immediately.

The direct witness of the Spirit of God with our spirits.

The entire sanctification of the soul from all sin.

The liability constantly to fall from grace, and be lost.

These doctrines Methodism has armed itself with from the beginning. They have been drawn from the armory of God—the Bible—and wielded with success. And in holding these doctrines there has appeared in them nothing that clashes, but perfectly harmonizes on all occasions. In Methodism there is not held any *secret doctrine*—which none but the elect are to meddle with—to be brought forward on certain occasions only, and then to be kept behind the curtain, while other doctrines more suitable for general use are dwelt upon, until the special occasion again returns. Methodism embraces nothing in doctrine that is not useful and proper, even in times of revival. Yea, revival is promoted by these doctrines, every one of them. And when sinners are converted through them, there is no need of labouring with them until they are nearly deranged, to get them to submit to what appears fallacious and paradoxical; but our doctrines are, in every step they take, identified with their experience.

The doctrines held by other denominations that are found to disagree with those of Methodism, have never had, evidently, a good effect upon those believing them. Persons entertaining doctrines antagonistical to ours, have been led by zeal in their cause to write books concerning Methodism, that "savoured not the things that be of God." They have apparently taken more pleasure in making statements against the influence of Methodism, than in spreading holiness. While others, again, have thought it necessary to assume the grounds of Methodist doctrines, and of Methodist forms, in order to the revival of God's work among them. But when Methodists have assumed the doctrines and forms of other denominations, have *they* succeeded *as well?* These remarks are made not to offend any, but to give the mind of the reader, if possible, a clearness of view of the more excellent way. The more Methodism is truly exposed to view, the more will it prosper; and any system of doctrine, in any Church, that requires secrecy to maintain it, the sooner it is driven from the Church, and buried in oblivion, the better.

The itinerant ministry is another peculiarity of Methodism, that has been exhibited quite largely in the world. This ministry has shown its credentials to be of the true evangelical stamp. Its preaching has been in the demonstration of the Spirit and of power. It has not, thus far, been *tongue-tied* to written sermons, to be read in coldness to an unmoved body of hearers. It has been free in truth, in tongue, and in travelling. It has not been bound by word nor by wages.

The preaching of the Methodist itinerant ministry has been the means of a work resembling that on the day of Pentecost, more than any other form of gospel preaching since apostolic days. By it devils have been cast out, and most wonderful reformations have taken place. The greatest revival of pure religion in the world has been brought about by it: thousands and millions of sinners, the century last past, has it succeeded in turning to the "wisdom of the just."

This ministry is a body of self-denying men. Leaving, on true missionary principles, a permanent home, relatives, friends, and pleasant associations, for hardships, trusting in Providence, they "go forth weeping, bearing precious seed," that they may "win souls" to deck their Redeemer's crown.

This ministry is supported by voluntary contributions, without the preacher's having a claim on the people by previous written agreement. This plan works well both ways: on the preacher it has a tendency to exercise his faith in God and to lead him to desire to be useful to the people, from heavenly motives; on the part of the people it is calculated to draw their benevolent feelings into voluntary exercise, to the mutual benefit of the preacher they support, and their own hearts.

This ministry has its starting place, under God, from among the people in the Church, and through their votes in class-meetings and in quarterly conferences. No ministry is less foreign from the people, and less liable to be considered oppressive to them, than that of Methodism.

Methodism, in its government and discipline, is just what its doctrines and free itinerant ministry lead to. They must all go together, or fall together.

The influence that Methodism, as it is, in all its parts, exerts, is beyond what can now be accurately defined. We are not to look for the effects of this influence within merely its own bounds. Other Churches are now what they would not have been, in piety and power, had Methodism never appeared. Methodism has to them been a battery, from which they have received light and fire. This should be a matter of rejoicing to Methodists, and all Christians. We receive blessings to give blessings away. And what Methodism has done for civilization it is impossible for us to estimate. Yet we have good reason to believe that these United States are much indebted, under God, to Methodism, for their superior greatness over other nations. In this respect Methodism is a responsible body. The union of these United States is much within the influence of Methodism. May God preserve both long to bless mankind, is the prayer of every true Methodist and American.

The position occupied by Methodism is thus seen to be indeed a peculiar one. All the "branches" of the Christian Church are not exactly—in freshness, vigour, and fruitfulness—alike, although of the same "Vine." They are not alike in affording favourable opportunities and gracious means in order to the salvation of sinners, and to "make their calling and election sure"; and it would be profitable to give our meditation in prayer for light on the subject.

The origin of Methodism, and the circumstances connected with it at the time, mark it also as a peculiar system, unlike the institutions that have originated with man. Divine power and wisdom were displayed in starting this sublime development of Christianity, as well as sustaining it in the after progress it

has made. This is clear from the fact that the instruments in its origin had no idea of what was about to take place through them. They looked with astonishment on the "strange" work that God was accomplishing through them. They wondered and trembled at seeing through the word they preached, by the Spirit imparted to them, men and women falling down like the slain in battle, crying, "Men and brethren what shall we do?" until evidently created anew in Christ Jesus unto good works. They kept in their journals a statement of facts of these mighty doings of God, in order at proper times to meet together and consult on their probable duty in the work, and to pray for aid and direction. And when preachers from the ranks of the common people, and often unlearned, were suddenly qualified and called, and made good proof of their ministry, they were about to stop them, and dared not, "for God was with them of a truth." The form of doctrine, the mould of government, discipline, and usages, came upon them unlooked for and without human forethought. The work of the Spirit moved them into forms of class-meetings and love-feasts. The same principles led out into the itinerancy, and other forms in Methodism; and all manifestly through the divine agency, as far at least as the main principles are concerned. . . .

Methodism, from the time of its origin to the present, has presented a universal adaptedness to all the wants of all classes, and conditions, and circumstances of men; and it embraces within its fold more variety of persons—in capacities, gifts, and versatile powers—than any other denomination. It is itself a field for the exercise of all the vast variety of powers and capacities of those within its wide embrace, supplying from its immense resources employment for all its members. In the class-meeting, love-feast, and prayer-meeting—those prudential means of grace—there are opportunities afforded for the exercise of every grade of capacity, to the edification of the body of Christ; and all the children of God, in order to spiritual experience and strength, must have, in some personally active way, "the gift stirred up that is within them." Methodism is, therefore, a system of gospel model, giving to every member a suitable place of usefulness within its communion. In it the poor, especially, have the gospel preached to them. And it is equally suitable to the rich: it opens a field of enterprise for their money. It is adapted to the ignorant; and many of this class, ready to perish, have been raised by it out of degradation to respectability and salvation. And the learned have enough to do within its pale; neither have they been cramped in their energies and acquired abilities through misgivings in reference to any of its peculiarities: and, blessed be God, he has afforded the Methodist Church as much sanctified learning as any other Church. It should be a matter of thankfulness, that while the common people and the illiterate are provided for among us, we have as learned Methodists as there are, in all probability, learned ones to be found in any other class. So that in our Zion every variety of aspect in human want is fully met, and every individual peculiarity, like the many parts of a complicated machine, is brought into particular utility with the general whole, in active usefulness for time and eternity.

In the probable *consequences* of Methodism flowing to future generations, there is a vast field thrown open. In prospect it is as mysterious and wonderful as it has been in the past. It will probably lose some of its less important features, but its doctrines and main principles, so manifestly from God, are of *self-subsisting energy;* and these will hold their place in the system until it shall reach the goal of time, the renovated earth and skies taking the place of the present mundane scene.

The kingdom of Christ "must increase" with the progress of constantly advancing time. This increase will be in a clearer and fuller development of all the essential principles of salvation, manifested perpetually to Christ's believing *Church,* and the augmentation of saving power exerted upon the *world,* until "a nation shall be born in a day." Christ's kingdom cannot stand still nor retrograde. The advancement made by the Church is the passing through scenes peculiar to its probation, which scenes of difficulties and impediments, peculiar to *their* own times and places, can never occur but *once.* In this onward march a period will come in which the Church shall have met and conquered every foe, and removed the covering of every obstacle. "Then cometh the end."

Chapter 22

The Catholic Crusade

THE 1850s saw the Catholic church expand at an unprecedented rate. Its striking increase in strength came not from native American sources but from immigration. During the decade the Catholic Irish fled to the United States in larger numbers than they ever had before or would afterward. The peak year was 1851, when the census recorded the entrance of over 220,000. The Irish were augmented especially by the immigrants from Bavaria and other Catholic parts of what today is Germany.

As members both of foreign and religious minorities, these newcomers clung hard to their faith. The Irish and German priests who led them, as well as the hierarchy which led the priests, felt that they had to be militant. They announced the absolutes of the Church of Rome with firmness. Outstanding in the hierarchy was the archbishop of New York, the Most Reverend John Hughes. On a Sunday evening in November 1850 he delivered a resounding lecture about "The Decline of Protestantism and its Cause." Excerpts are given here from the lecture as published in pamphlet form.

Archbishop Hughes told the faithful what they craved to hear. Instead of going into the doctrines of Catholicism, he dwelt on the basic posture of the church. He showed vividly how it contrasted with the posture of Protestantism. Protestantism might allow such an aberration, for instance, as "women's rights"; but Catholicism would never. According to Archbishop Hughes, if God had wanted women to have "rights" He would have bestowed them in the beginning. As it is, the archbishop predicts flatly, "They will not obtain them."

He points, with as much pride as the Reverend Mr. Williams did for the Protestants, to the success of Catholic missionary efforts throughout the heathen world. Speaking of the good work in Paraguay, for instance, he observes in a rhetorical question, "How strangely, and yet how instructively, has God manifested the distinction between truth and error?—for while

Protestantism has converted none, – Catholicism has converted all!" He goes on to predict the day when the entire United States, from the people to the president, will be converted to the Catholic faith. And he ends by urging his hearers to pray for the time when all the world is brought under the pastoral care of their church, the only true church.

Source: John Hughes, *The Decline of Protestantism and its Cause*
(New York, 1850), pp. 3–4, 22–28.

THE DECLINE OF PROTESTANTISM AND ITS CAUSE

The civilized world at the present day may be considered as divided into two great religious denominations; the one adhering to the Catholic faith, the other rallying under the general term of Protestantism. I am aware that there are other religious divisions, such as that of the Greek Church, and that of the followers of Mahomet; but I speak of nations the most enlightened and civilized of the present age, whether on the continent of Europe or on this hemisphere, and I conceive they can fairly be divided between those two denominations. What the Catholic Church is does not require any particular explanation. Its meaning is at once so simple, so comprehensive, so easily understood, that it were a waste of words to make the comprehension of it more clear than it already is to every mind. Not so, with Protestantism. That term, as ordinarily employed, is understood, in its popular sense, very clearly; nevertheless in any sense of science, or for the purposes of logical or theological accuracy, it is a word exceedingly ambiguous, vague and indefinite. Protestantism is a generic title, implying the *genus* without entering into any of the specific varieties which it is employed as a general term to designate. These two systems, working side by side, have occupied as well as divided the world between them for the last 300 years. One indeed had prevailed from the beginning of Christianity; whilst the other came into existence in the sixteenth century, proclaimed its mission, entered upon its work, and has subsisted since that period. . . .

In every country [Protestantism] is used as a state engine by the government; and here, where it is not so used, you can perceive the excesses and fanaticisms into which it runs. Look at the Northeastern part of this country, perhaps the most enlightened portion of it, the land which was first occupied by the stern Puritans. What is it now? A land of Socinians — a land of infidelity. The very pulpits, built for the purpose of preaching the doctrines of the Trinity, for instance, without any professed change from Protestantism, have been turned into places for preaching against the divinity of the Son of God! You have there the denial of the great truths which I have enumerated. You have even women, reared under the sweet influences of what should have been a Christian home, assembling now in "Congresses" and clamoring for "woman's rights"; claiming to be Christians, but forgetting their true dignity, as belonging to a sex rendered for ever glorious by the Virgin mother of the Incarnate God. Their Redeemer secured their privileges, which they overlook, and now under Protestantism they are contending for "woman's rights," measured by a base human standard. They will not obtain them.

You have your Father Millers also, who turned votaries of private interpretation, crazy with the idea that the last day has come, or was to have come four years ago. And who can stop him? Who among Protestants has the authority to say to him, "Unhappy man, you are not a Protestant if you say so, and you must cease"? He takes his Bible, and demonstrates from Daniel and the Apocalypse, that the world was to be consumed and brought to an end in the year 1846. Otherwise the Bibles were to be thrown in the fire as deceitful and fallacious.

So too with your Joe Smith and the Mormons; and where is there anything in Protestantism to prevent such impostors from sweeping away thousands of souls which Protestantism had undertaken to guide in the path to Heaven? The adherents of Protestantism, no doubt, preach from the pulpit obedience to the decisions of their ecclesiastical bodies, but of what authority are they? None at all. All is gone; the life is gone, the soul is gone, and the principle is gone, if there ever was any principle, except that which was calculated to produce endless divisions and contradictions among the advocates of Protestantism, and against those to whom God has been pleased to bequeath, as a legacy of

mercy and infinite love, one united system of divine Revelation.

During all this time to which I have referred, and in which the Catholic Church saw those several nations torn from her communion, as so many bright stars swept from the celestial firmament, she was not idle. She was making inroads upon the Protestant dominions, and converting their best men. But she did not stop there;—she sent forth her missionaries to replenish and recruit from Pagan lands those who should compensate for the havoc which Protestantism had made in her spiritual dominions. She brought South America and all its Indian tribes into communion with herself; and they have been preserved to her, and thereby placed in the path of continuous and progressive improvement. She sent her missionaries into China, and planted there the nucleus of what may one day turn out to be a beautiful and glorious portion of the Church of God. She sent them to Paraguay—not of your delicate stamp, not that class whose only object abroad appears to be to distribute tracts, and count even the number of their pages for the newspaper, even to the extent of millions;—but *her* missionaries seemed to be animated by the life and soul of truth, and an ardent love of the Church.

How strangely, and yet how instructively, has God manifested the distinction between truth and error?—for while Protestantism has converted none,—Catholicism has converted all! How beautiful, too, are some of the passages in the lives of many of the Catholic missionaries during the very period in which Protestantism was making its ravages in Europe. Who can imagine, for instance, a scene more touching than that exhibited on the tranquil rivers of Paraguay

—when the Jesuit missionaries finding the Indians shy, suspicious, and averse to personal intercourse, or any conversation with them, resorted to their canoes, and preached to the hearts of the savages, by chanting some of those beautiful and touching hymns which the Church has consecrated to the praise of God, or the sweet anthems composed in honor of the Mother of our Holy Redeemer. The Indians could not resist the influence of the harmony of these beautiful strains; they kept pace on the beach with the movements of the canoe; forgetting gradually their first diffidence and timidity, they were attracted to the presence and conversation of the missionaries. On one other occasion, in like manner, when one of two missionaries who had been separated from his only companion of the forest, returned to the place where he had left his brother, he found his body pierced with arrows. He had died a martyr to his faith; and when he saw that he was dying, he had opened his Breviary at the "Prayers for the departing"; and his surviving companion seeing all this, instead of flying for safety, intoned on the desolate rock, over the martyr's body, the *"Te Deum Laudamus";*—because from that moment he began to conceive stronger hopes that God would impart a blessing to that unhappy people, though they had shed the blood of their first missionary. HE had sent them; and in His hands one could be as powerful as both. Where has Protestantism produced any thing like this? Where have its missionaries exhibited any of those extraordinary manifestations of devoted faith and self-sacrifice, as well as divine approbation, which have distinguished the missionaries of the Catholic Church throughout all time? Nothing of the kind can be found. Protestantism acquired all it ever possessed in fifty years, in the heart of Christianity, amidst war and civil strife, and after that it became as if stricken with sterility. It could neither preserve itself nor its doctrines; and whether we number those who have unhappily gone farther from the truth, in following out its principles, or whether we count the multitudes disposed to return to Catholicism, there can be no hesitation in coming to the conclusion that Protestantism has declined, is declining, and is destined to decline; and probably before the end of a century from this day, there will remain of it throughout the civilized world but a spectacle of the wreck of what had been Protestantism. This is the probability; and it is on this account that the Church has never for a moment ceased to understand her mission and her purpose in regard to the errors of its advocates, as well as those of mankind in general. Protestantism pretends to have discovered great secrets. Protestantism startles our eastern borders occasionally on the intention of the Pope with regard to the valley of the Mississippi, and dreams that it has made a wonderful discovery. Not at all. Every body should know it. Every body should know that we have for our mission to convert the world,—including the inhabitants of the United States, the people of the cities, and the people of the country, the officers of the navy and the marines, commanders of the army, the Legislatures, the Senate, the Cabinet, the President, and all! We have received from God what Protestantism never received—viz., not only a commission but a *command* to go and teach all nations. There is no secret about this. The object we hope to accomplish in time, is to convert all Pagan nations, and all Protestant nations, even England with her proud Parliament and imperial sovereign. There is no secrecy in all this. It is the commission of God to his Church, and not a human project. God who, in his own inscrutable providence, permitted this great melancholy schism to take place, knows the time, the means, and the circumstances under which the return of many souls to unity, shall be accomplished. In the mean time, look over the list of great minds who have already relinquished high honors, and rank, and station, in the Church of England, and sought admission to the one true Church. Who, without a feeling of pride, can pronounce the name of the meek Spencer, who was willing to be despised and abject for Christ's sake,—who goes abroad among the poor, preaching to them, ministering to their wants, and asking them to offer up continual prayers for the conversion of his loved but erring England? Who can think of Newman, with all the strength of his mighty intellect, and all the sweet and tender affections of his pure soul, infused into every page of his writings, coming back and endeavoring as far as possible to repair on the side of truth the unintentional injury which he and his associates had done to the Church of Christ. Who can tell among ourselves the number of Protestants, and many of them ministers, who have already come, or are preparing to come back to Catholic unity. Now I can say for myself, that I have had much pleasant and fondly cherished intercourse with Protestants, and in all my life I never conversed with one who was entirely satisfied with his religion. I do not say, however, that, on this account, they were, as yet, ready to become Catholics. But on the other hand, those illustrious converts,

who have been liberated from the ambiguities of Protestantism, those noble auxiliaries, who have been brought up, as it were, in the camp of the enemy, such as Spencer, Newman, and others, from the moment they became Catholics found a fulness of measure equal to the desires of their souls—a provision of Heavenly things in the Church of God, suited and equal to the aptitudes and capacities of ransomed and regenerated humanity.

Why then should we not unite in prayer, that God will reconduct to the fold of Christ those upright, but as yet unhappily wandering brethren, who are wasting their strength, their lives, on the fields of Protestantism? Why not unite in prayer, that God will bring them all back into the sweet communion of the one true Church? We should pray for it. We must look for it. If it had not been for these awful errors of Protestantism, if all the nations had remained in the communion of the Church of God, it would seem that Christianity, by this time, would have absorbed all the nations of the earth. If the resources and labors of those several states of Protestantism mentioned in this lecture, had been united and directed to one common purpose, it seems to me that, under the ordinary blessing of God, Paganism, Mahometanism, and every species of darkness, would have vanished before the approach of the heralds of the Cross. Oh, why should we not pray that the day may be near when the missionary from London may meet the missionary from Rome, in the propagation of one and the same doctrine, teaching the subjects of heathenism, bringing all nations into one Church, and impressing upon them the belief in one Lord, one Faith, and one Baptism?

Chapter 23

The Dissidence of Dissent

RELIGION in antebellum America ran the gamut from the broadest, openest of denominations—such as Methodism, according to John Scarlett— to the most esoteric of sects. The dissenting sects were scattered throughout the country, though more started in upstate New York than anywhere else. Among them were the Millerites and the Mormons; we may recall that Archbishop Hughes spoke disdainfully of "Father Miller" as well as of "Joe Smith and the Mormons."

Perhaps the essence of sectarianism in America can be found in the United Society of Believers in Christ's Second Appearing, otherwise the Shakers. The rationale for Shaker doctrine appears clearly in F. W. Evans's *Compendium* of information about the sect. Issued in 1859, it represented the official views of the Shaker leadership of this decade.

Selections from two chapters are given here. The first, from "Mode of Worship," explains the justification for the ritual of dancing and "shaking" that has attracted so much public notice. The second, from "God Dual— Father and Mother," describes the scriptural sanctions, as seen by the Shakers, for their most controversial doctrine: that there was a female as well as a male Jesus Christ. They believed her to be embodied in the British mystic, Ann Lee, founder of the sect. To them she represented the Mother Spirit residing both in the Father and the Son. The reaction of the average American to this teaching can be imagined. Yet the Shakers suffered less persecution than some other dissenting sects, probably because they were so transparently harmless.

Source: F. W. Evans, *Shakers. Compendium of the Origin, History, Principles, Rules and Regulations, Government, and Doctrines*
(New York, 1859), pp. 90–93, 103–9.

MODE OF WORSHIP

1] It is pretty generally known that the Shakers serve God by singing and dancing; but *why* they practise this mode of worship is not so generally understood.

2] It should be recollected that "God is a Spirit," and can be worshiped only "in spirit and in truth." Without the presence of the Spirit there can be no true worship. Conviction of sin, godly sorrow, and repentance, are the first effects of the Spirit of God upon the conscience of a sinner. And when sin is fully removed, by confessing and forsaking it, the *cause* of heaviness, gloom, and sorrow is gone; and joy and rejoicing, and thanksgiving and praise, are then the spontaneous effects of a true spirit of devotion. And whatever *manner* the Spirit may dictate, or whatever the *form* into which the Spirit may lead, it is acceptable to Him from whom the Spirit proceeds.

3] All the *sabbaths* among the Jews, as hereafter set forth, were joyous festivals—times for men to do good to each other, by feeding the hungry, clothing the naked, etc.; for all to make each other happy, and thus rejoice before the Lord, "with music and dancing."

4] Dancing was a national custom among the Hebrews upon all extraordinary occasions of some great good, as a victory, etc. They expressed their satisfaction and happiness by *dancing*, as the Americans do by the abnegation of temperance, and the explosion of gunpowder.

5] When Israel had escaped the Egyptians, "all the women went after Miriam with timbrels, and with dances." The virgins of Israel held a yearly feast at Shiloh, with dances. When David killed Goliah there was dancing. "And David danced with all his might before the ark of the Lord."

6] Dancing is often mentioned by the seers, prophets, and prophetesses. "Thou hast turned my mourning into dancing." "Praise his name in the dance." "Praise him with the timbrel and dance." When the prophets spoke of the Millennial period and Church, it was with expressions such as, "Then shall the *virgin* rejoice in the dance, both old men and young together." "O virgin of Israel, thou shalt go forth in the dances of them that make merry." And Jesus, in speaking of the return of the prodigal son, included music and dancing as a part of the proceedings and rejoicing.

7] But so plain and simple a subject does not require much extension or amplification. Suffice it to say, that the Shakers believe the great *"sabbatical year"* of the world has come, wherein the long captive sinner is released; "the poor have the Gospel preached to them, without money and without price"; perpetual and universal brotherhood is established and proclaimed, each one (as Jesus said) going back to his inheritance in the earth: "Blessed are the meek, for they shall inherit the earth," and all things else, *in common,* as an everlasting Jubilee of jubilees, where the rich and the poor, the high and the low, the bond and the free, male and female, all become *one* in Christ Jesus; and *love* is the bond of their union.

GOD DUAL—FATHER AND MOTHER

. . . . .

25] An all-important, sublime, and foundational doctrine of the Shakers is the Existence of an Eternal Father and an Eternal Mother in Deity—the Heavenly Parents of all angelical and human beings. They claim that the *knowledge of God* has been *progressive,* from age to age, and from Dispensation to Dispensation.

26] In the first cycle, when spirituality in man was "as the waters to the ankles," God was known only as a great Spirit. In the *second* cycle, when spirituality was "as the waters to the knees," men began to inquire *who* and *what* God was, and received for answer, "I am that I am." You are not prepared to comprehend me further.

27] In the *third* cycle, when spirituality in the soul was "as the waters to the loins," God, for the first time, was revealed to man as *Father.*

28] And in the *fourth* cycle, when spirituality is becoming as a deep and broad expanse of waters, "that can not be measured" (see Ezek. xlvii.), God is also revealed in the character of *Mother* —an Eternal Mother—the bearing Spirit of all the creation of God, to whom the Shakers think reference is made in the Scriptures, particularly in the following extracts from the book of "Proverbs," under the appellation of *Wisdom:*

29] "The Lord possessed me in the beginning of his way, before his works of old. I was set up from everlasting, from the beginning, or ever the earth was. When there were no depths I was brought forth: when there were no fountains abounding with water. Before the mountains were settled, before the hills was I brought forth: while as yet He had not made the earth, nor the fields, nor the highest part of the dust of the world.

30] "When He prepared the heavens, I was there: when He set a compass upon the face of the depth: when He established the clouds above: when He strengthened the fountains of the deep: when He gave to the sea his decree, that the waters should not pass his commandment: when He appointed the foundations of the earth: then I was by Him, as One brought up with Him; and I was daily his delight, rejoicing always before Him."

31] As *Father,* God is the infinite Fountain of intelligence, and the Source of all power—"the Almighty, great and terrible in majesty"; "the high and lofty One, that inhabiteth eternity, whose name is Holy, dwelling in the high and holy place"; and "a consuming fire."

32] But, as *Mother,* "God is love" and tenderness! If all the *maternal* affections of all the female or bearing spirits in animated nature were combined together, and then concentred in *one individual human female,* that person would be but as a type or image of our Eternal Heavenly *Mother.*

33] The *duality* of God is expressed in the book of "Genesis" as follows: "Let us make man in our image, after our likeness. So God created man in his own image; male and female created He them; and called their name Adam."

34] From which, the Shakers insist, that it is the male and female in man that is peculiarly the *"image of God."* In this conclusion they further strengthen themselves from the Apostle Paul, who affirms that the order of the "Godhead," and the "eternal creative power of God," which would otherwise be invisible to man, are "clearly seen, by," through, and in, "the things that are made."

35] Consequently, if this be admitted, it follows, from the undeniable fact that all the things which God has "made" are *dual;* beginning with the *mineral* kingdom, which, from the "old red sandstone" to the very latest geological formation, exhibit the action of *two forces,* the positive and negative, which forms, in the *vegetable* kingdom, gradually resolve themselves into male and female types, from the fern to the polypus; and, in the *animal* kingdom, they are progressively developed from the polypus up to the simia tribes; and ultimately they culminate in *man* and *woman,* the image of God their Creator.

36] It seems scarcely possible to resist this evidence of a *dual order,* so "clearly seen" throughout all the domains of nature; or to admit it, without proving that *God also is* DUAL, Father and Mother, the image and likeness of man, whom He has made *male* and *female.*

37] "No carnal man hath seen God at any time," or witnessed an act of arbitrary, sovereign, creative power. The "eternal [creative] power" of God is only known to man through the perpetual operation of the originating and reproducing powers of male and female principles.

38] The Shakers believe that the distinction of sex is eternal; that it inheres in the soul itself; and that no angels or spirits exist who are not male and female.

39] From the fact that Adam (and Eve) "was the figure of him that was to come," they argue that the "second Adam, the Lord from heaven, a quickening Spirit," was also *dual,* male and female; and that they were the spiritual Father and Mother of Jesus, begetting, watching over, and bearing him in the regeneration, towards the *new birth,* into their own quickening spiritual element.

40] Every thing is begotten, travails, and is born into the elements of its parents. "That which is [begotten and] born of the flesh, is flesh; and that which is [begotten and] born of the Spirit, is spirit."

41] Jesus, being a male, could only reveal and manifest the *Father* in Christ and God. But when the *second* Adam appeared to Ann, and became her spiritual Parents, she, being a female, revealed and manifested the *Mother Spirit* in Christ and in Deity.

Chapter 24

Reflections of Faith

THREE aspects of American religion show themselves in this group of visual documents. The first is religion as a manifold institution, a strong social structure not only in itself but in its many subsidiaries. The picture "Means of the diffusion of Religion in the United States" gives us graphic evidence. The second is religion as an influence on the American myth. Its stamp was unmistakable: no one denied that the United States was a Christian country. Its legends often had a Christian turn to them and its heroes (the subjects usually of the legends) were either Christian to begin with or else were soon Christianized. The exception was the frontier hero such as Davy Crockett. A classic episode in antebellum mythology is Washington kneeling in prayer at Valley Forge in 1778. He may have knelt just as he may have chopped down that cherry tree, but if he did not kneel he was made to. The Christian impulse in the American people required it. Nor did the impulse flag. In 1860 the new Republican party sent an informal committee to Springfield to settle the question of Lincoln's religious beliefs.

The third aspect is religion as morality, and under that religion as reform. The greatest abuse of the era was drunkenness; against it the church mobilized its legions. The Currier lithograph illustrates something of the church's propaganda. It would be stretching the third phase too far to make it stand for the entire Puritan ethic of hard work, sober behavior, and devout belief; and yet a case can be made for it. We can see Puritan ethic manifest in other aspects of American life represented in this book, and certainly it is worth reminding ourselves that the church is where it started.

A fourth aspect of American religion is well represented neither here in the visual documents nor, so far, in the prose selections. It is the religious response, uneasy, troubled, finally bitter on both sides, to slavery in the South. For decades, in fact ever since the founding of the Republic, the great Protestant denominations had been a bond between North and South. But slavery split the two most powerful of them down the middle. In 1844 the slaveholders formed the Methodist Church South after Northern abolitionists had insisted that a Southern bishop free his slaves. The next year the Baptists followed. Their slaveholding wing formed the Southern Baptist Convention and by the end of the 1850s it had doubled its membership. The Episcopalians managed to avert a split but it was at a considerable cost of moral leadership.

Meanwhile, throughout the 1850s slavery was ardently defended in a host of pulpits in the South as well as an occasional one in the North. On the other hand, the radical wing of the Northern church housed some of the most fiery of the abolitionists. Yet even by the end of the decade a large number of Northern churchgoers were still uncommitted. They had not decided where they stood, and so an effort was made in both the pulpits of the North and South to woo them. One reflection of this attempt will be found in a later section of this book, dealing with slavery.

Source: Means of the Diffusion of Religion in the United States. Drawn by William Van Ingen and engraved by "C. Sch."
Reproduced from the Collections of the Library of Congress

The power of Protestantism is shown in this elaborate illustration. Its most potent institutions appear amid the scrollwork of the artist's fancy. The central one is of course the individual church, the meetinghouse for the godly. Its architecture looks mildly Gothic, its dimensions substantial. The activities it sheltered each week were, typically, much more diverse than those we see within a church today. Group worship led them of course, with two or three services on Sunday and a service on Wednesday night; but there were also apt to be women's and men's guild meetings, semisocial events for young people (no dancing, however, and no card-playing), and cultural affairs such as lectures. Many a local lyceum met in a church basement. Henry Thoreau once remarked dryly that he had lectured in the basement of an Amherst, New Hampshire, church and helped, he hoped, to undermine it.

The adjunct institutions reached out in several directions. Tent preaching, for instance, was concentrated in the smaller towns and the country; urban congregations tended to be too sophisticated, by now, to be comfortable with its fire and brimstone. It had reached its peak in the frontier camp meeting; but since the frontier was moving west of the Mississippi, the camp meeting was losing some of its appeal. Yet the tent meeting as such, conducted by the itinerant evangelist, would not wither till the mid-twentieth century. Within its canvas walls, his arms flailing, his voice hoarse, he would long remain an American phenomenon.

In a sense the tent meeting repre-

MEANS OF THE DIFFUSION OF RELIGION IN THE UNITED STATES

sented the missionary effort of the church. Since this illustration is concerned with America alone, it shows nothing of the vast work of foreign missions. But there is another indication of home missions, besides the tent meeting, in the sailors' church we see, the floating bethel. Even the Episcopal Church, most conservative of American denominations, had a bethel moored off Manhattan for some years before the Civil War. The bethel existed because it was an article of our folk faith that sailors were the most sinful of all workers. However, the church made an effort to reach other groups as well, the slum dwellers in the growing cities, for instance, and the immigrant farm workers.

Formal religious instruction was widespread. The Sunday School, chiefly but never exclusively for children, was a staple of the church. Everyone seemed to realize that the best time to claim anybody for Christ was when he was young. Here we see a mingled group of children and adults. To the right of this scene we glimpse the day school. Though this may have been a sectarian school, the chances are that it was a public school where a rather diffuse religious instruction could be given. Then as now, the relation between church and state was an uneasy one. Nevertheless, most parents wanted—as they saw it—God in the schools. It would be a century before school prayers, for instance, would be declared unconstitutional.

The Christian college is shown at the bottom of this plate. We can recall that more colleges were being established all the time and they were almost entirely denominational. Even Antioch College, while ahead of its era in several ways, showed the Christian influence. Though its president, Horace Mann, was a lay-

man eight out of its thirteen trustees were Protestant ministers. In the 1850s the question was not whether a college should be Christian but rather how Christian it should be. And the question was in point because the colleges of America, starting with Harvard in colonial days, were designed to produce ministers. As time went on they were also designed to produce teachers, lawyers, doctors, and more broadly educated adults; yet ministers were still apt to come first. Many of the college professors were ministers, as were many of the college presidents. Courses in religion were generally compulsory; so was daily chapel. The hand of God was not hard to detect on most campuses.

The last of the devices of diffusion we see is the printed word. It preached Christianity in the form of tracts, printed sermons, and religious books. Its coverage was astonishing. The book of sermons was to be found on many a publisher's list. But its popularity was nothing when compared with that of the publications of the two giants of religious publishing: the American Tract Society and the American Bible Society. The tracts were little religious leaflets, little printed homilies; and they were either sold for a few cents or given free. By 1850 the American Tract Society's most effective tract, *Quench not the Spirit,* had run to 908,000 copies. Other favorites of the American public were *The Lost Soul, Why are you not a Christian,* and *Procrastination.* All were printed by the hundred thousands.

The American Bible Society published the most appealing of all books. In one year in the mid-1850s the Society issued 240,776 Bibles and 427,489 copies of the New Testament by itself. By the time the Civil War began nearly every

American family had its Bible, whether by gift or purchase. According to the society's report of May 1856, it could find only one family out of every twenty-one without a Bible. Without doubt the Christian religion and its institutions suffused the fabric of American society.

Source: Gen. Geo. Washington in Prayer at Valley Forge. Painted by Lambert Sachs and lithographed by P. Kramer, for P. S. Duval & Co., 1854.
Reproduced from the Collections of the Library of Congress

We have fashioned our heroes to our own liking. If history failed to support us we ignored it. Half consciously perhaps, we developed myths and a national mythology. From time to time we altered our heroes but we never reversed them. We might modify the characteristics we emphasized in Washington or Lincoln or Franklin Roosevelt. Lincoln might supplant Washington as our hero of heroes. But we never turned our back on them to exalt, say, Benedict Arnold. Before the Civil War the American pantheon was largely occupied by the heroes of the Revolution. Most were military men. However, they were never soldiers alone. Though we wanted our heroes to be able to fight and command, at heart they had to remain civilians. We wanted them, further, to be unselfish men. We wanted them to work hard for the public good. We wanted them to be moral men; in the American pantheon no libertines were allowed. And we wanted them God-fearing.

George Washington was a nominal Episcopalian but hardly devout. By the time he died, religion in America was at a low ebb. The Protestant denominations were trying to revive enthusiasm; the Catholics were simply holding their own; and the deists were more popular among lively young Americans than any rationalists would be for another hundred years. Washington was in reality a man of his era. Our heroes, however, had to remain pious. By the 1850s, when religion had flooded back into American life, the need was still stronger to make our heroes Christian men.

The lithograph we have here is only one of its kind. In all of them Washington kneels in prayer but as a rule with head bowed. And sometimes the pathos is compounded by making him kneel in snow. Regardless, the point is that he is shown at prayer. The script beneath the title (deleted because it would be illegible here to the reader) gives the gist of the legend. The time in the version set down here is June 1778, shortly before the Revolutionary Army had to leave its winter encampment at Valley Forge. We read that a "respectable old Quaker by the name of Potts" happened to pass by the General's headquarters. He heard a voice and, peeking over some bushes, saw Washington praying fervently and audibly. He was thanking God for his previous blessings and humbly beseeching Him to grant success to this war for man's freedom.

The wood here is lush, leafy, almost Edenic. It reminds us that it was a bit more appropriate to show Washington worshipping in nature than in a church.

GEN. GEO. WASHINGTON IN PRAYER AT VALLEY FORGE

After all, as William Cullen Bryant wrote, "The groves were God's first temples." This landscape, however, is less a grove in the Gothic sense and more a thicket. In the jargon of art critics it is "picturesque" instead of "sublime." It follows a formula: for instance, with all these bushes and trees about, we can be sure without looking that there will also be some still water and at least one rock.

With its soft, fuzzy forms, this popular painting is a fine example of awkward art. Washington kneels in the dead center of the picture, eyes heavenward, while Quaker Potts raises his hand in a stagy gesture of surprise. He stands engulfed in the feathery foliage. Washington's posture is much more interesting. Whether by chance or design, his hands are not clasped in prayer; to us today he appears to be addressing God rather than beseeching Him. The scene is cluttered, the composition inept, with little feeling for perspective. But the people who bought it hardly ever cared.

Source: The Bible and Temperance. Lithographed and published by N. Currier, before 1856.
Reproduced from the Collections of the Library of Congress

In several respects—and not only in the matter of slavery—antebellum America appeared a hard and brutal country. One manifestation of its coarseness was the confirmed drunkard. If he was poor, he had his reasons for craving liquor. It was his main relief from the desperation of poverty: gin or whiskey stood waiting for him. There was also a fair amount of toping, for other reasons, among the men in the middle and upper class. We cannot measure it but we know that the tavern and distillery throve.

One plain testimony to the wide extent of drunkenness is the amount of opposition it generated. A few of the states, led by Maine, passed temperance laws. Anti-alcohol societies multiplied, the ancestors of the Women's Christian Temperance Union and the Anti-Saloon League of the twentieth century. They called themselves the cold-water legions. They printed their cold-water hymnals and sang soberly from them.

These societies represent the outstanding attempt of the American church to act as a vehicle for social reform. Drunkenness was not immoral but in the eyes of the church it was the next thing to it. The temperance crusade, so called, took religion as far as most Americans would let it go.

The lithograph reproduced here was a steadily salable item. In composition it antedated the 1850s but it probably continued to sell till the Civil War. The picture was part of a somber series on the degradation that drink could bring. The great exemplar of the genre was the English artist Hogarth's two series called *Beer Street* and *Gin Lane*. In "The Bible and Temperance" we have the effort of one of his feeble successors. The legend tells us that our drunkard has steadily degenerated. He has lost his job and reputation, has become idle and dissolute, and has dragged his family into poverty. Here his good wife has just finished laundering the small remnant of her clothes. The tub with its topping of suds

THE BIBLE AND TEMPERANCE

stands in the center of the floor while a few ragged garments hang on an improvised line. The wife listens, as do the children, while the minister comforts them by reading from the Bible. Meanwhile, the drunkard lies in a stupor on his bed. The moral needs no laboring.

This lithograph falls below the artistic standard of the general run of prints that Currier published. He did better after he teamed with Ives but he always had an eye for popular art. The picture is amateurish in every way. Notwithstanding, it carried its message and the message was plain. For that reason, and doubtless that alone, the lithograph kept its place in the stock that Currier sold.

ABSOLUTELY STUPID.

VI. *The Pleasures of Life*

Chapter 25

Democratic Zest

IN "Song of the Open Road" Whitman's vigorous, active enjoyment of life is seen at its clearest. He confronts life, all life, and embraces it. We are comrades in his cosmos, learning from him that it contains some evil as well as much good, some pain as well as much pleasure—and that we must appreciate it all. Besides Whitman's hearty acceptance of the world he sees around him, there is another significant strain in his poem. It is the delight in travel. On the literal level it is the kind of travel many Americans craved, the carefree journeying from place to new place. But it is also travel away from the confines of houses or the conditions that cage the spirit to the freedom of man's mind under the open sky.

Then too, "Song of the Open Road" can signify for us the interest in literature of the 1850s. Whitman was too much of an innovator for the man in the street, who liked jingles and sentimental ballads. Yet *Leaves of Grass* had an impact from the time of its first edition, in 1855. "Song of the Open Road" first appeared in the second and expanded edition, of 1856, and is reprinted below.

Source: Walt Whitman, *Leaves of Grass*
(Brooklyn, 1856), pp. 223–39.

SONG OF THE OPEN ROAD

1

Afoot and light-hearted I take to the open road,
Healthy, free, the world before me,
The long brown path before me leading wherever I choose.

Henceforth I ask not good-fortune, I myself am good-fortune,
Henceforth I whimper no more, postpone no more, need nothing,
Done with indoor complaints, libraries, querulous criticisms,
Strong and content I travel the open road.

The earth, that is sufficient,
I do not want the constellations any nearer,
I know they are very well where they are,
I know they suffice for those who belong to them.

(Still here I carry my old delicious burdens,
I carry them, men and women, I carry them with me wherever I go,
I swear it is impossible for me to get rid of them,
I am fill'd with them, and I will fill them in return.)

2

You road I enter upon and look around, I believe you are not all that is here,
I believe that much unseen is also here.

Here the profound lesson of reception, nor preference nor denial,
The black with his woolly head, the felon, the diseas'd, the illiterate person, are not
    denied;
The birth, the hasting after the physician, the beggar's tramp, the drunkard's stagger, the
    laughing party of mechanics,
The escaped youth, the rich person's carriage, the fop, the eloping couple,
The early market-man, the hearse, the moving of furniture into the town, the return
    back from the town,
They pass, I also pass, anything passes, none can be interdicted,
None but are accepted, none but shall be dear to me.

3

You air that serves me with breath to speak!
You objects that call from diffusion my meanings and give them shape!
You light that wraps me and all things in delicate equable showers!
You paths worn in the irregular hollows by the roadside!
I believe you are latent with unseen existences, you are so dear to me.

You flagg'd walks of the cities! you strong curbs at the edges!
You ferries! you planks and posts of wharves! you timber-lined sides! you distant ships!
You rows of houses! you window-pierc'd façades! you roofs!
You porches and entrances! you copings and iron guards!
You windows whose transparent shells might expose so much!
You doors and ascending steps! you arches!
You gray stones of interminable pavements! you trodden crossings!
From all that has touch'd you I believe you have imparted to yourselves, and now would
    impart the same secretely to me,
From the living and the dead you have peopled your impassive surfaces, and the spirits
    thereof would be evident and amicable with me.

4

The earth expanding right hand and left hand,
The picture alive, every part in its best light,
The music falling in where it is wanted, and stopping where it is not wanted,
The cheerful voice of the public road, the gay fresh sentiment of the road.

O highway I travel, do you say to me *Do not leave me?*
Do you say *Venture not—if you leave me you are lost?*
Do you say *I am already prepared, I am well-beaten and undenied, adhere to me?*

O public road, I say back I am not afraid to leave you, yet I love you,
You express me better than I can express myself,
You shall be more to me than my poem.

I think heroic deeds were all conceiv'd in the open air, and all free poems also,
I think I could stop here myself and do miracles,
I think whatever I shall meet on the road I shall like, and whoever beholds me shall like
        me,
I think whoever I see must be happy.

5

From this hour I ordain myself loos'd of limits and imaginary lines,
Going where I list, my own master total and absolute,
Listening to others, considering well what they say,
Pausing, searching, receiving, contemplating,
Gently, but with undeniable will, divesting myself of the holds that would hold me.

I inhale great draughts of space,
The east and the west are mine, and the north and the south are mine.

I am larger, better than I thought,
I did not know I held so much goodness.

All seems beautiful to me,
I can repeat over to men and women You have done such good to me I would do the same
        to you,
I will recruit for myself and you as I go,
I will scatter myself among men and women as I go,
I will toss a new gladness and roughness among them,
Whoever denies me it shall not trouble me,
Whoever accepts me he or she shall be blessed and shall bless me.

6

Now if a thousand perfect men were to appear it would not amaze me,
Now if a thousand beautiful forms of women appear'd it would not astonish me.

Now I see the secret of the making of the best persons,
It is to grow in the open air and to eat and sleep with the earth.

Here a great personal deed has room,
(Such a deed seizes upon the hearts of the whole race of men,
Its effusion of strength and will overwhelms law and mocks all authority and all argument
        against it.)

Here is the test of wisdom,
Wisdom is not finally tested in schools,
Wisdom cannot be pass'd from one having it to another not having it,
Wisdom is of the soul, is not susceptible of proof, is its own proof,
Applies to all stages and objects and qualities and is content,
Is the certainty of the reality and immortality of things, and the excellence of things;
Something there is in the float of the sight of things that provokes it out of the soul.

Now I re-examine philosophies and religions,
They may prove well in lecture-rooms, yet not prove at all under the spacious clouds and
        along the landscape and flowing currents.

Here is realization,
Here is a man tallied—he realizes here what he has in him,
The past, the future, majesty, love—if they are vacant of you, you are vacant of them.

Only the kernel of every object nourishes;
Where is he who tears off the husks for you and me?
Where is he that undoes stratagems and envelopes for you and me?

Here is adhesiveness, it is not previously fashion'd, it is apropos;
Do you know what it is as you pass to be loved by strangers?
Do you know the talk of those turning eye-balls?

7

Here is the efflux of the soul,
The efflux of the soul comes from within through embower'd gates, ever provoking
        questions,
These yearnings why are they? these thoughts in the darkness why are they?
Why are there men and women that while they are nigh me the sunlight expands my
        blood?
Why when they leave me do my pennants of joy sink flat and lank?
Why are there trees I never walk under but large and melodious thoughts descend upon
        me?
(I think they hang there winter and summer on those trees and always drop fruit as I
        pass;)
What is it I interchange so suddenly with strangers?
What with some driver as I ride on the seat by his side?
What with some fisherman drawing his seine by the shore as I walk by and pause?

What gives me to be free to a woman's and man's good-will? what gives them to be free
　　to mine?

8

The efflux of the soul is happiness, here is happiness,
I think it pervades the open air, waiting at all times,
Now it flows unto us, we are rightly charged.

Here rises the fluid and attaching character,
The fluid and attaching character is the freshness and sweetness of man and woman,
(The herbs of the morning sprout no fresher and sweeter every day out of the roots of
　　themselves, than it sprouts fresh and sweet continually out of itself.)
Toward the fluid and attaching character exudes the sweat of the love of young and old,
From it falls distill'd the charm that mocks beauty and attainments,
Toward it heaves the shuddering longing ache of contact.

9

Allons! whoever you are come travel with me!
Traveling with me you find what never tires.

The earth never tires,
The earth is rude, silent, incomprehensible at first, Nature is rude and incomprehensible
　　at first,
Be not discouraged; keep on, there are divine things well envelop'd,
I swear to you there are divine things more beautiful than words can tell.

Allons! we must not stop here,
However sweet these laid-up stores, however convenient this dwelling we cannot remain
　　here,
However shelter'd this port and however calm these waters we must not anchor here,
However welcome the hospitality that surrounds us we are permitted to receive it but a
　　little while.

10

Allons! the inducements shall be greater,
We will sail pathless and wild seas,
We will go where winds blow, waves dash, and the Yankee clipper speeds by under full sail.

Allons! with power, liberty, the earth, the elements,
Health, defiance, gayety, self-esteem, curiosity;
Allons! from all formules!
From your formules, O bat-eyed and materialistic priests.

The stale cadaver blocks up the passage—the burial waits no longer.

Allons! yet take warning!

He traveling with me needs the best blood, thews, endurance,
None may come to the trial till he or she bring courage and health,
Come not here if you have already spent the best of yourself,
Only those may come who come in sweet and determin'd bodies,
No diseas'd person, no rum-drinker or venereal taint is permitted here.

(I and mine do not convince by arguments, similes, rhymes,
We convince by our presence.)

11

Listen! I will be honest with you,
I do not offer the old smooth prizes, but offer rough new prizes,
These are the days that must happen to you:
You shall not heap up what is call'd riches,
You shall scatter with lavish hand all that you earn or achieve,
You but arrive at the city to which you were destin'd, you hardly settle yourself to satisfaction before you are call'd by an irresistible call to depart,
You shall be treated to the ironical smiles and mockings of those who remain behind you,
What beckonings of love you receive you shall only answer with passionate kisses of parting,
You shall not allow the hold of those who spread their reach'd hands toward you.

12

Allons! after the great Companions, and to belong to them!
They too are on the road—they are the swift and majestic men—they are the greatest women,
Enjoyers of calms of seas and storms of seas,
Sailors of many a ship, walkers of many a mile of land,
Habituès of many distant countries, habituès of far-distant dwellings,
Trusters of men and women, observers of cities, solitary toilers,
Pausers and contemplators of tufts, blossoms, shells of the shore,
Dancers at wedding-dances, kissers of brides, tender helpers of children, bearers of children,
Soldiers of revolts, standers by gaping graves, lowerers-down of coffins,
Journeyers over consecutive seasons, over the years, the curious years each emerging from that which preceded it,
Journeyers as with companions, namely their own diverse phases,
Forth-steppers from the latent unrealized baby-days,
Journeyers gayly with their own youth, journeyers with their bearded and well-grain'd manhood,
Journeyers with their womanhood, ample, unsurpass'd, content,
Journeyers with their own sublime old age of manhood or womanhood,
Old age, calm, expanded, broad with the haughty breadth of the universe,
Old age, flowing free with the delicious near-by freedom of death.

13

Allons! to that which is endless as it was beginningless,
To undergo much, tramps of days, rests of nights,

To merge all in the travel they tend to, and the days and nights they tend to,
Again to merge them in the start of superior journeys,
To see nothing anywhere but what you may reach it and pass it,
To conceive no time, however distant, but what you may reach it and pass it,
To look up or down no road but it stretches and waits for you, however long but it
    stretches and waits for you,
To see no being, not God's or any, but you also go thither,
To see no possession but you may possess it, enjoying all without labor or purchase,
    abstracting the feast yet not abstracting one particle of it,
To take the best of the farmer's farm and the rich man's elegant villa, and the chaste
    blessings of the well-married couple, and the fruits of orchards and flowers of
    gardens,
To take to your use out of the compact cities as you pass through,
To carry buildings and streets with you afterward wherever you go,
To gather the minds of men out of their brains as you encounter them, to gather the love
    out of their hearts,
To take your lovers on the road with you, for all that you leave them behind you,
To know the universe itself as a road, as many roads, as roads for traveling souls.

All parts away for the progress of souls,
All religion, all solid things, arts, governments—all that was or is apparent upon this
    globe or any globe, falls into niches and corners before the procession of souls
    along the grand roads of the universe.

Of the progress of the souls of men and women along the grand roads of the universe,
    all other progress is the needed emblem and sustenance.

Forever alive, forever forward,
Stately, solemn, sad, withdrawn, baffled, mad, turbulent, feeble, dissatisfied,
Desperate, proud, fond, sick, accepted by men, rejected by men,
They go! they go! I know that they go, but I know not where they go,
But I know that they go toward the best—toward something great.

Whoever you are, come forth! or man or woman come forth!
You must not stay sleeping and dallying there in the house, though you built it, or though
    it has been built for you.

Out of the dark confinement! out from behind the screen!
It is useless to protest, I know all and expose it.

Behold through you as bad as the rest,
Through the laughter, dancing, dining, supping, of people,
Inside of dresses and ornaments, inside of those wash'd and trimm'd faces,
Behold a secret silent loathing and despair.

No husband, no wife, no friend, trusted to hear the confession,
Another self, a duplicate of every one, skulking and hiding it goes,
Formless and wordless through the streets of the cities, polite and bland in the parlors,
In the cars of railroads, in steamboats, in the public assembly,
Home to the houses of men and women, at the table, in the bedroom, everywhere,

Smartly attired, countenance smiling, form upright, death under the breast-bones, hell
    under the skull-bones,
Under the broadcloth and gloves, under the ribbons and artificial flowers,
Keeping fair with the customs, speaking not a syllable of itself,
Speaking of any thing else but never of itself.

14

Allons! through struggles and wars!
The goal that was named cannot be countermanded.

Have the past struggles succeeded?
What has succeeded? yourself? your nation? Nature?
Now understand me well—it is provided in the essence of things that from any fruition
    of success, no matter what, shall come forth something to make a greater struggle
    necessary.

My call is the call of battle, I nourish active rebellion,
He going with me must go well arm'd,
He going with me goes often with spare diet, poverty, angry enemies, desertions.

15

Allons! the road is before us!
It is safe—I have tried it—my own feet have tried it well—be not detain'd!
Let the paper remain on the desk unwritten, and the book on the shelf unopen'd!
Let the tools remain in the workshop! let the money remain unearn'd!
Let the school stand! mind not the cry of the teacher!
Let the preacher preach in his pulpit! let the lawyer plead in the court, and the judge
    expound the law.

Camerado, I give you my hand!
I give you my love more precious than money,
I give you myself before preaching or law;
Will you give me yourself? will you come travel with me?
Shall we stick by each other as long as we live?

Chapter 26

National Art

LITERATURE and the fine arts formed the core of the high culture of the 1850s. Both fiction and nonfiction flourished, with more Americans buying books and magazines than ever before. Poetry was likewise popular, more popular (it may be guessed) than it is today. The call for a truly American literature was being sounded throughout the decade—and the literature appeared. The first great American writers published their work, though it must be admitted that it had a mixed reception. But any decade that saw the writing of Emerson and Thoreau, Hawthorne and Melville, and for that matter Longfellow and Oliver Wendell Holmes, could count itself blest.

The call for an American art seemed almost as loud as the call for literature. Its results were never so brilliant; notwithstanding, a group of painters produced a considerable body of work of permanent interest. The most notable were George Caleb Bingham, Asher Durand, and William Sidney Mount. Each was highly talented in his own way but none had the genius of the best American authors.

To create a national art two things were needed. The first was the artist, of course. He had to be a complete man, with the best possible "physical, intellectual, and emotional nature." The second was a mature and cultivated citizenry to appreciate his works. If these existed in this country—and they could—then an American art would appear rivaling that of the Greeks. Or so, at any rate, the Reverend W. S. Kennedy promised in an address on "Conditions of the Development of National Art."

It was picked up and printed in the September 1859 number of the *Journal* of the Cosmopolitan Art Association, which was the chief organization in the 1850s for the purveying of works of art. It is probable that Kennedy spoke for the great majority of his readers. To Americans at mid-century art could be enjoyed best, its beauty could be appreciated most, if it was good and true as well as beautiful. The address is reprinted in part below. Its rhetoric is high-flown but undeniably well intended.

Source: W. S. Kennedy, "Conditions of the Development of National Art,"
Cosmopolitan Art Journal, 3 (September 1859) : 150–52.

CONDITIONS OF THE DEVELOPMENT OF NATIONAL ART

Only the very best types of mankind, and the noblest nations, can produce distinguished art. An inferior people may have some special talent, for a specific department of art-exercise, such as the African's talent for song, or the Indian's tact in feather-work, or the Chinaman's delicate carving.

But no grand developments of art can be produced, either by a people of inferior intellect or by a people of natural ability but low civilization and little culture.

Art is the rare blossoming and fruitage of the mind, in the best circumstances. And therefore we need only look for it, or hope for it, among those nations of the highest intellectual capacity. History shows that no very advanced art has ever grown up outside of the flow of Caucasian blood. And from what has been we may infer what will be.

Taste, and emotion, and handicraft, are indeed as important in art as intellect; but these qualities generally co-exist with good intellect, and must be directed by it, in order to produce works of beauty. The artist must have the clear-seeing eye, exact, comprehensive, and penetrating, as well as the feeling heart, that may throb and leap when the vision of beauty falls upon it.

And, waiting upon the artistic eye and soul, strong and cunning to embody the glorious conceptions of the spirit, must be the hand of the well-made man.

And, therefore, the production of good art demands complete manhood, the best physical, intellectual, and emotional nature; and the nation that develops an art equal to that of Italy or Greece, must have the humanity, manhood and rank of nature equal to Greek and Roman.

If the lower instincts predominate, if a nation be of that low type which sensuality, or mammonism, or vain excitements, can satisfy, it is vain to look for any grand developments from it.

There must be strong intellect and moral elevation, and patient, working force, or no great works can be built up. There must be a foundation of great character upon which national art may rest. And, if a nation has reached the zenith of artistic development, as soon as its character declines its art must wane.

But not only must there be good manhood, blood, intellect, and character, the best humanity and natural ability; there must also be thorough culture and mature civilization for the production of high art.

The common impression that genius is independent of circumstances and surroundings, and that a first-class artist may spring up anywhere, and, irrespective of his age and nation, blaze out in glorious beauty, is a great error.

There are, indeed, a few noble souls, so richly endowed that they will shoot far ahead of their cotemporaries, and will so earnestly cast about for the means of sustenance and growth, that they flourish, rich and vigorous, where others starve.

Original genius is a wonderful endowment; but it is not self-sufficient, and cannot thrive and unfold unless there be some means of cultivation available, any more than a strong plant can grow and bloom upon the naked rock. It is the peculiarity of such genius to gather for itself whatever the age affords of culture and inspiration, and to use the materials about it, as no inferior nature could.

But no man nor school can be independent of the age, nor rise *very far* above it. . . .

Nothing great is ever produced until the popular thought and heart set toward it, and the people look and long for it, and get ready to welcome its advent.

When Liberty is to be born, a whole nation begins to pant for freedom. When a continent is to be discovered there is restlessness among the nations, and a widespread yearning for room and a field for pent-up energies and enterprise.

And so, the steam engine is not invented, till the heaving forces and rapid life of the people begin to feel that wind and horse power and all common motors are too weak and slow. The spinning jenny and cotton gin come only when more cotton crowns the fields and crowds the factories, and is wanted by the people, than can be cleaned and spun by simple handicraft.

Literature is created only when there is popular intelligence, or a reading public waiting for it.

And in like manner art appears, in fair development, only when popular taste and public appreciation, and a widespread love of the beautiful, foster art-talent, encourage artistic genius, and reward the artist's toil. . . .

The children must be taught to trace and admire the visible beauty of creation; to notice the noble forms and graceful lines, and glowing colors that adorn all the works of God.

The adult populace must be so impressed by the loveliness of Nature, that they shall cease to think of her merely as larder or provision store to feed the stomach; and shall pause occasionally in their life journey and toil to mark the scenery of the way, and enjoy the richness of hues, and grace of curves, that make every field a glorious picture.

And as the appreciation and enjoyment of natural beauty increase, there will grow up a stronger longing to reproduce and carry into our homes somewhat of the outer glory of creation.

And still further, will rise yearnings to enunciate the inner visions of the soul, and to body forth in tangible form, those dreams of loveliness that gather upon the soul's horizon and foretoken the Paradise to which we are bound.

And as these yearnings multiply, and this taste is cultivated among the people, there will arise an atmosphere of beauty and admiration for true art, such as shall foster whatever latent genius the nation possesses, and bring out the artists, that else had slumbered in obscurity, and build up gradually the fair structure upon which, at last, shall mount a

Raphael, an Angelo, or a Shakespeare, to stand forever in history as the highest exponent and glory of his nation.

This branch of my subject is so important and so comprehensive that I would fain dwell upon it, and indicate and urge the means by which our nation may cultivate itself and get ready for a great development of national art.

There is not yet, among our continent-conquering and wilderness-subduing people, leisure, and high culture, and chastened taste, adequate to nourish an art worthy of our nation.

But we have the natural endowments and character, and the incipient civilization and culture, the foundation and material for an art second to none in history. . . .

As indices of the art that is in process of gestation, and to be hereafter born of this nation, as also the means by which the taste and faculty are to be developed that shall form the national basis of our future art, I may mention the wide-spread love of eloquence and poetry that characterize our people; the universal passion for music; the floods of engraving that circulate in books and periodicals, and the vast patronage afforded to photography. Poets, orators, lecturers, singers, and players, wood-engravers, and photographers, to say nothing of portrait painters, all find their fortunes in America.

I am reminded that in all this there is very little high art, or appreciation of high art. And if we were an old nation, this gormandizing of cheap art, coarse, and superficial, would be discouraging and prove us incapable of emulating our European models.

But it is to be remembered that cheap art pleases the child; and that this passion for song and pictures, which patronizes the poorer artists so enormously, indicates the latent talent and huge appetite which foretoken the strong character that is to come out of this babe of the nations.

Let us get age, maturity, and the aesthetic culture for which I am pleading; let the agencies I have named, to which I may add such institutions as this Association, which seek to develop a taste for art-work among the masses, go on and be followed up by more advanced educators; and above all, let art-studies enter into our common schools and higher institutions, as they should, so that the faculties for the Beautiful may be developed and cultivated with the faculties for the True and the Good, let our nation learn to appreciate, love, and comprehend true art, and, unquestionably, great artists and great art will be born among us.

At first sight it would seem as if the severe analytic and dissecting habit of this age, which goes to nature with none of an artist's love, but only with a critic's eye and scalpel, bent only on constructing science, must take away the charm and mystery of nature which fosters art. And probably in an age of such scientific enthusiasm, when the anatomy and physiology of nature are specially sought, art cannot rapidly advance.

Yet nature will bear analysis and dissection, and when we have unclothed, and flayed, and anatomized her and learned all the mechanism of her frame and currents of her life and laws of her action, she will quietly resume her vestments and her beauty, spread again her robes of verdure over the fields that we have plowed; fringe with fir-trees the hills into which we have mined, and send her rills and rivers singing through the valleys, and her birds warbling through the forests, as sweetly as aforetime; gladdening her artists and rejoicing her poets as richly as before her inner mysteries were invaded.

Indeed, as a knowledge of anatomy assists the sculptor and painter, a scientific knowledge of nature may help the artist better to see her beauty.

Only when one goes to look at her as an artist, or to see her beauty, he must lay aside his dissecting eyes and take her whole and draped in her concrete loveliness as the Creator presents her.

And were it but for the pure and rich enjoyment of the study, we should be munificently rewarded for the labor of acquiring a correct and cultivated taste and an artist's capacity for looking upon nature. But when we consider that by such study we are to come into sympathy with all high art, and encourage and stimulate those who labor to produce the beautiful, and bring rare visions of it into our own homes, and halls, and sanctuaries, the motive expands, and the study becomes a key to new realms of beauty, and a power for advancing civilization and all highest culture.

Chapter 27

The Swedish Nightingale

MUSIC was a far more popular art than painting. Instruments were accessible to all. Many a family could not afford a piano, but enough could so that by the end of the 1850s there was a new piano for every 1500 persons. The melodeon, or reed organ, cost less; and more of them were bought in consequence. For the person who could not pay for a melodeon there was still a guitar. And there was always that universal if variable instrument, the human voice. Sheet music for it sold by thousands and thousands. Lowell Mason's books of hymns sold better than anyone else's; by 1858 his *Carmina Sacra* and its supplement had sold half a million copies. Stephen Foster's songs were heard everywhere. His "Old Folks at Home" and "My Old Kentucky Home" were both issued in the early 1850s. By November 1854 his publishers boasted that they had sold 90,000 copies of "My Old Kentucky Home" and 130,000 of "Old Folks at Home."

Most music was made at home but a national interest in the performing artist was growing. At least a few orchestras made tours; there would be more later. Meanwhile, for reasons of taste and economics both, the solo artist was most sought after. The most highly applauded performer of the fifties was a foreigner, the Swedish soprano Jenny Lind.

Of all the singers who appeared before American audiences prior to the war, the favorite was Jenny. Her voice had a remarkable clarity and appeal, winning even the most critical of listeners. She proved able to charm Broadway toughs as easily as frosty Philadelphians. Her American tour, under the management of P. T. Barnum, was as lengthy as it was successful. The journalist and critic C. G. Rosenberg chronicled it in *Jenny Lind in America* (1851). His account—a minor masterpiece of its kind—illustrates not only her personal attractiveness but also the nation's interest in music. The selections printed below are from Rosenberg's report of her first concert, given in New York; as the report opened, it was eight o'clock and the conductor had just made his entrance.

Source: C. G. Rosenberg, *Jenny Lind in America*
(New York, 1851), pp. 21–26.

NEW YORK

Scarcely had M. Benedict entered the orchestra, than the applause burst forth. After bowing, he took his post as conductor, and the overture to *Oberon* began. This was well played, but it was obvious that nothing was to have the attention of the audience this evening, save Jenny. Belletti then came forward and sang the "Sorgete" very admirably. He also received a token of their joy when he had finished, in a loud and vigorous demonstration, and after he had retired the principal object of attraction made her appearance.

Jenny Lind was now face to face with an American audience, and probably the largest audience before which she had ever sung. She was about to make her *debut* in the New World. I will not say that she "trembled," as the papers generally did say on the following morning, but she was certainly pale and considerably agitated, nor did the enthusiasm which burst forth at her appearance, tend at all to restore her tranquillity. The *Scena* * which she was about to sing, was the "Casta Diva," and as she commenced it, nothing could have been more evident than the excitement under which she was laboring. It had for the first few moments completely mastered her voice. The first notes she struck were uncertain and feeble, but as she proceeded confidence returned to her; and when she concluded the first part of the

* We here subjoin the Programme of this concert.

Air, it was obvious that her self-possession was recovered; and the warm burst of applause which she received, completely restored her to herself. She indeed sung the *Cavatina* so finely, that the audience were completely carried away by their feelings, and drowned the last portion of the air in a perfect tempest of acclamation. Scarcely had she concluded it, than a shower of *bouquets* was hurled upon the stage; while handkerchiefs were waved and cheers were given, which endured for several minutes.

After this, Benedict and Hoffman played their duet on the two pianos. This, ably as it was rendered, was barely listened to, and the multitudes in that large building applauded, at its termination, not so much the merit of the two executants, or the skill of the composer, as their retiring movement to make way for Jenny and Signor Belletti. In the duet, which she now gave with this gentleman, it was evident that she had no more fears for the result of her first appearance. She sang it deliciously, and the approbation of the audience broke out so vehemently that they were at length compelled to desist, and this from sheer exhaustion.

In the meantime, a singular scene had been going on in the rear of the building. It had been rumored that an attempt to gain admission was to be made from the side abutting on the Hudson, and, as it turned out, this rumor was well founded. The river was swarming with boats, filled with the hardest class

CASTLE GARDEN.
First Appearance
of
Mademoiselle Jenny Lind,
on
Wednesday Evening, 11th September, 1850.
Programme.
Part I.

Overture, (*Oberon,*)	Weber.
Aria "Sorgete," (*Maometto Secondo,*) . . .	Rossini.
Signor Belletti.	
Scena and Cavatina, "Casta Diva" (*Norma,*) . .	Bellini.
Mademoiselle Jenny Lind.	
Duet on two Piano Fortes, ...	Benedict.
Messieurs Benedict and Hoffman.	
Duetto, "Per piacer alla Signora," (*Il Turco in Italia,*)	Rossini.
Mademoiselle Jenny Lind and Signor Belletti.	

Part II.

Overture, (*The Crusaders,*)	Benedict.
Trio for the Voice and two Flutes, composed expressly for	
Mademoiselle Jenny Lind, (*Camp of Silesia*) , . .	Meyerbeer.
Mademoiselle Jenny Lind.	
Flutes, *Messrs. Kyle and Siede.*	
Cavatina "Largo al Factotum," *Il Barbiere,* . .	Rossini.
Signor Belletti.	
The Herdsman's Song, more generally known as The Echo	
Song, ... Mademoiselle Jenny Lind.	
The Welcome to America, written expressly for this	
occasion, by Bayard Taylor, *Esq.* . . .	Benedict.
Mademoiselle Jenny Lind.	
Conductor, ... M. Benedict.	

The Orchestra will consist of Sixty Performers, including the first Instrumental talent in the country.

Price of Tickets Three Dollars. Choice of places will be sold at Auction, at Castle Garden.

Doors open at six o'clock. Concert to commence at eight o'clock.

No checks will be issued.

Mdlle. Jenny Lind's Second Grand Concert, will be given at Castle Garden, on Friday evening, 13th instant.

Chickering's Grand Pianos will be used at the first Concert.

of customers, numbering considerably more than five hundred. They had absolutely besieged the Castle Garden by water. However, Mr. Matsell, the chief of the police, had effectually guarded against the chance of such an intrusion, by stationing a large body of his men to repel it, if attempted. In spite of this, a bold effort was made, and some of these strange lovers of melody landed, and had a struggle to maintain their position or enter the Hall,—which they would have in many cases effected, but for the vigilance of the police force.

The orchestra had now returned to the stage, and the overture to Benedict's opera of *The Crusaders* was its first performance in the second portion of the concert. This I will grant was listened to, and received a warm testimony of approbation from the audience. It, however, speedily calmed down when the star of the evening again appeared.

This time it was the Flute Song, by Meyerbeer, taken from the *Camp of Silesia,* which was rendered by her, and it is needless to say that her singing of this delicate inspiration of the German composer, again called forth the enthusiasm of those who were present, until the applause calmed down from the fatigue which it produced. Indeed, but for the intense anxiety on the part of the audience to hear the Echo Song, on which so much had previously been said, we have little doubt but that they would have insisted upon hearing the trio once more. This song she sings in her own native language, accompanying her voice, at the piano, with her own fingers. In it she imitates the herdsman calling his cattle, and the echoes of his voice, which are heard among the mountains. It completely and irrevocably sealed her triumph,—and when she came forward and

sang Her Greeting to America, it was listened to as that of the greatest singer who had ever crossed the water that separates it from the Old World. Bayard Taylor had originally written three verses. These, however, had been cut down to two, in order to give Jenny the opportunity of acquiring them in the brief space which she could give to this task. They run as follows:

> I greet with a full heart, the Land of the West,
>   Whose Banner of Stars o'er the world is unrolled;
> Whose empire o'ershadows Atlantic's wide breast,
>   And opes to the sunset its gateway of gold!
> The land of the mountain, the land of the lake,
>   And rivers that roll in magnificent tide—
> Where the souls of the mighty from slumber awake,
>   And hallow the soil for whose freedom they died!
>
> Thou Cradle of Empire! though wide be the foam
>   That severs the land of my fathers and thee,
> I hear, from thy bosom, the welcome of home,
>   For song has a home in the hearts of the free!
> And long as thy waters shall gleam in the sun,
>   And long as thy heroes remember their scars,
> Be the hands of thy children united as one,
>   And peace shed her light on the Banner of Stars!

Benedict had done all that a composer could do for them in the brief space of time which was given him to write the music. As a *piece de circonstance,* the song was exceedingly successful, and deserved the thunders of approbation which followed it. After retiring, she was again called for, and appeared to receive a perfect avalanche of *bouquets*. She then left the stage for the last time this evening, wearied out, yet delighted with a success so magnificently beyond any that had yet greeted a vocalist in America.

The audience, however, were not yet contented. They must see Barnum, and a loud cry commenced in every part of the hall for his appearance. After a few moments he made his appearance, and when silence was restored, addressed them, to announce one of Jenny Lind's own princely acts of charity. The brief speech which he then made, has so completely run the rounds of the whole American press, that it would be useless here to recapitulate it. Under the excitement of the moment, he said, that he "felt compelled to disregard the fact that Mademoiselle Lind had herself begged him not to mention on this evening one of her own noble and spontaneous deeds of beneficence. Her share of the proceeds of the concert would, he believed, be close upon $10,000, every cent of which she had declared her intention of devoting to charitable purposes." He then mentioned the manner in which she wished this large sum to be applied.

Three enthusiastic cheers were then given for the fair Swede, and three more for Barnum, after which the assembly began to separate.

Chapter 28

Social Life

TODAY the typical middle-class, middle-aged American has less social life than his antebellum ancestor. It is a safe guess that urban and suburban living both have narrowed his range of friendships. The varied sociability of the 1850s has been reduced to two rituals: the cocktail party, where he drinks and talks, and the dinner party, where he eats and talks – or, lately, the pot party. Before the Civil War, if he lived in the country, he would have joined in such assorted activities as church socials, barn raisings, husking bees, and family feasts. His wife would have had an equal share in social life. Though she would have left the barn raising to the men, she would have used the time for such feminine things as quilting bees. For both husband and wife much of the activity in those days blended work and play and so satisfied the Puritan ethic. The young people had parties of several sorts, some of them fairly boisterous.

In the city or town there was less work mingled with the social life than in the country but it was still vigorous. Outings, picnics, suppers, and so on were held in abundance. Even the poor, it can be guessed, found more social life before the war; immigrant or native, they probably enjoyed a sense of community seldom seen today except among the Black militants and the Appalachian mountaineers.

Though the effects of American Puritanism lingered into the 1850s, social pleasures were becoming nearly universal. One of the main things that people did at parties was play games. Adults, and especially but not exclusively young adults, made them the staple of many a gathering. One of the best indexes is that books on how to play games began to appear. One, prepared by some unsung hack writer, was printed by Philip J. Cozans in 1855. Called *Home Games for the People,* it has half a dozen parts. The selections given below come from the first part, on what the author calls "Games of Action." They were.

Among other things they serve to show that though sex was restrained in antebellum America, it was by no means completely smothered. Note the opening direction for the first game: "A player kneels down before a lady, concealing his face in her lap, as for the crying of forfeits." The name of the game? "Hot Cockles."

Source: Anon., *Home Games for the People*
(New York, 1855), pp. 9–10, 11–14.

GAMES OF ACTION

Hot Cockles.

Fortunately the principles of this game of our ancestors are more easily explained than its title, whose origin is lost in the midst of antiquity.

A player kneels down before a lady, concealing his face in her lap, as for the crying of forfeits. He then places one hand, with the palm uppermost, on his back. The rest of the company advance in turns, each administering to the open hand a slap. The task of the kneeler is to discover (without looking up) who it is has given the slap. Should he succeed, the detected player takes his place; if not, he continues to occupy it himself, till such time as he shall make a more fortunate guess.

The impatience of the victim, who, having received several slaps without divining the operator, hears ironical suggestions offered to him, such as, "the loan of a pair of spectacles," "a bedroom candle, as he really ought not to go to sleep *there*," a promise to "hit harder next time, that he may recognise the hand," &c., is very delightful indeed—*to the spectators*.

The Feather.

One of the players takes a bed-feather, a bit of cotton-down, or any light sub-stance coming under the comprehensive denomination of "fluff," which he tosses up in the centre of the assembled circle (who should be seated as closely together as convenience will admit of). He then blows upon it to keep it floating in the air. The individual to whom it comes nearest does the same in order to prevent its falling on his knees, or indeed any part of his person—an accident which would subject him to the payment of a forfeit.

One of the chief advantages of this simple but highly amusing game is, that steady serious people may be induced to engage in it. The gravity of their faces, blowing and puffing away at the contemptible feather, as if all their hopes were centred in evading its responsibility is truly edifying. Sometimes it happens (it being impossible to blow and laugh at the same time) that the "fluff," drops into the player's mouth at the very moment when he is concentrating all his energies in the effort to get rid of it. This is the signal for shouts of laughter, and for a forfeit demanded in just expiation of the player's greediness. We recollect seeing an eminent college dignitary in such a predicament—a spectacle not without its instructive tendencies.

Jack's Alive.

The players pass from one to another a lighted match or twist of paper, of which the flame has been blown out, saying (as they present it), *"Jack's alive!"*

The player in whose hands the last spark dies out pays a forfeit; for which reason, when "Jack" appears in a tolerably lively condition you do not hurry yourself to give it up. When, on the contrary, the sparks seem inclined to die out you lose no time in handing it to your neighbour, who is bound to receive it directly you have pronounced the requisite words.

This very simple game affords considerable amusement without in the least degree taxing the intellectual resources of the players.

The Wolf and the Lambs.

In this game, all the ladies of a company may participate, but only one gentleman at a time—who should be a man of dauntless courage and great powers of endurance.

This latter personage is called the *Wolf*. The principal lady takes the part of the *Shepherdess*. The others stand behind her in a single file, and constitute the *Flock*.

The aim of the Wolf is to catch the innocent lamb who may happen to be at the extremity of the flock. He, however, manifests his hostile intentions by the following terrible announcement!

"I am the Wolf! the Wolf! Come to eat you all up."

The Shepherdess replies, "I am the Shepherdess, and will protect my lambs."

The Wolf retorts, "I'll have the little white one with the golden hoofs."

This dialogue concluded, the Wolf attempts to make an irruption in the line of the flock. But the Shepherdess extending her arms, bars his passage. If he succeeds in breaking through, the lamb placed at the end abandons her post before he can catch her, and places herself in front of the Shepherdess, where she incurs no risk; and so on with the others in succession, till the Shepherdess finds herself the last of the row.

The game then finishes. The unlucky wolf pays as many forfeits as he has allowed lambs to escape him.

If, on the contrary, he has contrived to seize one of them, he does not eat her, but has the privilege of kissing her, and compels her to pay a forfeit.

This game, in company with cricket, skittles, steeplechasing and others, is more adapted to the open air than the precincts of an expensively furnished drawing-room.

Chapter 29

Wit and Humor

THE American has long been proud of his sense of humor. Deny him one and he bristles. Much of the humor was oral and so has evaporated. But even in the 1850s a good deal got into the cultural record. It survives in the comic pictures: the caricatures and cartoons, the humorous lithographs and engravings. It survives most of all in the written word. The professional authors of humor, led by the greatest of them, Mark Twain, would not abound till after the Civil War. Nevertheless, there was already a considerable amount of humorous writing on the market. There was the regional humor, usually set in stories or sketches. It came from New England, the Western frontier, and the South. Through its pages moved the teller of tall Kentucky tales or the Yankee yarn spinner. There was some social satire, as we shall see in the next selection. And there was a substantial aggregate of humor printed originally in the newspapers or magazines which defies categorizing.

Comic poetry became a favorite, with here and there a whole book of it appearing. For instance: *A Budget of Humorous Poetry*, edited anonymously and issued in 1859. Three poems from its pages are given below. The first is "Love in the Bowery" by F. A. Durivage. It reveals that New York was a good source for local color and it furnishes us with an idea of what the Manhattan dialect sounded like. In it a "fire laddie" ruefully remembers the girl who left him.

The other two poems are anonymous. "The Rail" is reprinted not only because of its dry humor but because it recaptures for us a once-standard story locale, the railway train. It gave us "smoking-room stories" as well as the occasional comic verse such as "The Rail." It also gave us, as the poem points out, cinders, noise, and brutal accidents. The last poem, "Reflections," is reprinted purely for the fun of it.

Source: *A Budget of Humorous Poetry,* ed. anon.
(Philadelphia, 1859), pp. 25-27, 197-99, 293-95.

LOVE IN THE BOWERY

> The course of true love didn't never
> run smooth.—SHAKESPERE—*Bowery
> Edition.*

I SEEN her on the sidewalk,
  When I run with No. 9:
My eyes spontaneous sought out hern—
  And hern was fixed on mine.
She waved her pocket handkerchief,
  As we went rushin' by—
No boss that ever killed in York
  Was happier than I.
I felt that I had done it;
  And what had won her smile—
'Twas them embroidered braces,
  And that 'ere immortal tile.

I sought her out at Wauxhall,
  Afore that place was shet—
Oh! that happy, happy evenin',
  I recollex it yet.
I gin her cords of peanuts,
  And a apple and a "wet."
Oh! that happy, happy evenin',
  I recollex it yet.

I took her out to Harlem—
  On the road we cut a swell,
And the nag we had afore us
  Went twelve mile afore he fell.
And though ven he struck the pavement,
  The "Crab" began to fail,
I got another mile out—
  By twisting of his tail.

I took her to the Bowery—
  She sat long side of me—
They acted out a piece they called,
  "The Wizard of the Sea."
And when the sea-fight wos fetched on,
  Eliza cried "hay! hay!"
And like so many minutes there
  Five hours slipped away.

Before the bridle halter,
  I thought to call her mine—
The day was fixed when she to me
  Her hand and heart should jine.
The rum old boss, the father, swore
  He'd gin her out her hand,
Two hundred cash—and also treat
  To number 9's men stand.

But bless me! if she didn't slip
  Her halter on the day;
A peddler from Connecticut,
  He carried her away.
And when the news was brought to me,
  I felt almighty blue;
And though I didn't shed no tear,
  Perhaps I cussed "a few."

Well, let it pass—there's other gals,
  As beautiful as she;
And many a butcher's lovely child
  Has cast sheep's eyes at me.
I wears no crape upon my hat,
  'Cause I'm a packin sent—
I only takes a extra horn,
  Observing, "LET HER WENT!"

THE RAIL

I met him in the cars,
  Where resignedly he sat;
His hair was full of dust,
  And so was his cravat;
He was furthermore embellished
  By a ticket in his hat.

The conductor touched his arm,
  And awoke him from his nap;
When he gave the feeding flies
  An admonitory slap,
And his ticket to the man
  In the yellow-lettered cap.

So, launching into talk,
  We rattled on our way,
With allusions to the crops
  That along the meadows lay—
Whereupon his eyes were lit
  In a speculative ray.

The heads of many men
  Were bobbing as in sleep,
And many babies lifted
  Their voices up to weep;
While the coal-dust darkly fell
  On bonnets in a heap.

All the while the swaying cars
  Kept rumbling o'er the rail,
And the frequent whistle sent
  Shrieks of anguish to the gale,
And the cinders pattered down
  On the grimy floor like hail.

When suddenly a jar,
  And a thrice-repeated bump,
Made the people in alarm
  From their easy cushions jump;
For they deemed the sounds to be
  The inevitable trump.

A splintering crash below,
  A doom-foreboding twitch,
As the tender gave a lurch
  Beyond the flying switch—
And a mangled mass of men
  Lay writhing in the ditch.

With a palpitating heart,
  My friend essayed to rise;
There were bruises on his limbs
  And stars before his eyes,
And his face was of the hue
  Of the dolphin when it dies.

I was very well content
  In escaping with my life;
But my mutilated friend
  Commenced a legal strife—
Being thereunto incited
  By his lawyer and his wife.

And he writes me the result,
  In his quiet way as follows:
That his case came up before
  A bench of legal scholars,
Who awarded him his claim,
  $15,000!

REFLECTIONS

Upon receiving a copy of my first poem
  published in a village newspaper.

Ah! here it is! I'm famous now—

An author and a poet!
It really is in print! Ye gods!
  How proud I'll be to show it!

And gentle Anna! what a thrill
　　Will animate her breast,
To read these ardent lines and know
　　To whom they are addressed!

Why, bless my soul! here's something
　　　strange,
　　What can the paper mean,
By talking of the "graceful brooks,
　　That *gander* o'er the green?"
And here's a T instead of R,
　　Which makes it "Tippling rill;"
"Will seek the *shad*" instead of shade,
　　And "*hell*" instead of "hill."

"They look so—" what? I recollect
　　'Twas "sweet" and then 'twas "kind,"
And now to think the stupid fool
　　For "*bland*" has printed "blind?"
Was ever such provoking work?
　　'Tis curious, by the by,
How anything is rendered blind
　　By giving it an eye.

"Hast thou no tears"—the T's left out—
　　"Hast thou no ears" instead;
"I hope that thou art dear" is put
　　"I hope that thou art dead."
Who ever saw in such a space
　　So many blunders crammed?
"Those gentle eyes bedimmed" is spelt
　　"Those gentle eyes be d—d!"

"The color of the rose" is "nose,"
　　"Affection" is "affliction;"
I wonder if the likeness holds
　　In fact as well as diction?
"Thou art a friend," the R is gone:
　　Whoever would have deemed
That such a trifling thing could change

A "friend" into a "fiend!"
"Thou art the same" is rendered "lame,"
　　It really is too bad;
And here because an "I" is out,
　　My "lovely *maid*" is "mad!"
They drove her blind by poking in
　　An eye—a process new;
And now they've gouged it out again,
　　And made her crazy, too.

"Where are the muses fled, that thou
　　Shouldst live so long unsung,"
Thus read my version—here it is—
　　"Shouldst live so long *unhung!*"
"The fate of woman's love is thine,"
　　An H commences "fate;"
How small a circumstance will change
　　A woman's love to hate!

I'll read no more! what shall I do?
　　I'll never dare to send it;
The paper's scattered far and wide—
　　'Tis now too late to mend it.
Oh, fame! thou cheat of human bliss—
　　Why did I ever write?
I wish my poem had been burnt
　　Before it saw the light.

Let's stop and recapitulate:
　　I've damned her eyes, that's plain—
I've told her she's a lunatic,
　　And blind and deaf and lame!
Was ever such a horrid hash
　　In poetry or prose?
I've said she was a fiend, and praised
　　The color of her nose.
I wish I had that editor
　　About a half a minute—
I'd "bang" him to his heart's content,
　　And with an "H" begin it.

Chapter 30

Fudge Doings

ABOVE and beyond the local-color comedy, the funny stories, and the waggish verse was a more sophisticated type of humor which appeared in print. It was urban rather than rural, Eastern rather than Western, Northern rather than Southern. Its drolleries were quieter, its tone more sedate. The note it struck was one of social satire.

We can see one of the best examples in *Fudge Doings* (1855). The author was Donald Mitchell, an antebellum essayist who could write either sentimentally or wittily with admirable effect. Under the pseudonym of Ik. Marvel, he composed a series of sketches of the new American rich. There would be many more of the rich after the Civil War, but *Fudge Doings* illustrated the fact that they were already thrusting themselves forward. The Fudge family has enough raw, new money to indulge in the vanities which delight the satirist.

In the chapter "Wishes, Ways, and Means," slightly abridged below, we have in Mitchell's portrait of Mrs. Fudge an early version of one of the stock figures of comedy, the female social climber. The portraits of her children are sharply drawn—there are some nice touches to Wash. Fudge and his sister Wilhelmina Ernestina—but they cannot compare with the one of Mrs. Fudge. Furthermore, she is the center of the family and most of the absurd action originates with her.

In this chapter, as elsewhere in the book, she is consequently the star, shining with a steady glow of genteel vulgarity.

Source: Ik. Marvel [Donald Mitchell], *Fudge Doings*
(New York, 1855), pp. 52–59.

WISHES, WAYS, AND MEANS

Mrs. Fudge has a purpose. Ever since she ceased to be a Bodgers, and began to be a Fudge, she has cherished this purpose. Ever since she left Newtown for a life in the city; ever since she eschewed the Baptist persuasion for the refinements of Dr. Muddleton's service; ever since she pestered her husband into a remove from Wooster street to the Avenue, a gigantic purpose has been glowing within her. That purpose has been to erect herself and family into such a position as would provoke notice and secure admiration. There may be worthier purposes, but there are few commoner ones. Mrs. Fudge is to be commended for the pertinacity with which she has guarded this purpose, and measurably for her success.

Wealth Mrs. Fudge has always religiously considered as one of the first elements of progress: she is not alone in this; she can hardly be said to be wrong. Mr. Solomon Fudge is a rich man. I could hardly have adduced a better proof of it, than by my statement of the fact that he is a large holder of the Dauphin stock. None but a substantially rich man could afford to hold large stock, either in the Dauphin or the Parker Vein Coal Companies. Such humble corporations as pay dividends (which they earn) are generally held by those poor fellows who need dividends. Mr. Fudge needs no dividends. Coal companies generally pay no dividends.

Mrs. Fudge, for a considerable period of years, has made the most of her wealth. She is, however, a shrewd woman; Uncle Solomon is a prudent man; she has, therefore, made no extraordinary display. She has kept a close eye upon equipages, hats, cloaks, habits, churches, different schemes of faith and of summer recreation. She is "well posted" in regard to all these matters.

Unfortunately—I say it with a modest regret—a certain Bodger twang belonged to my aunt, which the prettiest velvet cloak, or the most killing of Miss Lawson's bonnets, could never hide. *I* regard it as a native beauty, redolent of the fields; *she*—I am sorry to affirm it—does not regard it at all. It has, however, I am convinced, stood in the way of her advancement.

For five years she may be said to have occupied the same position; the seasons hardly counted upon her; they were certainly not counted by her. She enjoyed a certain prestige of wealth; as much, at any rate, as could be forced into laces and withdrawn readily from the stockbroker's capital. Her children held ignoble positions, either in the nursery or at school. At one time, indeed—I think it was during the cholera-season—she came near ruining her prospects in life by gaining the reputation of a domestic woman. She has since, however, very successfully counteracted this opinion.

I have spoken of the children of Mrs. Fudge. Children are an ornament to society; greater ornaments, frequently, than their parents. With a city education, and with the companionships that grow up in a city school, they possess a foot-hold, as it were which could never have belonged to Phœbe Bodgers. Mrs. Fudge understands this; she has had an eye to this matter, in the course of her son's schooling: her daughter she has watched over with the same motherly care.

Respectable little girls have not unfrequently been invited home to tea by Wilhelmina Ernestina, at the instance of the mamma of Wilhelmina Ernestina. The same little girls, of good family, have been invited out to ride with the mamma of Wilhelmina Ernestina. The mamma has taken great pleasure in talking with such little girls; and has kindly amused them by instituting comparisons of her furniture, or her dress, or her tea-service, with the furniture, and dress, and tea-service with which the little girls of good family are familiar at home. From all this, Mrs. Fudge has derived some·very valuable hints.

In short, Wilhelmina Ernestina is a perfect treasure to Mrs. Fudge. Her point-lace pantalets attracted considerable attention while they were still living in an obscure mansion of Wooster street. Wilhelmina has, moreover, a passably pretty face. It has a slight dash of bravado, which, considering the uses to which it is to be applied, is by no means undesirable. She is just now upon the point of "coming out"; and, as much depends upon her action and success at this particular period, her mother and myself naturally regard her movements with a good deal of anxiety. I shall take pleasure in recording, from time to time, in the course of these papers, her perils and her triumphs.

Her son, George Washington, more familiarly known to the family as Wash. Fudge, is a promising young man. He is an ornament to the street: he is immensely admired by two very young girls over the way, much to their mother's mortification.

I shall venture to draw a short sketch of his appearance and habits: the sketch will not, however, be a *unique*. Several portraits of him already exist; Mrs. Fudge herself possesses two in oil and three in Daguerreotype. He has, moreover, bestowed several upon young ladies about town, to say nothing of a certain Mademoiselle who became enamored of him—to use his own story—and who holds a highly respectable position in the choir of a distinguished opera troupe.

Wash. Fudge has had some twenty years' experience of life—mostly town-life. He is, therefore, no chicken. This is a favorite expression of his, and of his admirers. He dresses in quite elegant style. I doubt somewhat, if such waistcoats and pantaloons as ornament Wash. Fudge can be seen on any other individual.

He was entered at Columbia College: there was not a faster man in his class. His mother advised association with such young gentlemen as appeared to her—from the catalogue—to be desirable companions. She even contrived a few oyster-suppers in the basement, to which they were invited. The affair, however, did not succeed. The young gentlemen alluded to did not return the civilities of young Fudge. Miss Wilhelmina Ernestina, although set off in her best dress, and playing some of her richest bits of piano practice, did not seem to do execution on a single one of the young gentlemen above alluded to.

Wash. Fudge decided Columbia College to be a bore; he determined to leave the faculty. The determination was happy and mutual.

He now devoted himself to dancing, billiards, and flat cigars. His progress was very creditable. Mrs. Fudge took a great deal of very proper pride in the jaunty and dashing appearance of her son Washington. She had not a doubt of his growing capacity to do great execution upon the lady-members of New York society: he had already, indeed, given quiet proofs of his power in this way by certain dashing flirtations in small country-places. A trip to Paris was naturally regarded by Mrs. Fudge as a great opportunity for perfecting himself in the designs which he had in view. A trip to Paris was therefore determined on, somewhat to the demurral of Mr. Solomon Fudge, but much to the satisfaction of his son and heir.

Mrs. Fudge flattered herself that the Miss Spindles, and Pinkertons, and other young females of distinguished families, would find him perfectly irresistible on his return. She saw herself the envied mother of one of the most delightful young men about town—to say nothing

of the accomplished and fascinating Wilhelmina Ernestina. She saw, furthermore, her advances upon the fashion of the town sustained by the flattering attentions of young gentlemen of distinction, and by such overflowing receptions as would for ever bury all recollection of the Bodger blood.

I wish calmly to ask if Mrs. Solomon Fudge is to be blamed for all this? Are not great numbers of mothers anxious and hopeful in the very same way? Nay, do they not continue anxious and hopeful from year to year, trusting in Providence, money, and management, to secure their ultimate rescue from the shades of second-rate society? Is it not reasonable to expect that six years of coaching, at the very pick of the hours; adroit charities to well-known city institutions; persistent listening to the Rev. Dr. Muddleton; positive familiarity with Miss Lawson, will in time, effect their purpose; and that the stout Mrs. Solomon Fudge will, supported on the wings of Wilhelmina and George Washington, soar to the utmost height of society and of ton?

Chapter 31

The Old and the New

TRUE, America was a brisk, businesslike country. By far the greatest part of the energy of the 1850s went to increasing what we now call the gross national product. Notwithstanding, there was a growing amount of time for relaxation. Though it can never be correctly calculated, the chances are that the inexpensive pleasures, the relaxations of the poor but not the poor alone, spread up and down the social scale. And the pleasures that cost money, the pleasures enjoyed in the middle and at the upper end of the social scale, swelled at a startling rate. We can remind ourselves again that between the Panic of 1837 and the Panic of 1857 lay two decades of almost uninterrupted prosperity.

The pleasures of rural life, abundant in the 1850s, have now found their way into American folklore. They stand for an age when even pleasure seemed heartier than it is now. Two of the lithographs which follow show us country joys. The third shows us the polka, which represents a more advanced and often suspected entertainment. Its home was the city. It symbolizes the wicked new ways of enjoying oneself that today's parsons still cluck at.

A picture of Jenny Lind can stand for the enjoyment of all the fine arts but of music in particular. So can two of the illustrations for previous sections, "Farewell Old Cottage" and "Willie we have Missed you," for they come from the covers of the sheet music of the 1850s.

A summer scene from Coney Island—not yet thronged with sweating swimmers or hot-dog and cotton-candy booths—tells us that the water is being rediscovered. Though the bathers are more heavily clothed for high summer than today's girls in January, they still show the slow eroding of Puritanism. The classic Puritan was supposed to detest all enjoyments, especially those involving the senses. He cast an especially suspicious look at bathing, whether in ocean, lake, or stream. He suspected (and he was right) that the bathing suits would shrink from decade to decade. He knew in his heart that we would end by splashing together as naked as the Japanese.

There remained a good many other pleasures that the Puritan still interdicted. In the antebellum South and in the rural North, dancing and card-playing were the Devil's own devices. No decent churchman countenanced them. And no one thought of allowing such entertainment in the church basement any more than he would have thought of conducting a Black Mass in the church itself.

The final illustration in this group represents a different mode. Here the pleasure is one of the mind, for this picture of the silly rich in New York is a satirical one. It is intended to arouse not a laugh but a dry smile, as it offers us a look at the foolish excesses of reform and novelty. Like satire in general or caricature in particular, it is aimed at making us self-conscious. We are losing our primal innocence when we smile at an illustration such as this one, regardless of whether it flatters our prejudices or not.

Source: Fall Games—The Apple-Bee. Drawn by W. Homer.
Harper's Weekly, November 26, 1859.

The harvest festivals were among the most ancient of social pleasures adopted by the Americans. Older than antiquity, they still suited the boisterous American temperament. Their culmination each year was the Thanksgiving which the Pilgrims had instituted, but most farming communities had a variety of celebrations, formal and informal. Harvest home and the husking bee were good examples.

Here in this busy, crowded drawing we see an apple bee in full tilt. The setting is the spacious kitchen of a middle-class farmhouse, with gourds hanging on the wall and onions strung overhead. This is not a party for any one age group: we find wrinkled grandmothers as well as little children. But the accent is undeniably on youth and there is a certain air of sexual revelry. The folk-belief we see illustrated is that if a girl will peel an apple and then throw the peel over her shoulder, it will form into the initials of the man she is going to marry.

At the far left of the picture a trio of oldsters watch with gathered brows. The grandfather seems to frown only at the man near him who operates the apple corer-peeler. However, the two grandmothers look way across the room at a young couple enthusiastically kissing. The young man is the aggressor but he is getting no resistance. Another couple is kissing next to the fireplace but not with the same vim. The cores and peelings fall into a barrel before the intent operator. In front of the barrel are two children kneeling. The boy plays with a jack-o'-lantern, the mark of another fall festival, Halloween.

The center of interest is the young woman tossing an apple peel behind her

FALL GAMES—THE APPLE-BEE

196

and looking over her shoulder to see what initials it will make. She turns casually, gracefully. The young woman on the left who watches too strikes a sophisticated note we would not quite expect in this kitchen, for her shoulders are bare and around her neck she wears an ornamental cross. Her attire is the opposite of that worn by the girl on the other side, who sits pensively in the shadow but also watches the apple peel fall. Further to the right a pretty girl sits facing us; she and her swain stop their peeling to watch as well. Though the girl's face is characterless the young man's is sharp, lively, and aggressive. Behind him, at the rear of the kitchen, somebody's uncle or father hoists a glass of cider and gazes at it like a connoisseur.

The picture is full of movement and vitality, as well it might be. For it reveals the apprentice work of Winslow Homer, who would become one of the eminent painters of the postwar era. The contrast of light and shade is vivid; we cannot be sure where the light in the foreground comes from but the fact does not bother us. The composition is just asymmetrical enough to please the eye. And its structure promises well for the young artist. The movement of the picture is a whirling one, suitable for a party or festival. The direction is counterclockwise and is set by the upflung arm of the girl in the center.

Minor parts of the patterns repeat themselves, to our satisfaction. For instance: the faces of the two girls on the right, one in light, the other in shadow. And at the left of the picture, the faces of the two grandmothers, each matching the other in censoriousness.

Source: American Country Life: Pleasures of Winter. Drawn by F. F. Palmer and lithographed by N. Currier, 1855.
Reproduced from the Collections of the Library of Congress

In spite of some exceptions the pleasures of the poor were often few and grimy, changing seldom over the generations. They have left little trace. The pleasures of the American middle class, on the other hand, and of the American rich have left clear signs behind them. The country life we see pictured here is that of the affluent farmer, probably, or perhaps of the city merchant who lives at the edge of town. No drudge in any case, he owns a handsome house, a farm with outbuildings and apparently a tenant house too, and doubtless employs not only a hired man but the Negro servitor we see before us.

The family is well dressed, in token of the increasing prosperity of the antebellum period. The horses of those days were as much a status symbol as the automobiles of today, so it is worth noting that here we see a matched pair of highsteppers. In the background behind them, old Dobbin draws a sledge loaded with logs but the sleek horses hitched to the sleigh look expensive.

The artist, Palmer, was one of Currier's hacks. He has nicely caught the mixture of detail and sentiment which, as Currier was learning, sold so well. The landscape is frosted with sugar; the air looks invigorating. The Negro smiles

as the little boy prepares to toss a snowball at him. The center of the picture's interest is the sleigh and the servant. They are framed by the branching trees at one side and the front of the house at the other. Behind them the scene stretches out into the distance. Palmer has managed to get a sense of wintery vastness by spotting his vista with one object beyond the other. Near the horizon we can barely see a group of people skating on the pond. They too are enjoying winter, and cheaply.

Palmer is at his best in catching the expression on the Negro's face. Here he comes up almost to the standard of the brilliant Long Island genre artist of the 1840s and fifties, William Sidney Mount. But the expressions on the other faces are pure cliche. The features of the two children and their mother all look as if formed of wax. Notwithstanding, the group is patently in the process of enjoying itself and amiably modifying the Puritan ethic.

Source: Cover for "The Celebrated Varsovienne" Lithographed by J. H. Hufford and published by Oliver Ditson & Co., 1857.
Reproduced from the Collections of the Library of Congress

The fastest way to hell, according to a good many scandalized observers, was the polka. First of all, it was a foreign dance, Bohemian originally; and all Continental importations were suspect to good Americans. Still more to the point, it was a lively, bouncing one, in which the man put his arm around his far from reluctant partner while she held her hand on his shoulder. It was widely believed that the quick tempo and the partial embrace stimulated the passions. A few measures of the polka and even the nicest girl was ready to surrender all that she held dear. Or that was the general impression, anyway.

Here on the cover of a popular piece of sheet music the artist shows us the polka in one of its less inflammatory moments. Either through guile or lack of skill, he gives us none of the sense of galloping movement that made the polka popular in the 1850s. The couple before us seems to be footing it rather sedately in fact. The girl turns her head modestly aside though she looks mildly interested. The man looks down with the sober expression that Count de Gurowski found so characteristic of Americans when at play. The two are turning their heads together in one of the motions of the dance but the artist, Hufford, can catch little of the action in spite of his attempt to show the swinging coattails of the man.

The others at the party either smile slightly or look expressionless: nowhere can we detect the glint of rising lust. Yet sex is not absent. The girl's shoulders are bare; the man's breeches are fashionably tight. The clothing the people wear looks upper-class. The most esoteric touch of style is the monocle which the artist has given the principal man. No American male would wear one, so this is a covert advertisement of the foreign decadence which remained one of the polka's most effective allurements.

The chiaroscuro of Hufford's picture appears routine. The lights and darks

COVER FOR "THE CELEBRATED VARSOVIENNE"

alternate unimaginatively. The girl's white gown contrasts with her partner's black evening-dress. The wide doorway frames the dancers in the brilliantly lighted room. The furnishings on either side help to define the picture and, though sketchy, give the proper evidence of prosperity.

Source: Jenny Lind. Lithograph of Sarony, 1850.
Reproduced from the Collections of the Library of Congress

The fine arts never flourished in the 1850s as did industry or agriculture—after all, this was America—but they prospered more than ever before. Music was the most popular of the fine arts. People sang and played at home and also enjoyed hearing performers more skilled than they themselves. These performers were native Americans for the most part, but the most spectacular one during the decade was foreign, the Swedish singer Jenny Lind, described earlier.

Her success was the more widespread because she toured America under the unexpected auspices of the most flamboyant promoter of his time, P. T. Barnum. Barnum treated Jenny with great propriety, however. He saw in her a chance to make himself respectable, so though her tour was a smashing success it had no air of the circus about it. The total paid for all admissions to her opening concert, in New York, was nearly $25,000. She completely mastered her audience there and then went on to comparable triumphs in Boston, Philadelphia, Baltimore, Washington, Richmond, Charleston, New Orleans, Natchez, Memphis, St. Louis, Nashville, Louisville, Cincinnati, Wheeling, and Pittsburgh. It was a royal progress.

She gave her applauding audiences a mixture of airs from Italian or German operas and lieder such as "The Echo Song" and "The Bird Song." Here, costumed as "The Daughter of the Regiment" in Donizetti's opera of that name, she flourishes the flag of victory while gazing placidly away from us.

The artist has made Jenny's face prettier than nature did but he has preserved a sweetness of expression which many remarked who saw her on her American tour. His composition is symmetrical and rather dull. Jenny stands exactly in the center of it, with one foot forward to balance her raised arm. The mountainous scenery is appropriate enough for the opera but the arrangement of it is standard "picturesque," down to the customary blasted tree at the left margin. However, the artist's technique is unusual. Unlike so many of his fellows, he does not draw every leaf on a tree nor every stone in a brook. His style has a certain dash. The leaves are indicated in masses, for example; the water beneath the little footbridge is simply suggested. It would be a long day before innovation meant as much to the popular lithographers, such as Sarony, as to the serious artists but here at any rate was a foretaste of it.

JENNY LIND.

Source: Scene at Coney Island—Sea Bathing Illustrated.
Frank Leslie's Illustrated Newspaper, September 20, 1856.

Among pleasures old and new, bathing and swimming were as ancient as time. But in America they were not rediscovered till the middle of the nineteenth century. Of course there had always been little boys who stripped and plunged in during the hot summer. But bathing as a recreation was a latecomer to the American scene. Even in the 1850s it remained a captive to American Puritanism, as we can see by a glance at the illustration. Both men and women wear enough clothing to inhibit even the stoutest swimmer. Here as a matter of fact we see no real swimming. A bald-headed man is doing a dog paddle while in front of him someone may be sloping back to shore. But most of the figures simply sit in the water or stand next to the edge of the beach. The two ladies in the foreground are not only clothed from head to foot but are protected from the sun by a parasol. Only their tender feet are bare.

Turning to the family in the center of the picture, we see that the father's hat has blown off in the sea breeze, and his wife and child watch his all-too-comic effort to recapture it. Behind the family there is a bath house and next to it a makeshift pavilion where several spectators sit enjoying the prospect. A jauntily dressed idler leans against the pavilion and cocks an eye at the well muffled bathing girls.

The scene is drawn boldly and vividly, with an attention not only to such things as the stressed perspective but also to social touches. The artist shows his awareness of social criticism as well as of the usefulness of comic relief. His drawing is aimed at a broad audience and clearly reaches it. The girl holding her foot, the man chasing his hat, the idler against the shed: all these catch the eye of the beholder. The picture shows no refinement and only passable technical skill. However, it does what it sets out to do: make us look at the scene.

The picture is actually the result of the new, enterprising journalism of the Englishman who called himself Frank Leslie and started his magazine in December 1855. The changing culture of New York afforded him an ideal source for illustrations, and he was determined to make his a picture paper. He also handled national news, as well as sports and fashions. He soon showed a shrewd eye for the sensational, with the result that his weekly boomed. By the third year it was claiming a circulation of 100,000. Its success soon spawned imitators headed by *Harper's Weekly,* established in 1857. But they never caught the flavor of the original. Among today's magazines *Life* is probably closest to *Leslie's*.

SCENE AT CONEY ISLAND—SEA BATHING ILLUSTRATED.

SCENE AT CONEY ISLAND—SEA BATHING ILLUSTRATED

Source: Halloo! Turks in Gotham! Artist: W. A. or A. W., from
Bloomerism in Practice.
The Harry T. Peters "America on Stone" Lithography Collection,
The Smithsonian Institution

The pleasures of satire seem manifold but surely one of the chief ones is poking fun at reformers. In the America of the 1850s cartoons and caricatures were being more widely distributed than ever before. Americans had become inordinately proud of their sense of humor and fed it with anything they could. A favorite subject for various artists was the women's rights movement. The austere ladies who led the movement were often ridiculed. One of them was Elizabeth Oakes Smith. She was doubly vulnerable as both a feminist and an abolitionist. Here in this lithograph we glimpse the result of a lecture of hers; it is Plate 7 of a series called "Bloomerism in Practice."

She has completely converted the New York matron who prances before us, and the matron in turn has converted her complaisant husband and her little boy. She wears Turkish harem dress (or what the artist thought was Turkish harem dress) while her husband wears bloomers. Invented at the start of the decade by Mrs. Amelia Bloomer, they were worn in public only by the most advanced females. Mrs. Turkey and her little boy smoke Turkish cigars of course, though her husband merely sniffs the smoke. Their sex roles are, inevitably, reversed. Mrs. Turkey has a pair of daggers and perhaps a pistol stuck in her belt; Mr. Turkey goes armed only with a fork and spoon and carries a cooking pot. His only military item seems a dagger-stickpin in his shirt.

The artist has caught the facial expressions nicely. Mrs. Turkey looks sharp, bold, and shrewish; the little boy stares arrogantly at his father; and Mr. Turkey smiles indulgently at his offspring. As the Turkey family crosses the street a local Turkish merchant watches them from the doorway of his establishment. The building forms part of the background for the picture, with the handsome new Trinity Church forming the rest.

The picture is full of movement. The two main figures step to the left with the parasol pointing the way. The boy turns in the other direction and so he acts as a complement. The dog is pointed to the left, but it has its feet firmly planted so that the force is in the opposite direction. The composition is competently designed. The slanted parasol connects the lines both of the store building and of the church, as well as filling in the space between them. The parasol is topped by a crescent and, on looking closely, we see that Trinity Church is too. The cross is gone from its steeple, fit sign of the fact that the reformers want to abolish Christian customs and substitute the abominations of the East.

Pl. 7.

HALLOO! TURKS IN GOTHAM!

Mrs. Turkey having attended Mrs. Oaks-Smith's Lecture on the Emancipation-Dress *, resolves at once to give a start to the* New Fashion *and in order to do it with more* Effect *, she wants* Mr. Turkey *to join her in this bold* Attempt.

(on. 288d)

HALLOO! TURKS IN GOTHAM!

VII. *The Peculiar Institution*

Chapter 32

Abolition on the March

WITH the passing of each year the controversy over slavery grew more bitter. In the South hardly a voice was raised against slavery during the entire 1850s; only its defenders could be heard. In the North the average American tried to ignore it. He had no wish to be reminded of the Negroes' cruel plight. He had his own life to live: a job to do, a family to raise and educate, a church to belong to, and—for that matter—a social life to enjoy. But the abolitionists refused to let him alone. Their arguments filled the air; their manifestos and meetings multiplied. In their angry zeal they matched the most ardent Southern proponents of slavery.

The average Northerner, to all appearances, was not yet ready either to espouse abolition or support a war with the Southern states. He was getting gradually closer, however, year by year. How far the antislavery movement had progressed could be seen from a landmark speech by the antislavery leader Wendell Phillips. He gave it in Boston on the twentieth anniversary of the notorious Boston riot of October 21, 1835, when a mob had threatened the abolitionists, chief among them William Lloyd Garrison, with actual violence while the officials of Boston watched with tolerant eye. Now the case was different. The right of the abolitionists to meet and make themselves heard was plainly established. Abolition itself was still to come but the right to press for it was, certainly in Boston, not to be denied.

It was a night of triumph for the veteran reformers who listened to Phillips's burning account of the efforts, two decades earlier, to paralyze the movement. The meeting, held in Stacy Hall, was first addressed by Garrison. Among other things, he read accounts from the newspapers of October 1835 which harshly criticized the abolitionists. When Phillips spoke, he measured the gains made by the crusade. With a characteristic mixture of piety and moral arrogance he excoriated the old enemies of abolition while lauding its old friends. He scorned the hapless mayor of twenty years before, and he eulogized not only Garrison but the group of Boston women who had determined at the time to meet as the Female Antislavery Society. He praised the man, Francis Jackson, who had opened his home to the women when they were refused a public hall. He condemned an opposition meeting in Faneuil Hall which the mayor had permitted and even presided over.

Phillips recalled the criticisms of twenty years before in terms that to us may sound familiar; he recalled the charges of the enemies of dissent. The dissenters were accused, like the dissenters of today, "of harsh language and over-boldness, and great disparagement of dignities." Time had made the criticism of 1835 sound pointless; progress had indeed taken place. Nevertheless, it was now 1855 and Phillips gave the rest of his speech to urging his audience on to the work still ahead. Much more remained to be done.

Source: Wendell Phillips, "Speech before the Antislavery Meeting Held in Stacy Hall, Boston, on the Twentieth Anniversary of the Mob of October 21, 1835"
Speeches, Lectures, and Letters (Boston, 1863), pp. 213–14, abridged; 216–27, abridged.

SPEECH BEFORE THE ANTISLAVERY MEETING

Mr. President: I feel that I have very little right on this platform to-day. I stand here only to express my gratitude to those who truly and properly occupy it, for what we all owe them—the women and the men—who stood by our honor, and so nobly did our duties, when we forgot it and them twenty years ago.

At this hour, twenty years ago, I was below in the street;—I thank God I am inside the house now! I was not in the street as one of the mob, but as a spectator. I had come down from my office in Court Street to see what the excitement was. I did not understand antislavery then; that is, I did not understand the country in which I lived. We have all learned much since then; learned what antislavery means,—

learned what a republican government really is,—learned the power of the press and of money, which I, at least, did not know then. I remember saying to the gentleman who stood next to me in the street: "Why does not the Mayor call out the regiment?" (I belonged to it then.) "We would cheerfully take arms in such a case as this. It is a very shameful business. Why does he stand there arguing? Why does he not call for the guns?" I did not then know that the men who should have borne them were the mob; that all there was of government in Boston was in the street; that the people, our final reliance for the execution of the laws, were there, in "broadcloth and broad daylight," in the street. Mayor Lyman knew it; and the only honorable and honest course open to him was, to have said, "If I cannot *be* a magistrate, I will not *pretend* to be one."

I do not know whether to attribute the Mayor's disgraceful conduct to his confused notion of his official duties, or to a cowardly unwillingness to perform what he knew well enough to be his duty. A superficial observer of the press and pulpit of that day would be inclined to consider it the result of ignorance, and lay the blame at the door of our republican form of government, which thrusts up into important stations dainty gentlemen like Lyman, physicians never allowed to doctor any body but the body politic, or cunning tradesmen who have wriggled their slimy way to wealth,—men who in a trial hour not only know nothing of their own duties, but do not even know where to go for advice. And for the preachers, I am inclined to think this stolid ignorance of civil rights and duties may be pleaded as a disgraceful excuse, leaving them guilty only of meddling in matters far above their comprehension. But one who looks deeper into the temper of that day will see plainly enough that the Mayor and the editors, with their companions "in broadcloth," were only blind to what they did not wish to see, and knew the right and wrong of the case well enough, only, like all half-educated people, they were but poorly able to comprehend the vast importance of the wrong they were doing. The mobs which followed, directed against others than Abolitionists, the ripe fruit of the seed here planted, opened their eyes somewhat. . . .

The Mayor played a most shuffling and dishonorable part. For some time previous, he had held private conferences with leading Abolitionists, urging them to discontinue their meetings, profess-ing, all the while, entire friendship, and the most earnest determination to protect them in their rights at any cost. The Abolitionists treated him, in return, with the utmost confidence. They yielded to his wishes, so far as to consent to do nothing that would increase the public excitement, with this exception, that they insisted on holding meetings often enough to assert their *right* to meet. Yet, while they were thus honorably avoiding everything which would needlessly excite the public mind, going to the utmost verge of submission and silence that duty permitted,—while the Abolitionists, with rare moderation, were showing this magnanimous forbearance and regard to the weakness of public authority and the reckless excitement of the public,—the Mayor himself, in utter violation of official decorum and personal honor, accepted the chair of the public meeting assembled in Faneuil Hall, and presided over that assembly,—an assembly which many intended should rouse a mob against the Abolitionists, and which none but the weak or wilfully blind could avoid seeing must lead to that result. In his opening speech to that factious meeting, the Mayor, under oath at that moment to protect every citizen in his rights, and doubly bound just then by private assurances to these very Abolitionists, forgot all his duty, all his pledges, so far as to publicly *warn them of the danger of their meeting,*—a warning or threat, the memory of which might well make him tremblingly anxious to save Garrison's life, since of any blood shed that day, every law, divine and human, would have held the Mayor guilty. . . .

I never open the statute-book of Massachusetts without thanking Ellis Gray Loring and Samuel J. May, Charles Follen and Samuel E. Sewall, and those around me who stood with them, for preventing Edward Everett from blackening it with a law making free speech an indictable offence. And we owe it to fifty or sixty women, and a dozen or two of men, that free speech was saved, in 1835, in the city of Boston. Indeed, we owe it mainly to one man. If there is one here who loves Boston, who loves her honor, who rejoices to know that, however fine the thread, there *is* a thread which bridges over that dark and troubled wave, and connects us by a living nerve with the freemen of the Revolution,—that Boston, though betrayed by her magistrates, her wealth, her press, and her pulpits, never utterly bowed her neck, let him remember that we owe it to you, Sir, [Mr. Francis Jackson,] who offered to the women not allowed to meet here, even though the Mayor was in this hall, the use of your house; and one sentence of your letter deserves to be read whenever Boston men are met together to celebrate the preservation of the right of free speech in the city of Adams and Otis. History, which always loves courage, will write it on a page whiter than marble and more incorruptible than gold. You said, Sir, in answer to a letter of thanks for the use of your house:

If a large majority of this community choose to turn a deaf ear to the wrongs which are inflicted upon their countrymen in other portions of the land,—if they are content to turn away from the sight of oppression, and "pass by on the other side,"—so it must be.

But when they undertake in any way to impair or annul my right to speak, write, and publish upon any subject, and more especially upon enormities which are the common concern of every lover of his coun-

try and his kind,—so it must not be,—so it shall not be, if I for one can prevent it. Upon this great right let us hold on at all hazards. And should we, in its exercise, be driven from public halls to private dwellings, one house at least shall be consecrated to its preservation. And if, in defence of this sacred privilege, which man did not give me, and shall not (if I can help it) take from me, this roof and these walls shall be levelled to the earth,—let them fall, if they must. They cannot crumble in a better cause. They will appear of very little value to me, after their owner shall have been whipped into silence.

This was only thirty days after the mob. I need not read the remainder of that letter, which is in the same strain. . . .

At that Faneuil Hall meeting, one of "the family" was present,—one of that family which was never absent when a deed of infamy was to be committed against the slave,—a family made up mostly of upstart attorneys, who fancy themselves statesmen, because able to draw a writ or pick holes in an indictment. Mr. Thomas B. Curtis read the resolutions; and then followed three speeches, by Harrison Gray Otis, Richard Fletcher, and Peleg Sprague, unmatched for adroit, ingenious, suggestive argument and exhortation to put down, legally or violently,—each hearer could choose for himself,—all public meetings on the subject of slavery in the city of Boston. Everything influential in the city was arrayed against this society of a few women. I could not but reflect, as I sat here, how immortal principle is. Rev. Henry Ware, Jr. read the notice of this society's meeting from Dr. Channing's pulpit, and almost every press in the city woke barking at him next morning for what was called his "impudence." He is gone to his honored grave; many of those who met in this hall in pursuance of that notice are gone likewise. They died, as Whittier so well says,

> their brave hearts breaking slow,
> But, self-forgetful to the last,
> In words of cheer and bugle glow,
> Their breath upon the darkness passed.

In those days, as we gathered round their graves, and resolved that, the "narrower the circle became, we would draw the closer together," we envied the dead their rest. Men ceased to slander them in that sanctuary; and as we looked forward to the desolate vista of calamity and toil before us, and thought of the temptations which beset us on either side from worldly prosperity which a slight sacrifice of principle might secure, or social ease so close at hand by only a little turning aside, we almost envied the dead the quiet sleep to which we left them, the harvest reaped, and the seal set beyond the power of change. And of those who assaulted them, many are gone. The Mayor so recreant to his duty, or so lacking in knowledge of his office, is gone; the Judge before whom Mr. Garrison was arraigned, at the jail, the next day after the mob, is gone; the Sheriff who rode with him to the jail is gone; the city journals have changed hands, being more than once *openly* bought and sold. The editor of the *Atlas,* whose zeal in the cause of mob violence earned it the honor of giving its name to the day,—"the *Atlas* mob" many called it,— is gone; many of the prominent actors in that scene, twenty years ago, have passed away; the most eloquent of those whose voices cried "Havoc!" at Faneuil Hall has gone,—Mr. Otis has his wish, that the grave might close over him before it closed over the Union, which God speed in his good time;—but the same

principle fills these same halls, as fresh and vital today, as self-fixed and resolute to struggle against pulpit and press, against wealth and majorities, against denunciation and unpopularity, and certain in the end to set its triumphant foot alike on man and everything that man has made.

Here stands to-day the man whom Boston wealth and Boston respectability went home, twenty years ago this night, and gloried in having crushed. The loudest boasters are gone. He stands to-day among us, these very walls, these ideas which breathe and burn around us, saying for him, "I still live." If, twenty or twice twenty years hence, he too shall have passed away, may it not be till his glad ear has caught the jubilee of the emancipated millions whom his life has been given to save! . . .

I find that these people, who have made this day famous, were accused in their own time of harsh language and over-boldness, and great disparagement of dignities. These were the three charges brought against the Female Antislavery Society in 1835. The women forgot their homes, it was said, in endeavoring to make the men do their duty. It was a noble lesson which the sisters and mothers of that time set the women of the present day,—I hope they will follow it.

There was another charge brought against them,—it was, that they had no reverence for dignitaries. The friend who sits here on my right (Mrs. Southwick) dared to rebuke a slaveholder with a loud voice, in a room just before, if not then, consecrated by the presence of Chief Justice Shaw, and the press was astonished at her boldness. I hope, though she has left the city, she has left representatives behind her who will dare rebuke any slave-hunter, or any servant of the slave-power, with the same boldness, frankness, and defiance of authorities, and contempt of parchment.

Then there was another charge brought against their meetings, that they indulged in exceedingly bold language about pulpits and laws and wicked magistrates. That is a sin which I hope will not die out. God grant we may inherit that also.

I should like to know very much how many there are in this hall to-day who were out in the street, as actual mobocrats, twenty years ago. I know there are some here who signed the various petitions to the City Government to prevent the meeting from being held; but it would be an interesting fact to know how many are here to-day, actually enlisted under the antislavery banner, who tore that sign to pieces. I wish we had those relics; the piece of that door which was long preserved, the door so coolly locked by Charles Burleigh,—it was a touching relic. We ought to have a portion of that sign which the Mayor threw down as a tub to the whale, hoping to save some semblance of his authority,—hoping the multitude would be satisfied with the sign, and spare the women in this hall, —forgetting that a mob is controlled only by its fears, not by pity or good manners.

But, Mr. President, it is a sad story to think of. Antislavery is a sad history to read, sad to look back upon. What a miserable refuse public opinion has been for the past twenty years!—what a wretched wreck of all that republican education ought to have secured! Take up that file of papers which Mr. Garrison showed you, and think, Republicanism, a Protestant pulpit, free schools, the model government, had existed in our city for sixty years, and this was the

result! A picture, the very copy of that which Sir Robert Peel held up in the British Parliament, within a month after the mob, as proof that republicanism could never succeed. It is a sad picture to look back upon. The only light which redeems it is the heroism that consecrated this hall, and one house in Hollis Street, places which Boston will yet make pilgrimages to honor.

The only thing that Americans (for let us be Americans to-day, not simply Abolitionists),—the only thing for which Americans can rejoice, this day, is, that *everything* was not rotten. The *whole* head was not sick, nor the *whole* heart faint. There were *ten men*, even in Sodom! And when the Mayor forgot his duty, when the pulpit prostituted itself, and when the press became a pack of hounds, the women of Boston, and a score or two of men, remembered Hancock and Adams, and did their duty. And if there are young people who hear me to-day, let us hope that when this special cause of antislavery effort is past and gone, when another generation shall have come upon the stage, and new topics of dispute have arisen, there will be no more such scenes. How shall we ever learn toleration for what we do not believe? The last lesson a man ever learns is, that liberty of thought and speech is the right for all mankind; that the man who denies every article of our creed is to be allowed to preach just as often and just as loud as we ourselves. We have learned this,—been taught it by persecution on the question of slavery. No matter whose the lips that would speak, they must be free and ungagged. Let us always remember that he does not really believe his own opinions, who dares not give free scope to his opponent. Persecution is really want of faith in our creed. Let us see to it, my friends, Abolitionists, that we learn the lesson the whole circle round. Let us believe that the whole of truth can never do harm to the whole of virtue. Trust it. And remember, that, in order to get the whole of truth, you must allow every man, right or wrong, freely to utter his conscience, and protect him in so doing.

The same question was wrought out here twenty years ago, as was wrought in the protest of fifty or a hundred Abolitionists, when an infidel (Abner Kneeland) was sent to Boston jail for preaching his sentiments. I hope that we shall all go out of this hall, remembering the highest lesson of this day and place, that every man's conscience is sacred. No matter how good our motives are in trying to gag him! Mayor Lyman had some good motives that day, had he only known what his office meant, and stayed at home, if he felt himself not able to fill it. It is not motives. Entire, unshackled freedom for every man's lips, no matter what his doctrine;—the safety of free discussion, no matter how wide its range; —no check on the peaceful assemblage of thoughtful men! Let us consecrate our labors for twenty years to come in doing better than those who went before us, and widening the circle of their principle into the full growth of its actual and proper significance.

Let me thank the women who came here twenty years ago, some of whom are met here to-day, for the good they have done me. I thank them for all they have taught me. I had read Greek and Roman and English history; I had by heart the classic eulogies of brave old men and martyrs; I dreamed, in my folly, that I heard the same tone in my youth from the cuckoo lips of Edward Everett;— these women taught me my mistake. They taught me that down in those hearts which loved a principle for itself, asked no man's leave to think or speak, true to their convictions, no matter at what hazard, flowed the real blood of '76, of 1640, of the hemlock-drinker of Athens, and of the martyr-saints of Jerusalem. I thank them for it! My eyes were sealed, so that, although I knew the Adamses and Otises of 1776, and the Mary Dyers and Ann Hutchinsons of older times, I could not recognize the Adamses and Otises, the Dyers and Hutchinsons, whom I met in the streets of '35. These women opened my eyes, and I thank them and you [turning to Mrs. Southwick and Miss Henrietta Sargent, who sat upon the platform] for that anointing. May our next twenty years prove us all apt scholars of such brave instruction!

Chapter 33

Appeal to the Uncommitted

WRITING in a tone of reasonableness founded on the rocklike certainty that he was right, Samuel Davies Baldwin addressed his book *Dominion* to the doubtful. Printed in Nashville in 1858 by the Southern Methodist Publishing House, it represented the effort by many Christians to find Biblical support for Negro slavery—or, as Baldwin put it sweetly, "a state of supervision as servants." He used all the techniques of biblical scholarship he could to reinforce his argument. The ardent upholder of slavery had no need of Baldwin's book though he probably found it convenient. But there were many other people, north and south, who craved guidance; and Baldwin tried to provide it. Those in the South dared not seek it publicly; those in the North could be open about their need.

Stripped down, Baldwin's thesis is that God ordained the sons of Ham to be slaves to the sons of Shem and Japheth. And Negro slavery in America is infinitely better than slavery anywhere else. In fact the slave is lucky that he is here. "In our country four millions of negroes, the offspring of three hundred thousand slaves, have an existence far preferable to that of their race in its native land." And when they die thousands of them will go to heaven, as they never could have in heathen Africa.

When slavery has been threatened in America, God has intervened to preserve it, most notably through the introduction of cotton planting into the South. The hand of God is also shown in the unanimity with which the South supports slavery. There are seventeen non-slaveholders to each slaveholder, and yet they all agree on "the propriety of the institution."

Slavery gets the credit for producing "Uncle Tom, the intelligent and enlightened hero of bondage." No free Negro could be as impressive. But the clinching argument involves not only Uncle Tom but all his brethren: they like slavery. As Baldwin observes blandly, "Providence has kept the negro race in a state of singular satisfaction with its lot in the South." To

Baldwin the Negro's contentment is entirely understandable, for he "labors leisurely, is free from solicitude, and is seldom sick; and when he dies, he is blessed with the consolations of religion."

Source: Samuel Davies Baldwin, *Dominion*
(Nashville, 1858), pp. 96–102.

POLITICAL RIGHTS OF JAPHETH

There are thousands who know not what to say or believe. Many think Hamitic slavery should be circumscribed within its present bounds, and be left to die of inanition. But is such a theory consistent with the universal law of love? If Hamitic service is a Divine gift, why restrict it to other limits than those assigned by Providence? If restricted here, it will inevitably develop itself in far worse forms to the human family elsewhere. Its products are in pressing demand, and this demand will stimulate the supply. In our country four millions of negroes, the offspring of three hundred thousand slaves, have an existence far preferable to that of their race in its native land. But for slavery, these had never existed. Thousands of them are on their way to heaven, and but for slavery they had never known God. In British slave countries they perish by millions, and exhibit no regular increase, while here they multiply and prosper. As, therefore, Hamitic bondage will certainly extend in spite of navies and philanthropists, it is a dictate of humanity, as a choice between evils, that slavery should be under the control of a humanized people, such as our countrymen have shown themselves to be. Carolina is more humane than Brazil, and Texas than Guiana or Buenos-Ayres.

The dissolution of our country would not prevent Hamitic slavery, but rather send it lawlessly and wild to seize and engraft itself in every suitable climate. The law of love demands of us, where we cannot eradicate evils, to keep things from growing worse; and since Hamitic slavery will expand, it is benevolent to let it do so under the watchful eye of a humanizing legislation, rather than beneath the reckless control of exasperated covetousness. Our mission is to benefit the world rather than a few; to soften the asperities of all races, rather than provoke outrage; and to mollify ills we cannot eradicate. True benevolence would keep Hamitic bondage under the stars and stripes, rather than under the triple head of Cerberus.

But again: the law of God demands the multiplication of our race; and as this can be obeyed only through adequate means of support, and as such support must primarily proceed from the cultivation of the soil, it follows that governments are obligated to devote principal attention to the increase of agricultural products. In the United States, as a consequence of Hamitic tillage, the Hamites have increased from thousands to millions, while the subsistence of thousands of others has depended upon their toil. Obedience to the

Divine law of population has, therefore, been secured through Hamitic service. As a tree is known by its fruit; as sin is not the seed of holiness; and as disobedience to one law of God cannot result in direct obedience to another; and as Hamitic service does result in direct obedience to God's law, it follows that it is not in opposition to his will or law. But it is said that it would have been better for all parties had the Hamites never been brought to the United States. This assertion is a bold one, and as thoughtless as bold. Had Hamitic service never been introduced, then millions who now live, and who have lived, would, from the very nature of things, never have lived at all. To prevent the existence of human beings is the dogma of the dog in the manger. The white race here has increased as fast as the nature of things would admit, and yet there is room in America for countless millions more. But this proscribing policy would shut millions from existence because of their color. To prevent the existence of millions is *actually depriving them of life,* and deliberate deprivation of human life, whether by the policy of governments or churches, is tantamount to murder in the *first degree.* Such wholesale prevention of human life is by no means in accordance with the law of love. That law will not permit us to exclude Hamitic increase, nor allow us to fence our borders against all but those of our own *caste.*

The Hamites in the United States who are not in a state of supervision as servants, do not materially increase in multitude, yet in servitude they do; so that nature, teaching us the will of God, demonstrates that such bondage is the very best estate they can be in for a *season,* and that it is more in accordance with the law of love than any other policy that can be pursued.

Again: Providence permanently blesses those governments only who keep his law. But he has blessed the South beyond all people upon earth. The material wealth of the South, in *proportion to its white population,* far surpasses that of any people that ever lived on earth. There was a period in its history when Hamitic service seemed about to prove a real disaster; but just at that juncture Providence interposed and prevented the severance of the races by introducing the culture of the cotton plant, making "cotton king of commerce." Thus a Divine blessing was bestowed on the South; a blessing endorsing the propriety of holding Hamites to service.

Again: when the question of this service was pressed to the utmost in our national councils, and the South was greatly troubled, Providence once more interposed by enhancing the universal market value of Hamitic products, thus tightening the links of union between the races. And yet again: the empire of Britain once threw her whole influence with that of the North, against the South, to crush out Hamitic service. But now she is made providentially to feel such a pressure on her own prosperity by the necessities for Hamitic produce, that she is softly taking her massy feet from our heart, and giving encouragement to our hands, and also acknowledging her emancipation philanthropy to be a failure.

God has blessed the South with political unanimity of sentiment on the necessity of letting Hamitic service remain. He installed it with the American Constitution, and has carried it forward with the flight of our ensign. The white population of the South, in 1850, was 6,222,418, and the actual number of slaveholders was 347,525: the proportion of non-slaveholders being as 17 to 1. Here the balance of power against the actual holder is immense, and it could overwhelm the system in a moment, were it disposed. But vast as is this preponderance of might, there is the most unparalleled unanimity of sentiment as to the propriety of the institution. But such extraordinary unity of thought, doctrine, and action among a people *fully conversant with the system and with the Bible,* cannot be regarded in any other light than as purely providential.

God has, again, shown the benevolence of the Southern institutions by permitting counter experiments. The British empire emancipated negroes in the flourishing island of Jamaica, close by us. This example tested the European doctrine of the law of love, and found it false and fanatical, and injurious to all parties. Jamaica, under a system of Hamitic bondage *far inferior to ours,* was yet a highly prosperous country; but after an experiment of *only twenty* years, we find that its productiveness has decreased from millions to thousands; population has dwindled immensely; and barbarism, idleness, and vice have succeeded to order, plenty, and activity. The true doctrine of the law of love can result neither in barbarism, nor in diminished population, nor in poverty; so that the conclusion is resistless, that British emancipation has violated that very law of love it proposed to obey. Predicating its course on the asserted political equality of all races, it assumed that Deity was cruel if it denied the doctrine. Discarding a difference of rights instituted by the Lord, it arrogated a benevolence above that of the Divinity, and now experiences the re-

ward of its error. The British experiment is a lesson taught before our eyes. It is an exposition of the law, presenting both sides of its issues. It establishes the fact that God's law is founded in benevolence, and that its fruits of obedience are beneficial to all parties.

The experiment of liberating negroes has also been tried, and while a *few* have done nobly, their condition, generally, is not as comfortable nor as moral as that of the slaves. This experiment is accumulating a vastly inferior race, which no private benevolence nor public legislation have been able to exalt above a second-class people. "Uncle Tom," the intelligent and enlightened hero of bondage, is a fruit of slavery, to which the free blacks have never produced a rival.

Another experiment, of less noble nature, has also been tried. It is that of stealing slaves from the South, and transporting them to the North; and with what results? Much capital has been thus benevolently wasted, much trouble has been experienced, and many tears uselessly wasted. The negro has been carried to a climate too frigid for his constitution, and his industry has added neither to his aggregate wealth, population, intelligence, nor virtue. He is far worse in circumstances, and farther from developing the ends of his being, than when in the more agreeable and prolific South. With a contempt for "poor white folks," (to use his own familiar words,) and with the faith that *liberty* and *freedom from work* are synonymous terms, he despises honest poverty and labor; but seldom toils, and often steals. So unsatisfactory have been the results of negro-stealing to philanthropists, that they are opening their own eyes to the crude fruits of their costly experiment, and would let it alone, did not pride of opinion still urge a sluggish robbery for the sake of honesty and piety. The stealing experiment has proved a failure, and has thus again providentially endorsed the South.

Once more: Providence has kept the negro race in a state of singular satisfaction with its lot in the South. While mobs and insurrections and nullification have been of constant recurrence among the white race, the negro has given but very few examples of dissatisfaction since the organization of the confederacy; and those examples were never general. Plots of insurrection have always been revealed by negroes themselves, and usually have been found instigated and promoted by thieves of the white race. In the field or the city, in the cabin or the church, in the prayer-meeting or the dance, the negro is ever the cheerful singer or the mirthful performer. With food, raiment, and shelter while in health, with medicine, physicians, and sympathy in sickness, his material and religious mercies are superior to those enjoyed by three-fourths of the human family. He plots no insurrection, he frames no general combinations, but abides in a state of peace. He labors leisurely, is free from solicitude, and is seldom sick; and when he dies, he is blessed with the consolations of religion. When we therefore take a large survey of the results of Hamitic service in America, and mark the singular and often vast interpositions of Providence to sustain it, and to bless it perpetuators, we can but feel that God is for it, and that it accords with the worldwide application of the law of love to a fallen race.

The argument of the opposition undertakes to prove that Hamitic service is against the law of love; and that, by consequence, God could not righteously confer a right to it upon Japheth. We have replied, that God did formally grant it; and that it is not against the law of love, since it was conferred on the Hebrews; and if it was consistent with love in their case, it is so in that of Shem and of Japheth; and that Providence has asserted its consistency with benevolence by preserving the institution of Hamitic service in America through all vicissitudes, and by making it a great political blessing to the Hamites, and to the world at large.

Finally, the whole argument of the opposition is this: "Christianity is hostile to Hamitic slavery, making it in turpitude equal to piracy, because Christianity says, 'Thou shalt love thy neighbor as thyself.' "

The answer is, this argument proves too much for its correctness; for God's constitution for the Hebrews admitted the righteousness of Hamitic slavery, and it affirmed as its main law the very same thing Christianity does, viz., "Thou shalt love thy neighbor as thyself." The great law is the same in both codes; and if Hamitic service was right in one code, in view of the law of love, on the same premise it may be just in the other code. From this conclusion there can be no escape.

Chapter 34

The Hireling and the Slave

POETRY was turned into highly popular propaganda through the efforts
of William Grayson. A cultivated South Carolinian, he put into verse one of
the outstanding ideas of the South. It was that the black bondslave was much
better off than the white wage slave. In its resentment of criticism by Northern and English abolitionists, the South had turned increasingly to this de-
fense. The starving children in the slums of Boston or Liverpool, the argument ran, deserved far more pity than the pickaninny playing on the plantation. The Negro slave had security and considerate treatment as his lot,
more than could be claimed for the Massachusetts millhand or Yorkshire
spinner.

Grayson's *The Hireling and the Slave* appeared in 1854 and was quickly
reprinted and widely quoted. It was prefaced with a brief by Grayson in
prose. The poem itself is in heroic couplets, the most fashionable form for
eighteenth-century England. Grayson read with relish among the poets of
that era. His poem is a long one, as were a number of notable eighteenth-
century poems, but his audience would not have wanted him to omit a line.
Grayson adroitly mingled satire with sentiment. For the technique of verse
satire he drew on both John Dryden and Alexander Pope. For suggestions
on the handling of sentiment he went to Oliver Goldsmith's "The Deserted
Village." In fact, if he modeled his piece on anything, it was Goldsmith's
poem.

Grayson adopts Goldsmith's basic structure, which is a contrast between
a village once populous and peaceful and the same village now deserted.
Goldsmith's villain is the rise of British commerce. It has allowed one
wealthy man to buy the whole village and expel the villagers. They now
live miserably in the city, while their village has become an empty, over-
grown part of a single man's domain. Goldsmith's sentimental picture of the
old days and his strictures on the new both are reflected in *The Hireling*

and the Slave. Grayson paints the plantation as pastoral; its Negroes enjoy their work and play. But he portrays the hireling and his brood as the victim of the grimmest wrongs: his very children may labor like animals in the coal mine, dragging the coal cart on their hands and knees.

Grayson's work, excerpted below, ends with an exhortation to the master to take good care of the slave: "The negro's hand, to useful arts incline,/His mind enlarge, his moral sense refine."

Source: [W. J. Grayson] *The Hireling and the Slave*
(Charleston, 1854), v–vii; 19; 20–21, abridged; 23–24, abridged; 59–61, abridged; 80, abridged; 84–85, abridged.

THE HIRELING AND THE SLAVE

The malignant abuse lavished on the Slaveholders of America, by writers in this country and England, can be accounted for, but in one way, consistently with any degree of charitable consideration for the slanderers. They have no knowledge of the thing abused. They substitute an ideal of their own contriving for the reality. They regard Slavery as a system of chains, whips and tortures. They consider its abuses as its necessary condition, and a cruel master its fair representative. Mr. Clarkson took up the subject, originally, as a fit one for a college exercise in rhetoric, and it became a rhetorical exercise for life to himself and his followers. With these people the cruelty of Slavery is an affair of tropes and figures only. They have shown as little regard for truth, fairness and common sense, as they would do to gather all the atrocities of their own country committed by husbands and wives, parents and children, masters and servants, priest and people, and denounce these several relations in life in consequence of their abuses.

The labourer suffers wrong, abuse and cruelty in England, but, they say, it is against the law, against public opinion; he may apply to the Courts for redress; these are open to him. Cruelty to the Slave is equally against the law. It is equally condemned by public opinion; and as to the Courts of Law being open to the pauper hireling, we may remember the reply of Sheridan to a similar remark,—yes, and so are the London Hotels—justice and a good dinner, with Champagne, are equally within his reach. If, in consequence of the evils incident to hireling labour—because there are severe, heartless, grinding employers and miserable starving hirelings, it were proposed to abolish hireling labour, it would be quite as just and logical as the argument to abolish Slavery because there are sufferings among Slaves, and hard hearts among Masters. The cruelty or suffering is no more a necessary part of the one system than of the other. Notwithstanding its abuses and miseries, the Hireling System works beneficially with white labourers; and so also, notwithstanding hard masters, Slavery, among a Christian people, is advantageous to the negro. To attempt to establish the hireling system with Africans, would be as wise as to endeavour to bestow the constitutional government of England on Ashantee or Dahomey. In both cases there would be an equal amount of abstract truth and practical absurdity.

How small the choice, from cradle to the
    grave,
Between the lot of Hireling and of Slave!
To each alike applies the stern decree,
That man shall labour; whether bond or
    free,
For all that toil, the recompense we claim—
Food, fire, a home and clothing—is the
    same. . . .
  The manumitted serfs of Europe find
Unchanged this sad estate of all mankind;
What blessing to the churl has freedom
    proved,
What want supplied, what task or toil
    removed?
Hard work and scanty wages still their lot,
In youth o'erlaboured, and in age forgot,
The mocking boon of freedom they deplore,
In wants, cares, labours never known before.
  Free but in name—the slaves of endless
    toil,
In Britain still they turn the stubborn soil,
Spread on each sea her sails for every mart,
Ply in her cities every useful art;
But vainly may the Peasant toil and groan,
To speed the plough in furrows not his own;
In vain the art is plied, the sail is spread,
The day's work offered for the daily bread;
With hopeless eye, the pauper Hireling sees
The homeward sail swell proudly to the
    breeze,
Rich fabrics, wrought by his unequalled
    hand,
Borne by each breeze to every distant land;
For him, no boon successful commerce yields,
For him no harvest crowns the joyous fields,
The streams of wealth that foster pomp and
    pride,

No food nor shelter for his wants provide,
He fails to win, by toil intensely hard,
The bare subsistence—labour's least reward.
  In squalid hut—a kennel for the poor,
Or noisome cellar, stretched upon the floor,
His clothing rags, of filthy straw his bed,
With offal from the gutter daily fed,
Thrust out from Nature's board, the Hireling
    lies—
No place for him that common board sup-
    plies,
No neighbour helps, no charity attends,
No philanthropic sympathy befriends;
None heed the needy wretch's dying groan,
He starves unsuccor'd, perishes unknown.
  These are the miseries, such the wants, the
    cares,
The bliss that freedom for the serf prepares;
Vain is his skill in each familiar task,
Capricious Fashion shifts her Protean mask,
His ancient craft gives work and bread no
    more,
And want and death sit scowling at his
    door. . .
  There, unconcerned, the philanthropic eye
Beholds each phase of human misery;
Sees the worn child compelled in mines to
    slave
Through narrow seams of coal, a living
    grave,
Driven from the breezy hill, the sunny glade,
By ruthless hearts, the drudge of labour
    made,
Unknown the boyish sport, the hours of
    play,
Stript of the common boon, the light of day,
Harnessed like brutes, like brutes to tug and
    strain
And drag, on hands and knees, the loaded
    wain:
There crammed in huts, in reeking masses
    thrown,
All moral sense and decency unknown,
With no restraint, but what the felon knows,
With the sole joy, that beer or gin bestows,
To gross excess and brutalizing strife,
The drunken Hireling dedicates his life:
There women prostitute themselves for
    bread,

There tearless mothers view their infant
dead,
Childhood bestows no childish sports or toys,
Age, neither reverence nor repose enjoys,
Labour, with hunger, wages ceaseless strife,
And want and suffering only end with life;
In crowded huts, contagious ills prevail,
Dull typhus lurks and deadlier plagues assail,
Gaunt famine prowls around his pauper
prey,
And daily sweeps his ghastly hosts away;
Unburied corses taint the summer air,
And crime and outrage revel with despair.
   Dragged from the cottage, conscript peas-
   ants go,
To distant wars, against an unknown foe,
On fields of carnage, at ambition's call,
Perish—the warrior's tool, the monarch's
   thrall. . . .
   Not toil alone, the fortune of the Slave!
He shares the sports and spoils of wood and
   wave;
Through the dense swamp, where wilder
   forests rise
In tangled masses, and shut out the skies,
Where the dark covert shuns the noontide
   blaze,
With agile step, he threads the pathless maze,
The hollow gum with searching eye explores,
Traces the bee to its delicious stores,
The ringing axe with ceaseless vigour plies,
And from the hollow scoops the luscious
   prize.
   When Autumn's parting days grow cold
   and brief
Light hoar frosts sparkle on the fallen leaf,
The breezeless pines, at rest, no longer sigh,
Bright, pearl-like clouds hang shining in the
   sky;
And on strong pinions, in the clear blue
   light,
Exulting falcons wheel their towering flight,
With short shrill cry, arrest the cheerful flow
Of song, and hush the frightened fields
   below.
When to the homestead flocks and herds
   incline,
Sonorous conchs recall the rambling swine,
And from the fleecy field, the setting sun

Sends home the Slave, his easy harvest done;
In field and wood he hunts the frequent
   hare,
The wild hog chases to the forest lair,
Entraps the gobbler; with persuasive smoke
Beguiles the 'possum from the hollow oak;
On the tall pine tree's topmost bough espies
The crafty coon—a more important prize—
Detects the dodger's peering eyes that glow
With fire reflected from the blaze below,
Hews down the branchless trunk with prac-
   tised hand
And drives the climber from his nodding
   stand;
Downward, at last, he springs, with crashing
   sound,
Where Jet and Pincher seize him on the
   ground,
Yields to the hunter the contested spoil,
And pays, with feast and fur, the evening
   toil.
   When calm skies glitter with the starry
   light,
The boatman tries the fortune of the night,
Launches the light canoe; the torch's beam
Gleams like a gliding meteor on the stream;
Along the shore, the flick'ring fire-light
   steals,
Shines through the wave, and all its wealth
   reveals;
The spotted trout its mottled side displays,
Swift shoals of mullet flash beneath the blaze;
He marks their rippling course; through cold
   and wet,
Lashes the sparkling tide with dext'rous net;
With poised harpoon the bass or drum as-
   sails,
And strikes the barb through silv'ry tinted
   scales. . . .
   Why peril then the negro's humble joys,
Why make him free, if freedom but destroys?
Why take him from that lot that now bestows
More than the negro elsewhere ever knows—
Home, clothing, food, light labour, and
   content,
Childhood in play, and age, in quiet spent,
To vex his life with factious strife and broil,
To crush his nature with unwonted toil,
To see him, like the Indian tribes, a prey

To war or peace, destruction or decay? . . .
  Let then the master still his course pursue,
"With heart and hope" perform his mission
      too;
Heaven's ruling power confest, with patient
      care,
The end subserve, the fitting means prepare,
In faith unshaken, guide, restrain, command,
With strong and steady, yet indulgent hand,
Justly, "as in the great Taskmaster's eye."
His task perform—the negro's wants supply,
The negro's hand, to useful arts incline,
His mind enlarge, his moral sense refine,

With gospel truth, his simple heart engage,
To his dull eyes, unseal its sacred page,
By gradual steps, his feebler nature raise,
Deserve, if not receive, the good man's
      praise;
The factious knave defy, and meddling fool,
The pulpit brawler and his lawless tool,
Scorn the grave cant, the supercilious sneer,
The mawkish sentiment, and maudlin tear,
Assured that God, all human power bestows,
Controls its uses, and its purpose knows,
And that each lot, on earth to mortals given,
Its duties duly done, is blest of Heaven.

Chapter 35

Irrepressible Conflict

MUCH of antebellum culture can be interpreted in terms of institutions. The family, the church, the school: these are prime examples. They continue down to the present day, and Americans in general believe that their influence has been benign. Not so, of course, for the institution of Negro slavery. Its influence has been baleful from the beginning. However, the South of the 1850s stood united as never before in defending it. Even today we could probably find a few defenders of it, mainly but not exclusively in the Southern states.

No view of American life during the decade would be complete without taking slavery into account. Most generalizations about American life of that time must include the automatic exception: it was different for the Negro in the South.

The pictorial documents printed here represent the chief responses of the decade to slavery. The first, "The Flag of our Union," represents the view which millions of people in the North and probably a numerical majority in the South still clung to—the view that somehow the Union could be maintained. The view that some compromise could be found to keep the South as part of the United States. The second document shows a slave sale. There is no arguing with it. The visceral impact of the picture is enormous and, at least in the long run, no compromiser could escape its message. The third document, a pair of cartoons, emblemizes the reaction of the South to criticism of slaveholding. The Southern slave is carefree and secure, while the white wage slave of the North and of England is a miserable wretch.

The final document is fantastic. It makes wicked fun of Mrs. Stowe and the abolitionists, in an allegory filled with the demons of the imagination. If there is, or was, such a thing as the American Dream, this picture shows us the opposite of it. It is one weird token of the civil war to come.

Source: Cover for "The Flag of our Union: A National Song."
Lithographed by H. Hoff and published by Wm. Hall & Son,
1851.
Reproduced from the Collections of the Library of Congress

The great majority of Americans in the North gave every evidence of hoping that the Union would continue. The Southern separationists called loudly for disunion but in all probability many of their fellow Southerners failed to agree. Though the Southern slaves could not make themselves heard, it is difficult not to believe that they wanted anything, including the Union, that might make them free.

This urge to maintain the Union still permeated much of American culture in the 1850s. There were even songs about it and the cover of one of them is shown here. The North and South are portrayed as sisters, equal in everything. Both hold the flag, with a fancy arrangement of interlocking arms. The sisters look much the same, though the South wears a slit dress with a low neckline while the North is more conservatively covered. The North gazes at the South; the South gazes at the flag. The world is their pedestal. Behind them stretch the cities of the United States, all amply endowed with churches—we can see their steeples rising above other buildings.

Hoff's lithograph is the standard hackwork of the time. The faces of the two sisters are devoid of bone structure and the figures seem boneless too beneath their classical dress. The American eagle stretches his wings, in a conception of sheer banality, to complete the circle of the stars and give the picture a frame.

Source: The Slave Sale. Ca. 1855
The Harry T. Peters "America on Stone" Lithography Collection,
The Smithsonian Institution

The impulse in the North was either to ignore slavery or condone it. But lithographs like "The Slave Sale" brought home the utter brutality of one human being buying or selling another. Much of the North remained Puritan, so the spectacle of a slave girl being forced to submit to her master seemed especially outrageous. In terms of depth psychology, it touched a basic chord in the American character: the guilty white, by violating the black, projected some of his guilt on the black. Another of the highly distasteful spectacles in slavery was the splitting up of Negro families at the whim of circumstance.

Here in this crowded, sardonic lithograph the artist has combined compassion with satire. The sight is harrowing. A slave girl, obviously as light in color as a mixed inheritance can make her, is about to be sold to a brutal, middle-

COVER FOR "THE FLAG OF OUR UNION: A NATIONAL SONG"

228

THE SLAVE SALE. CA. 1855

aged planter. And the spectator's comment is, "he has got the girl body & soul, unless God help her." But the comment is put in the mouth of a jackanapes, an overseer with whip in hand and an expression of mirthful lechery. Two planters listen to him. One tilts his head to look at the girl; the other, with his hand on the head of a sullen Negro child he may have bought, smiles in grim agreement. A female slave who may be the girl's mother apparently makes an appeal to the former owner of the girl to keep her, but she is ignored.

We also see a family being destroyed. A young Negro stands on the auction block while a young woman, doubtless his wife, sobs at her mother's lap. The auctioneer rests his hand on the Negro's head in an inspired gesture which suggests that he is merely showing off a piece of property. It may be that the group of slaves in the foreground makes another family which is also in danger of being dispersed.

The artist gives an edge to his picture by sketching two signs on the wall of the slave mart. One says that the slaves are being sold to furnish funds "for Salem Chapel" and thereby reminds us of the relation of the American church to slavery. The other advertises a reward for the return of a runaway female slave, "alive or dead." This was the sort of advertisement which shocked Charles Dickens when he visited the South and which he quoted in *American Notes*.

In topic and treatment the picture testifies to the influence of Harriet Beecher Stowe's great book, for at the bottom, barely visible, are the words "Vide Uncle Tom's Cabin."

The picture is a panorama, with many competing elements even though the center of interest is the slave girl being sold. Most of the figures are individualized. The faces are caricatured but not grossly so except for the overseer's. The attitudes look free though some of the gestures seem a bit stagy. To the uncommitted Northerner this picture could have made a very moving appeal.

Source: Slavery as it Exists in America / Slavery as it Exists in England. Published by J. Haven, 1850.
Reproduced from the Collections of the Library of Congress

The answer—heated, contemptuous, or caustic—that the South gave the abolitionists was the same in the 1850s that it had been in the 1840s. It was that the lot of the chattel slaves in the South was idyllic compared to that of the wage slaves in the North. Or in England, to repeat; for the South was much annoyed at the attacks on its "peculiar institution" by the English abolitionists. Here the attack focuses on England.

In the pair of cartoons the one on slavery in America shows us a group of grinning blacks. They dance around, exuding merriment, while two Northern visitors and two Southern planters comment. The Northerners exclaim in surprise. The first wonders why he ever criticized the South before visiting it. The second marvels, as he watches the happy scene, "Is this the way that Slaves are treated at the South!" The first planter replies that such treatment (with "some few exceptions") is normal. He

SLAVERY AS IT EXISTS IN AMERICA / SLAVERY AS IT EXISTS IN ENGLAND

adds that after four or five in the afternoon his own slaves are free to enjoy themselves in "any reasonable way." The second planter remarks that the visitors will now tell a different story when they return to the North. He adds gratuitously that the South must stand up for its rights even at the risk of the Union.

The cartoon on slavery in England shows nothing but misery. On the wall of the cloth factory in the left background, a starving operative has set a sign advertising his wife for sale. In the left foreground a weazened worker explains to his childhood friend "Farmer" that mill operatives generally die at forty. In the center a gaunt female clasps her hands, exclaiming at what the factory does to her and her children. To the right Tom assures Bill that he is going to run away from the factory to work in the coal mines. After all, he will have to put in only fourteen hours a day in the mines as compared to his seventeen-hour day at the factory. In the lower righthand corner still another operative, mortally ill, thanks God that his days of slavery will soon be done.

In the distance we can see the tents of a military encampment and soldiers on guard ready to shoot any mill operative who makes trouble. To the right of the encampment two fat men glower at the miserable operatives. One is a churchman holding a record of tithes which the poor must pay to support the Church of England. The other is the tax gatherer, ready to screw the last farthing from the poor while taking not a penny from the rich.

The art work is amateurish. Time has turned the cartoon on the happy Negro slaves into a caricature. But this kind of visual document made an appeal something like that of a television film-clip. And the place where the cartoon was issued is worth noting: it is not Mobile or Atlanta but Boston. Slavery still had friends in the North.

Source: A Dream: Caused by the perusal of Mrs. H. Beecher Stowe's popular work *Uncle Tom's Cabin.* Lithographed by C. R. Milne and published by J. C. Frost and G. W. Hall, 1855.
Reproduced from the Collections of the Library of Congress

The dream, the nightmare, the phantasmagoria we see results from a reading of Mrs. Stowe's *Uncle Tom's Cabin.* She said that she first observed slave life when she went on a visit to Kentucky. Kentucky did not forget the compliment, and we observe that this picture was lithographed and issued in Louisville.

The specific suggestion for "A Dream" came from an early seventeenth-century picture, Jacques Callot's "Temptation of St. Anthony." But the artist, Milne, also drew on the rich and weird European tradition of the apocalyptic scene. The scene is usually the Last Judgment or Hell. The manner tends to be morbidly extravagant. The tradition flourished in the Middle Ages and the Renaissance, with as its foremost exponent Albrecht Durer; but it continued down into the nineteenth century. At the very time that Milne was at work in Louisville, Gustave Doré was at work in Paris.

A DREAM: CAUSED BY THE PERUSAL OF MRS. H. BEECHER STOWE'S POPULAR WORK *UNCLE TOM'S CABIN*

233

Medieval gargoyles and grotesques crowd Milne's picture; devils of all shapes and sizes spit fire or work their wicked way.

The picture is brilliant in spite of its derivative nature. The Archfiend, chained but still horrendous, presides over the scene. He is weaponed with fire and snake. Below him a dusky English abolitionist grins under his broad-brimmed Quaker hat. His banner reads "Women of England to the Rescue," for the artist has not overlooked Mrs. Stowe's triumphal trip to England in 1853. She needs to be rescued—the imps of hell are drawing her into a cavern marked "Underground Railway." Regardless of her desperate plight she looks impassive as she holds aloft a copy of her book.

Near the left margin of the picture one portly devil reads her nefarious record to her while another clasps his hands in wonder. At the right side of "A Dream" we watch the legions of hell, in full armament, apparently firing at their fellow fiends. Those fiends want to spirit her away on the Underground Railway to nameless tortures, while the legions aim simply to burn her as they are burning the captive woman they already hold. In the background other devils, unmolested, are busy burning copies of Mrs. Stowe's book. However, *Uncle Tom's Cabin* can attract even some of the imps of hell; despite the cannonading one imp in the lower center of the picture bends to read it.

The picture is crammed with movement. Nearly everyone or everything is doing something. Only a few figures are shown at rest and they watch the devils' dance in sardonic satisfaction.

. . . For most of America, and that meant white America, the 1850s were a good decade, abundant in opportunity, full of resources, confident in tone. For white America this was indeed the promised land. For Negro America it was far from that, of course, and only the civil war would begin to mend matters. Meanwhile, in spite of all the good things which the 1850s offered, the war was coming closer all the time.

Secondary Sources

BOOKS about the 1850s are surprisingly few. Fred Lewis Pattee's *The Feminine Fifties* (1940) is a charming, discursive study of the literature, popular as well as classic, of the decade. E. Douglas Branch's *The Sentimental Years* (1924) covers the period from 1836 to 1860. It offers a broad view of antebellum life, describing among other things the literature, fine arts, reform movements, and religious trends of the time. Carl Bode's *The Anatomy of American Popular Culture, 1840–1861* (1959) takes up the fine arts one by one and the various kinds of printed works popular during the period, describes them, and suggests their relationship to the American character. It has been reprinted in paperback as *Antebellum Culture* (1970).

Selected portions of four other books are useful for background. Oliver Larkin's *Art and Life in America* (1949) is a panoramic work with a section, pages 147–231, on the years from 1830 to 1870. Frank Luther Mott's *Golden Multitudes* (1947) and James Hart's *The Popular Book* (1950) are both studies of American best sellers. Pages 88–142 in Mott and 85–139 in Hart contain some information about popular works of the 1850s. Carl Bode's *The American Lyceum: Town Meeting of the Mind* (1956; paperback 1968) approaches the period through its lecturing; he examines the relation of the lyceum to other elements in antebellum cultural history.

Acknowledgments

NEARLY all the printed materials came from copies in the Library of Congress, which for the study of American civilization is patently the best library in the world. The pictorial materials come either from the Prints and Photographs Division of the same library or else from the extensive archives of the Smithsonian Institution. I was helped with the problems of the pictorial materials by Mrs. Anne Golovin at the Smithsonian and Mr. Milton Kaplan at the Library of Congress.

For other assistance I turned to the McKeldin Library at the University of Maryland, particularly to Miss Betty Baehr of its staff, and to the Enoch Pratt Library of Baltimore, one of the best public libraries in the country.

Clerical and research help came from, most of all, my daughter Barbara but also from Miss Lorraine Janus of the University of Maryland's English Department, from Mrs. Bernie Smith, and from Mr. Walter Hageter. Additional help in typing came from Mrs. Dorothy Garrett and Mrs. Sharon Landolt.

C. B.

University of Maryland
College Park, Maryland